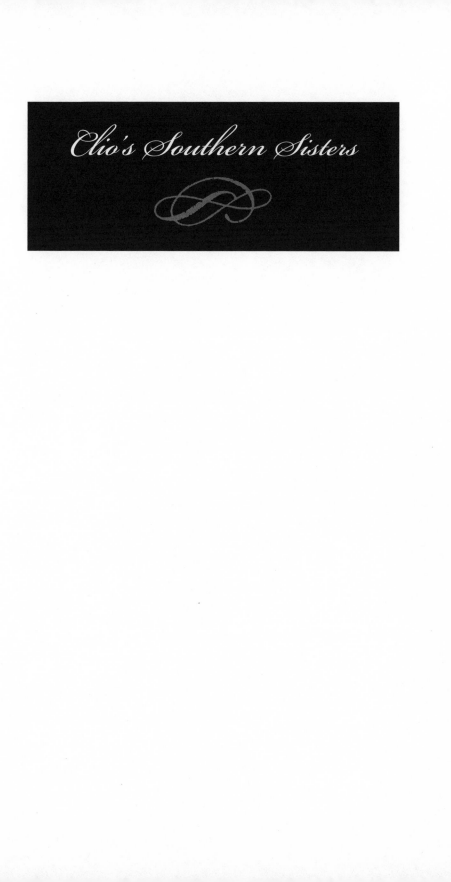

Clio's Southern Sisters

Southern Women

A series of books developed from the Southern
Conference on Women's History sponsored by the
Southern Association for Women Historians.

Series Editors

Betty Brandon
Michele Gillespie
Nancy A. Hewitt
Wilma King
Theda Perdue
Martha H. Swain

Clio's Southern Sisters

Interviews with Leaders of the Southern
Association for Women Historians

Edited by
Constance B. Schulz
and Elizabeth Hayes Turner

University of Missouri Press
Columbia and London

Library of Congress Cataloging-in-Publication Data

Clio's southern sisters : interviews with leaders of the Southern Association for
Women Historians / edited by Constance B. Schulz and Elizabeth Hayes Turner.
        p. cm. — (Southern women)
     Includes index.
     ISBN 0-8262-1541-6 (alk. paper)
     1. Women historians—Southern States—Interviews.   2. Southern Associ-
ation for Women Historians—Biography.   3. Southern States—Historiog-
raphy.   4. Women—Southern States—Historiography.   5. Women's studies—
Southern States—History.   6. United States—Historiography.   7. Women—
United States—Historiography.   I. Schulz, Constance B.   II. Turner,
Elizabeth Hayes.   III. Series.
     E175.45.C585   2004
975'.0072'02275—dc22

                                                            2004012423

∞ This paper meets the requirements of the
American National Standard for Permanence of Paper
for Printed Library Materials, Z39.48, 1984.

Designer: Jennifer Cropp
Typesetter: Crane Composition, Inc.
Printer and binder: Thomson-Shore, Inc.
Typefaces: Palatino, Bickham, Bernhard, and Cancione

Photo credits: A. Elizabeth Taylor courtesy The Woman's Collection, Texas
Woman's University; Anne Scott by Les Todd; Arnita Jones by Laura Dillon;
Rosemary Carroll by George Henry; Carol Bleser by Robert Duckworth; Jo Ann
Carrigan by William Rucker Carrigan.

This book is dedicated to the
women in this volume, whose courage
and determination opened doors and
provided leadership for others in the
historical profession.

Contents

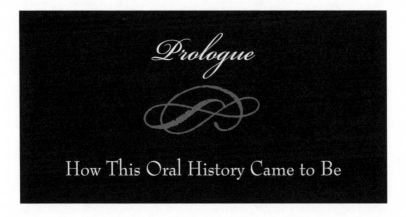

Prologue

How This Oral History Came to Be

"Human beings are unable to resist celebrating any anniversary divisible by twenty-five," wrote archivist and educator Timothy L. Ericson.[1] Historians have been justifiably skeptical of celebratory commemorative events, wary that the fallible memory of the celebrants retains that which is good and admirable and conveniently discards or downplays pettiness, discouragement, or the occasional failure that marked the progress toward these numerical milestones. Yet at the same time, we value these occasions as a means of drawing our more ahistorical neighbors into our own fascination with the past and its relationship to the present. In particular, we use milestones to construct narratives about our own histories within a profession, and to ensure that the records and memories of our professional past are preserved.

So it was with the Southern Association for Women Historians (SAWH) in 1990 as the executive board looked ahead to 1995 and the twenty-fifth

1. Timothy L. Ericson, "Anniversaries: A Framework for Planning Public Programs," in *Advocating Archives: An Introduction to Public Relations for Archivists*, ed. Elsie Freeman Finch (Metuchen, NJ: Scarecrow Press for the Society of American Archivists, 1994), 66.

anniversary of the meeting of a group of women in a small space next to the boiler room in the basement of the Kentucky Hotel in Louisville in 1970. The board created a Twenty-fifth Anniversary Task Force, chaired by Barbara Brandon Schnorrenberg. Among its suggestions for the 1995 celebration was the idea to conduct oral history interviews with founders of the SAWH. What better way to celebrate what had been accomplished than to record the memories of the founders, leaders, and followers who had made the association a success?

Thus was born the original Oral History Project from which this volume has grown. By 1992 there was some urgency; although many of the organization's founders were still relatively young, a few of the pioneer women scholars important to the history of women in the South were known to be in poor health. With a limited budget, Pamela Dean, a historian with the T. Harry Williams Center for Oral History at Louisiana State University, agreed to begin the project immediately by interviewing A. Elizabeth Taylor at the Southern Historical Association meeting in Atlanta in November 1992. Dean also interviewed Mollie C. Davis at that meeting. Then the project stopped while the association sought financial support to complete it.

It was fortunate that these initial interviews were conducted, because within a short time, Taylor had died. The Twenty-fifth Anniversary Task Force had developed a list of a dozen representative women who had helped to lead the organization during its first twenty years. Dean estimated that interviewing the women, not all of whom were even in the South, using professional oral history consultants could cost as much as $16,000. This sum was far beyond the resources of a small organization whose annual budget was less than half that amount. So the association turned, as women in voluntary associations have so often done, to its members. Gifts from a few individual members were matched by the executive board to provide seed money.

The Applied History M.A. Program at the University of South Carolina (now known as the Public History Program), provided a ready source of graduate students interested in learning how to do oral history who could conduct interviews or prepare transcriptions. The chair of the history department, Peter Becker, agreed to provide additional funds to create a graduate assistantship position. From 1993 to 1996, two graduate assistants, enrolled in the public history track in museum administration, provided steady, reliable support. Both of them delighted in the opportunity to meet and interview women whose work they were reading in their graduate seminars. They spent many hours conducting preliminary research in the SAWH records deposited at the Southern Historical Collection in the University of North Carolina Library at Chapel Hill, preparing the initial list of interview questions; transcribing interviews, checking the transcripts; corresponding with the interviewees regarding permissions and approval of the transcripts, gathering photographs and resumes, and keeping project records.

Initially, the sole intent of the project was to collect and preserve the memories of the women who had created this important professional organization; as historians we thought it our responsibility to record and preserve our own history. But during the interviews, as one woman after another recounted what it meant to her to become a historian in the South in the middle of the twentieth century, it became clear that these memories of their experiences should reach a broader audience. A preliminary proposal to edit the transcripts into a publishable manuscript was first presented to the SAWH executive committee in June 1994 at the Third Southern Conference on Women's History in Houston; the committee enthusiastically endorsed the idea. Beverly Jarrett, director of the University of Missouri Press, expressed an early interest in the project and urged us to move forward with a manuscript proposal. Both the SAWH board and reviewers who read the manuscript for the press made helpful suggestions for improvements.

The tasks suggested by those early reviewers have consumed another ten years. Schulz conducted three additional interviews: second interviews with Carol Bleser in the fall of 1996 and with Anne Scott in January 2001, and a belated first interview with Elizabeth Jacoway in January 2003. Elizabeth Hayes Turner became coeditor in 2000 and took on the substantial task of editing the complete interview transcriptions into publishable form.

Our intent was to preserve as much as possible the characteristic voice of each speaker, but Turner edited sharply in some cases to keep the discussion moving and on track. As in any conversation, there are pauses, digressions, and tangents, and where these did not apply to the subject at hand, they were removed. Likewise, when information was incomplete, or where confusion might arise, full titles and names of persons, organization, and institutions were added. Turner checked dates and provided accurate facts about which the interviewees had been unsure or had disagreed. She also silently corrected grammatical constructions that might have led to misunderstanding. Given the background of our interviewees as writers and public speakers, there were remarkably few of these! All changes made during the editing process have been reviewed and approved by the women whom we interviewed. Throughout the interview, transcription, and editing phases of the project we have tried to adhere to the highest oral history standards.[2] Readers interested in hearing the actual voices of the women whose stories fill this book can find recordings of all the original interviews and the complete transcripts in the SAWH Records at the Southern Historical Collection, the University of North Carolina at Chapel Hill.[3]

The long process through which this book has come to fruition presented us with an interesting historical problem during the last year of editorial work. The SAWH is now approaching the thirty-fifth anniversary of its founding. Ought we to recognize the women who led the organization in the last decade of the twentieth century, many of them active and important scholars who are transforming the field of women's history? Should we bring the story up to date by conducting more interviews? In rewriting the history of the SAWH, we have tried to acknowledge the influential role of this new generation of historians whose energetic commitment has continued to transform the organization as well as the scholarship to which it is dedicated. Nevertheless, upon reflection, we decided that this new generation of leaders had quite different experiences. Trained in graduate schools in the 1970s or later, when the history of women as a field of study and the growing acceptance of women in the historical profession had made considerable progress, their stories will have a different flavor and focus than those collected here. We believe we can safely leave it to the planners of the SAWH fiftieth anniversary celebration in 2020 to begin a new oral history project to capture those memories of the way in which the historical profession, and the women who became an increasing part of it during the late twentieth century, addressed new questions about our complex past.

The interviews that form the core of this book are thus the result of a collaborative process that has involved a number of historians for over a decade. Because of the way that the project began, and the questions that guided the interviews, the narratives are primary source documents that tell about the changes over time within a specific organization: the South-

2. Our guides to these practices, first for the graduate student assistants, and then for ourselves, can be found in the following: Donald A. Ritchie, *Doing Oral History* (New York: Twayne Publishers, 1995); Willa K. Baum, *Oral History for the Local Historical Society*, 3rd ed. (Nashville: American Association for State and Local History, 1987); Willa K. Baum, *Transcribing and Editing Oral History* (Nashville: American Association for State and Local History, 1981); Cullom Davis, *Oral History: From Tape to Type* (Chicago: American Library Association, 1977).

3. Two of the original interviews, conducted with women who have since left the historical profession and whose narratives (while interesting) necessarily departed from the purposes both of the original oral history project and of the more focused theme of this book, have not been included in the final manuscript.

ern Association for Women Historians.[4] But they are much more than that. They are the personal stories of a diverse group of women who chose the discipline of history as their life's work. The women who have shared their own histories with us in this volume give evidence, often in strong and effective language, of the experiences that shaped their entry into the historical profession. All of them received their Ph.D.s before 1975. All of them worked with male professors, and most of them wrote dissertations on subjects other than women's history. All of them offer vivid descriptions of the point at which they experienced the shift in their lives and in the lives of those around them that led toward a new day for women in the history profession. Some found that discrimination followed them like a shadow, and the pain of those days remains with them still. Others sought their graduate education in institutions where women were welcomed and where major professors valued their work and encouraged their success.

When they entered the job market many of these young scholars found, to their dismay, that some employers flatly refused to consider them because they were women. Lost job opportunities were linked in tangled ways to the prevailing image of women as less desirable colleagues, as intellectually weaker, as "different" from male professors. The women whose narratives you are about to read helped to launch the 1970s examinations of the status of women in such associations as the American Historical Association (AHA), the Organization of American Historians (OAH), and the Southern Historical Association (SHA) which revealed that women were not accorded equal participation. Because they had lost out to men in presenting papers at conferences, in having their work published in journals, in reviewing books, and in serving on committees, they were determined to bring about change for themselves and their women students. Having experienced the ways in which women historians *were* excluded, suffering from an "invisibility" that ultimately hurt their chances for employment and promotion, they saw the organization they helped to build as a means of "making the invisible *academic* woman visible."[5] As female scholars who studied the history of women, frustrated that their work lacked "legitimacy" because the subject was not valued by male historians who held the power to hire, to promote, and to award fellowships and prizes for written work, they created their own prizes, and they dedicated those prizes to the study of women's history in the South.[6]

4. For the questions asked, see the appendix.
5. The phrase is borrowed from Anne Firor Scott, *Making the Invisible Woman Visible* (Urbana: University of Illinois Press, 1984).
6. For an extended discussion of the difficulties women historians faced, see Jacqueline Goggin, "Challenging Sexual Discrimination in the Historical Profession:

These memories thus deserve an audience of women everywhere who are committed to the study of an inclusive past. They reflect the ideals and the realities, the experiences and the exasperation, the accomplishments and the hindrances that marked the move of women historians in the American South, and the study of southern women's history, from a peripheral to a central place in the historical profession.

Women Historians and the American Historical Association, 1890–1940," *American Historical Review* 97 (June 1992): 769–802. For histories of women historians, see Eileen Boris and Nupur Chaudhuri, eds., *Voices of Women Historians: The Personal, the Political, the Professional* (Bloomington: Indiana University Press, 1999); Joan Wallach Scott, "American Women Historians, 1884–1984," in *Gender and the Politics of History* (New York: Columbia University Press, 1988), 178–98; and in particular for women historians in the South, the perceptive and detailed introductory essay by Anne Firor Scott, ed., *Unheard Voices: The First Historians of Southern Women* (Charlottesville: University Press of Virginia, 1993), 1–71.

Acknowledgments

In this, as in any enterprise, there are always others who have given of their time, their energy, and their expertise. This oral history is no exception. In fact, many have helped, encouraged, and furthered this project along. From the beginning, the collection of oral interviews was aided by a team of historians committed to recording the voices and histories of the women who opened doors in the historical profession. We wish to thank Pamela Dean for her early and very timely interviews. We give thanks to Victoria Kalamaris, Toni Smart, and Kelli Walsh for their interviews, editing, and research. And we wish to thank the presidents and secretary-treasurers of the Southern Association for Women Historians for their leadership, guidance, and support: Catherine Clinton, Amy McCandless, Jacqueline Rouse, Sandra Treadway, Jane Turner Censer, Stephanie Cole, Michele Gillespie, and Melissa Walker.

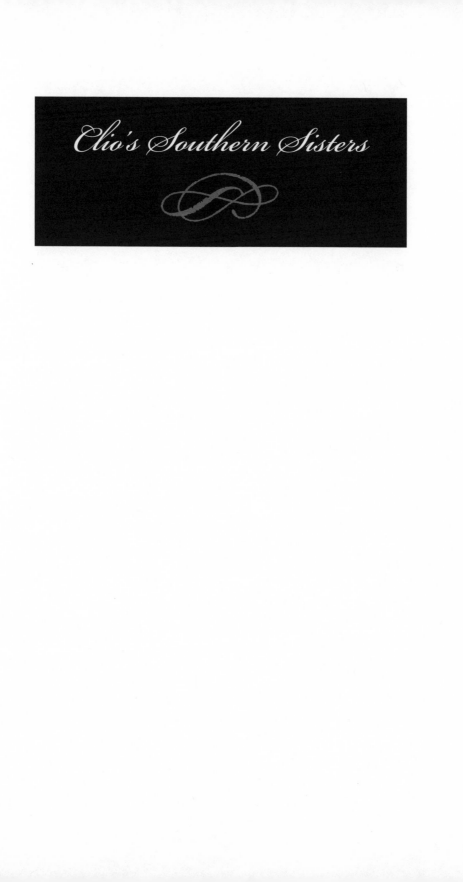

Clio's Southern Sisters

The Context

The Women's Rights Movement and the Origins and Development of the Southern Association for Women Historians

Constance B. Schulz and Elizabeth Hayes Turner

It is no accident that the Southern Association for Women Historians enjoys the founding date 1970.[1] The historians who founded, supported, and led the SAWH participated in a movement of women into the mainstream of American academic and professional life during the 1960s and 1970s. Their movement was a result, as has so often been true for women, of a determination to organize, and to draw on the power inherent in many individuals working toward common goals. The feminist movement in the 1960s influenced women historians along with other professional women in the larger struggle for gender equality, racial equality, and civil rights.

For the most part, the path that historians followed was carved out within their profession, first in national historical organizations, then in their own regional associations. Southern women historians were inspired by the example set in New England in 1930 by the Berkshire Conference of

1. Unless otherwise noted, the sources for this introductory history are the interviews in this volume and the Southern Association of Women Historians Records, the Southern Historical Collection, Wilson Library, the University of North Carolina at Chapel Hill.

Women Historians. They were influenced by the successes of women historians in the Coordinating Committee on Women in the Historical Profession (CCWHP) and later by its coassociation, the Conference Group on Women's History (CGWH). Together the CCWHP and the CGWH concentrated on raising the consciousness of the leadership of the American Historical Association (AHA) and the Organization of American Historians (OAH) about both women as historians and women's history. Finally, building on the example of a few women historians of the South—Mary Elizabeth Massey, LaWanda Cox, A. Elizabeth Taylor, and Anne Firor Scott, who had paved the way as individuals in scholarship and in leadership roles within the Southern Historical Association (SHA)—southern women historians demanded a larger role within their region's principal professional association.

The "caucus" of southern women historians that met and organized on a rudimentary level in 1970 struggled to maintain its foothold. At first the caucus functioned primarily as a center for sharing information; however, the group soon gained momentum through organized activities which laid the basis for creating a more structured organization. In 1975 the organization became the Southern Association of Women Historians. It would soon become a regular presence within the SHA. It functioned in two ways: it prodded the SHA to incorporate its women members more fully into the work of the association by gathering data about women's presence in SHA publications and leadership, and it began to highlight the scholarly work of women historians in a separate presentation at the SHA annual meeting.

Within a short time, the SAWH's activities expanded outside the immediate boundaries of its affiliation with the SHA. In keeping with the organization's dual mission of promoting the historical study of women in the South and encouraging the professional growth of women historians within the South, SAWH leadership began raising money for an endowment fund to support awards for scholarly achievement. SAWH followed the example of the Berkshire Conference and instituted a triennial professional southern conference on women's history. It sponsored scholarly publications. It became, in only twenty-five years, a full-fledged professional association with a profound influence on the development and legitimization of the field of southern women's history. The interviews in this book tell that story in wonderfully full anecdotal detail. But it is worth summarizing beforehand how it all came about.

In the minds of many historians the most important pieces of legislation for equalizing employment opportunities for women were the Equal

Pay Act of 1963 and the Civil Rights Act of 1964.[2] The latter forbade discrimination in employment on account of race, but inclusion of the word *sex* added a whole new category of protection. The addition was offered as an amendment from the floor by Virginia Congressman Howard W. Smith in an attempt to defeat the bill, but supporters of women's equality took the wording seriously. The indefatigable Congresswoman Martha Griffiths shamed many of the members of the committee into accepting women as a protected category and pushed the bill through to a vote. Griffiths, formerly a member of the National Woman's Party, was amazed by the fact that members of the House told jokes, laughed, and ridiculed the very real discrimination experienced by women. When she spoke to the members of Congress, she pointed out that black women might be turned away from jobs on account of their sex as well as their race, and certainly white women could be as well. "Your mothers, your wives, your widows, your daughters, your sisters . . . will be the last hired and the first fired. Why are you doing this?" she railed. "Add sex."[3] In the Senate, Republican Everett Dirksen tried to eliminate the word *sex* from the bill, but he was stopped in his tracks by the efforts of Griffiths, Senator Margaret Chase Smith, and members of the National Woman's Party. Moreover, President Lyndon Johnson supported the amendment and signed the bill into law on July 2, 1964. When congressmen and senators finally "got it," if only out of self-interest, women had a tool with which to begin to seek employment equity.[4]

Passage of the Civil Rights Act of 1964 was just the beginning, however. Tools, to be effective, must be used, and at first the Equal Employment

2. Flora Davis, *Moving the Mountain: The Women's Movement in America since 1960* (Urbana: University of Illinois Press, 1999), 39–43; Carl M. Brauer, "Women Activists, Southern Conservatives, and the Prohibition of Sex Discrimination in Title VII of the 1964 Civil Rights Act," *Journal of Southern History* 49 (February 1983): 37–56.

3. Martha Griffiths, interview, in *A Century of Women: Work and Family*, Turner Broadcasting System, 1994; Davis, *Moving the Mountain*, 42–44.

4. Title VII of the Civil Rights Act of 1964, Equal Employment Opportunity, Section 703:

"It shall be an unlawful employment practice for an employer

(1) to fail or refuse to hire or to discharge any individual, or otherwise to discriminate against any individual with respect to his compensation, terms, conditions, or privileges of employment, because of such individual's race, color, religion, sex, or national origin; or

(2) to limit, segregate, or classify his employees or applicants for employment in any way which would deprive or tend to deprive any individual of employment opportunities or otherwise adversely affect his status as an employee, because of such individual's race, color, religion, sex, or national origin."

Opportunity Commission (EEOC), created by the Civil Rights Act, was more willing to pursue cases of racial than of sex discrimination. As with many laws, enforcement depended on the willingness of individuals to report illegalities and sue for legal protection. As few working women found promotion in their job situations, as newspapers continued to print help-wanted ads divided by male and female, and as single mothers found themselves denied training in corporate programs *because* they were mothers, it became clear that women needed their own organizations to combat deeply ingrained attitudes of sex discrimination and demand equal employment opportunities.[5]

In 1966, with creation of the National Organization for Women (NOW), an opportunity for combat emerged. Founded by Betty Friedan and three hundred charter members, NOW dedicated itself to taking sex discrimination cases before the EEOC—and to court. NOW offered women another means to help break down gender barriers. Other groups followed: the Women's Equity Action League (WEAL), Federally Employed Women, the National Federation of Business and Professional Women. They and others began to clamor for equal opportunities in education, work, and politics, with promising early results. Executive Order 11375, signed by Lyndon Johnson, forbade sex discrimination by the federal government or by its contractors. WEAL, encouraged by legal remedies already in place, filed sex discrimination complaints against three hundred colleges and universities for not hiring and promoting women. NOW moved in the same way against thirteen hundred corporations that had contracts with the government. Faced with the loss of federal funding, universities, colleges, and corporations were forced to reconsider their hiring and promotion practices. Meanwhile radical feminists began to challenge the entire gender-based structure of society, pushing traditional thinking about women and men beyond conventional boundaries and into the realm of absolute equality.[6]

By 1970, a multiplicity of organizations had emerged to face issues of exclusion and sex discrimination in occupations and professions. Somewhere between 80,000 and 100,000 women joined associations for support, for consciousness-raising, or for the purpose of fighting against

5. Julia Kirk Blackwelder, *Now Hiring: The Feminization of Work in the United States, 1900–1995* (College Station: Texas A&M University Press, 1997), 180–82.
6. Sara Evans, *Personal Politics: The Roots of Women's Liberation in the Civil Rights Movement and the New Left* (New York: Vintage, 1980), 212–32; Judith Hole and Ellen Levine, *Rebirth of Feminism* (New York: Quadrangle Books, 1971), 30–44; Cynthia Fuchs Epstein, "Ten Years Later: Perspectives on the Women's Movement," *Dissent* 22 (Spring 1975): 169–79.

discrimination. In 1971, the National Women's Political Caucus (NWPC) added its support to enforcement of the Civil Rights Act *and* to the adoption of an Equal Rights Amendment (ERA). By challenging the Democratic and Republican parties to increase the number of women delegates to national conventions, to include women's issues in the party platforms, and to deliver support to female candidates, NWPC modeled for many other groups tactics and strategies that would help them fight male intransigence toward women's issues and male reluctance to include women in power sharing. The lessons to women's professional organizations were being taught at the national level. Following this, in 1972 came Title IX of the Higher Education Act, which made it illegal to discriminate against women in educational institutions. Thus legal codes offering protection to women workers, combined with political action and feminist consciousness, imparted to women a newfound inspiration to defy existing systems of entrenched sexism and gender discrimination.[7]

Women aspiring to enter the professions were among those who found that they had suffered severely because of sex discrimination. Law schools, medical schools, veterinary colleges, and university graduate programs often put quotas on the number of women admitted. As late as 1970, women still faced discrimination in admittance to graduate schools and in hiring and promotion in universities. By 1975 most of these disabilities for women had been removed, and by 1980 women were earning one-fourth of all doctorates and other professional degrees. This meant that hospitals, law firms, and universities had to keep an open mind about hiring and promoting women both because of the law and because the pool of women applicants was growing. However, while sex discrimination declined in graduate school admissions policies, women scholars still found themselves disadvantaged compared with men in the academic job market and in departments of history. By 1981 fewer than 50 percent of full-time faculty women were tenured, compared with 70 percent of men.[8]

As women scholars began to study the lives of women in the past,

7. Blackwelder, *Now Hiring,* 182; Carol Hymowitz and Michaele Weissman, *A History of Women in America* (New York: Bantam Books, 1978), 368–69; William H. Chafe, *Women and Equality: Changing Patterns in American Culture* (New York: Oxford University Press, 1977), 145–68; Glenda Riley, *Inventing the American Woman: An Inclusive History* (Wheeling, IL: Harlan Davidson, 1995), 348–9; Davis, *Moving the Mountain,* 211–20.

8. Blackwelder, *Now Hiring,* 186; Nancy Woloch, *Women and the American Experience* (Boston: McGraw Hill, 2000), 542; William H. Chafe, *The Unfinished Journey: America since World War II,* 2nd ed. (New York: Oxford University Press, 1991), 435; Davis, *Moving the Mountain,* 219.

even their subject matter conspired against equality for professional women historians. Feminists already in academia noted the paucity of courses dealing with women's issues. Prior lack of protection seems to have had a profound effect on the writing of women's history because most historians who wanted to contribute to this field were women. In a profession dominated by men, who legitimated the topics of importance, women's history was considered by many as nonsubstantive history. Until professional women historians could feel safe in writing women's history—until they could count on publications, job promotion, tenure, and respectability—women's history languished. New curriculum approaches in the 1970s also began to change the situation, and intellectual content that included and focused on women became a reality on college campuses, in part due to the efforts of seven Washington feminists who wrote a bill to provide funds for women's studies and to revise textbooks that excluded or derided women's achievements. The bill, called the Women's Educational Equity Act, was never passed outright, but thanks to Senator Walter Mondale, it was absorbed into the Senate's 1973 education bill as an amendment. In 1977 the National Women's Studies Association was founded. Thus universities became central to the feminist revolution, expanding courses dealing with women and hiring faculty for women's studies programs. By 1990, women's studies courses could be found in two-thirds of all universities; the number of women's studies programs swelled to over 300 with 30,000 course offerings.[9] Although men as well as women could teach such courses, and a few did and still do, the new women's studies programs offered increasing opportunities for hiring and promotion of women faculty.

In the midst of national trends to end sex discrimination through legislation, to increase women's consciousness-raising efforts, and to acknowledge the economic realities of women in the workforce, a growing number of professional women formed associations devoted to the promotion and advancement of women in the professions. The first activists to do this were within the American Sociological Association in 1969. One year later, four advisory bodies and five independent women's caucuses had emerged to observe, monitor, and report on the status of women in their disciplines. By 1971 fifty such associations existed. It was in this atmosphere that women historians, mostly from the South and mostly working in southern colleges and universities, founded the Southern Association for Women Historians.[10]

9. Davis, *Moving the Mountain*, 212–14, 223.
10. Ibid., 220.

The expansion of American higher education in the 1960s had led to a short-term growth in the demand for college and university teachers in all disciplines and in the growth of graduate programs in history. The result was a significant expansion by the late 1960s in the number of young women who entered and completed Ph.D. programs in history. Like women in the larger society, these young women quickly realized that their opportunities to participate fully in the life of their chosen profession did not correspond to their increasing presence in that profession. The primary professional associations—the American Historical Association, and the Organization of American Historians—had long been dominated by male professors. The Berkshire Conference of Women Historians, founded in 1930 to meet the special needs of the women who taught at the "Seven Sisters" colleges in New England, had begun its expansion into a national and international women's history organization, but it still seemed focused on its own region. By the late 1960s, women historians had begun to demand that the historical profession as a whole provide women opportunities to participate: through equal treatment in the job market; as presenters of papers at professional meetings; as reviewers of books and authors in the scholarly journals; and as committee members and leaders in their organizations.

The first truly national organization of women historians resulted from the determination of a few women to back those demands with action. Berenice A. Carroll circulated an invitation to interested women to gather at the annual meeting of the American Historical Association in Washington, D.C., in December 1969; Carroll had also drafted a petition calling on the AHA council to take steps to improve the status of women in the historical profession. At that 1969 meeting the AHA did appoint a Committee on the Status of Women (it became a permanent committee in 1971), charging it with studying issues related to women in the profession in order to recommend future action. While praising this encouraging step, the twenty-five women meeting in response to Carroll's invitation nevertheless decided to form an independent organization, which they named the Coordinating Committee on Women in the Historical Profession (CCWHP), "in order to reflect the group's concern with both the status of women in the profession and the development of women's history as a scholarly field."[11] By 1975, the latter determination to support the emergence of a new historical field led to the creation of a closely linked

11. Hilda Smith, Nupur Chaudhuri, and Gerda Lerner, *A History of the Coordinating Committee on Women in the Historical Profession—Conference Group on Women's History* (CCWHP-CGWH, 1989), 7–8

but separate group with an organizational structure and name of its own, the Conference Group on Women's History (CGWH).

The demand of women historians for a voice in existing professional associations, and an interest in forming new historical organizations specifically for women, was not limited to the national level. Women on the West Coast created the West Coast Historical Conference in 1969 (later renamed the West Coast Association of Women Historians.)[12] Southern women historians shared the same concerns voiced at the AHA and on the West Coast. They found a glimmer of hope in the success of a few women historians who had reached the presidency of the Southern Historical Association (Ella Lonn in 1946, Kathryn Hanna in 1953, and Mary Elizabeth Massey in 1972) or who had served recently on the executive council of the SHA (Mary Elizabeth Massey from 1959–1961, A. Elizabeth Taylor in 1963–1964, and Elsie M. Lewis in 1969).[13] From the founding of the SHA in 1935 until 1972, only three women had been elected president and ten elected to the SHA's executive council. Women actually were better represented on the council in the 1930s than in the 1940s, 1950s, and 1960s. By 1970 no woman had served on the *Journal of Southern History* board of editors since Nannie Tilley in 1952. The incidence of women serving on the SHA executive council, board of editors, and as chairs of important committees did not improve much during the decade of the 1970s. Between 1970 and 1981 one woman, LaWanda Cox, was named to the board of editors; only four women served on the executive council (A. Elizabeth Taylor, Anne Firor Scott, Memory F. Mitchell, and LaWanda Cox). No women chaired the nominating, program, or membership committees. Women were better represented on the award committees. This paucity of women scholars in important decision-making bodies was not unique to the SHA, but could be found in the AHA as well, proving the need for a second wave of feminism to combat entrenched sexism and to open doors for professional women historians.[14]

12. Ibid., 9–10.
13. See Mary Elizabeth Massey's presidential address to the annual meeting of the SHA in Hollywood-by-the-Sea, Florida, November 1972, "The Making of a Feminist," *Journal of Southern History* 39 (February 1973): 3–22. At the time she was professor of history at Winthrop College, Rock Hill, South Carolina. See also Carol Bleser, ed., "The Three Women Presidents of the Southern Historical Association: Ella Lonn, Kathryn Abby Hanna, and Mary Elizabeth Massey," *Southern Studies* 20 (Summer 1981): 101–21.
14. Jacqueline Goggin writes, "In 1930, 16 percent of academic women historians were full professors; in 1970, there were none. From World War II through the 1960s, recognition of women in the AHA also declined. Fewer women presented papers at annual meetings, fewer served on committees, and women were not elected to office in the same proportion as earlier years. . . . greater recognition for women was dashed on the rocks of entrenched sexual discrimination. Forty-five years would pass before

Several of the women who had been present in Washington, D.C., at the initial CCWHP "caucus" in December 1969 organized an ad hoc gathering in November 1970 at the annual meeting of the SHA in Louisville, Kentucky. Some of the thirty women who attended later remembered that organizational meeting "next to the boiler room" in the basement of the Kentucky Hotel as a turning point in their professional lives as women historians. At that meeting, the group set itself two broad, long-range goals: to seek out information on grants, opportunities for fellowships, and recruitment of women into the profession; and to "get some kind of women's history courses into the curriculum of our schools."[15] A small group of volunteers—Mollie C. Davis, Constance Ashton Myers, Barbara Brandon Schnorrenberg, and Charlotte M. Davis—agreed to work to keep the "Caucus of Women Historians" alive by sending out a newsletter and undertaking other tasks as they arose. It should be noted that Myers also had a role in the CCWHP steering committee, and Mollie Davis would become a cochairwoman of CCWHP in 1973; thus, from the beginning the SAWH was a part of the national coordination of women historians through the CCWHP. Mollie Davis and Charlotte Davis edited the newsletter ("Not Nepotism" they assured readers in their first issue), collected members' dues (two dollars) to cover postage of the newsletter, and arranged with SHA General Secretary-Treasurer Bennett H. Wall for a room for a meeting of interested women at the next annual meeting of the Southern (SHA). From these informal beginnings an agenda emerged:

1) the need to study the general status of women in the profession in the South. After the release by the AHA in 1970 of the "Rose Report," the influential first publication of the AHA Committee on the Status of Women chaired by Willie Lee Rose, southern women realized they too needed detailed information about the names, numbers, and status of women in history departments and history graduate programs in the region.

2) a focus on the status of women within the SHA. "Caucus" members saw themselves as an integral part of the SHA and wanted to work with

---

another woman would be elected president" ("Challenging Sexual Discrimination in the Historical Profession: Women Historians and the American Historical Association, 1890–1940," *American Historical Review* 97 [June 1992]: 802). See also, Bennett H. Wall, "The Southern Historical Association, 1935–1970: A Compilation of Officers and Other Data," *Journal of Southern History* 36 (August 1970): 389–99. The Sydnor Award Committee was chaired in 1972 by LaWanda Cox and in 1978 by Emma Lou Thornbrough; A. Elizabeth Taylor chaired the Ramsdell Award Committee in 1973 and Carol Bleser chaired it in 1974. Bennett H. Wall, "The Southern Historical Association, 1970–1979: A Compilation of Officers and Other Data," *Journal of Southern History* 45 (August 1979), 413–19.

15. SAWH *Newsletter* 1, no. 1 (April 1971).

its leadership to create a permanent committee in the association on the state of women, even as they supported the independence of their own organization. The first issue of the *Newsletter* had initially congratulated the SHA: "Since 1935 we have had two women presidents, a number of women on the executive council, three times a woman chaired the nominating committee, and of course at the moment we have a woman vice president [Mary Elizabeth Massey]."[16] The *Newsletter* regularly encouraged its readers to become more active in the SHA by paying its dues, voting in its elections, and attending its annual meeting. Nevertheless, women remained underrepresented on scholarly paper panels, as book reviewers, and in other roles in the association, and statistical reports on these issues became regular features of the SAWH.

3) encouragement of scholarship on women, to be facilitated through a systematic study of archival and manuscript sources for such scholarship available in the South, and the sharing of information on research in progress by and about women.

To achieve these ambitious goals a more formal organizational structure was needed. Between 1972 and 1985, the fledgling organization grew rapidly from an informal caucus to a well-organized association. In 1972–1973 Barbara Schnorrenberg became secretary-treasurer, a post she held until 1986, giving the new organization the much-needed stability of a permanent contact address. At the November 1975 SHA meeting in Washington, D.C., the Caucus of Women Historians of the Southern Historical Association adopted a set of bylaws, drafted by Rosemary Carroll, and a new name, the Southern Association of Women Historians. A companion proposal to raise the dues to $5 was rejected; they remained at $2 until 1977, when they were raised to $3.50, where they remained until 1985 when a new set of bylaws was adopted. These 1985 bylaws augmented the previous simple structure of an elected governing committee of president, vice president, and secretary-treasurer by the addition of new elective offices of first and second vice presidents and a managing editor. The new bylaws also expanded the simple committee structure of program, nominations, and local arrangements committees with the creation of new committees on publicity, awards, finance, audit, and membership. After 1985 an executive committee of officers was authorized to carry on SAWH business between annual November meetings. At that time, the organization's name was changed to the more inclusive Southern Association *for* Women Historians, reflecting a determination to admit to membership all historians in or outside of the

16. Ibid.

South, whether male or female, who supported its goals of advancing the status of women in the historical profession in the South and stimulating interest in the study of southern women's history.

The structure created in 1974 and expanded in 1985 gave the SAWH the flexibility to provide a growing range of information and services to its members. SAWH meetings became an established feature of the SHA annual meetings. At Atlanta in 1979, SAWH initiated its first annual meeting address with a talk by A. Elizabeth Taylor. Rather than following the practice of many organizations of a presidential address, each SAWH president instead invited a leading scholar of the history of women to give a lecture. Over the years those sessions attracted a growing audience of men and women. Several of the women whose interviews follow considered the lectures to be a key element in the growth in respectability and importance both of the SAWH and of the scholarship on southern women that the lectures featured.

The *Newsletter*, published three times a year, expanded to include information about jobs and funding opportunities; news of the activities of other women's professional historical organizations, national and regional; and shared news of members. It also provided a forum for women faculty and graduate students to seek matching papers to create scholarly session proposals and for archives and manuscript repositories to announce the acquisition and opening of important records and collections for studying women's history.

Three additional goals were added to the SAWH agenda in this second period of its growth. Joining with the CCWPH, and the standing committees on the status of women in the AHA and the OAH, the SAWH committed itself to passage of the ERA. In 1979 SAWH leadership was instrumental in putting a successful resolution for support of the ERA on the agenda at the annual SHA business meeting. When the SHA voted (because of what it considered prohibitive hotel costs) to move its 1980 meeting from Washington, D.C., to Atlanta, Georgia, SAWH president Judith F. Gentry wrote a strenuous letter of objection to meeting in a non-ERA state. Ultimately, the ERA was unsuccessful in a number of southern states, but the issues associated with the final push for its passage were embraced by many southern women historians through political action by the SAWH. It should be noted, as illustrated in the interviews below, that a few SAWH officers and members disagreed with this stance; their opposition was not to the ERA, but to the politicization of an organization which they regarded as primarily concerned with scholarship and women's role in the academy.

As the job market for academic historians declined in the early 1970s, and the percentage of women in graduate history programs continued to rise, SAWH members became increasingly concerned about the importance of mentoring and encouraging women graduate students. Shortly after the adoption of the 1985 bylaws, the committee structure was expanded to include a graduate student committee. This committee sponsored receptions for graduate students at the annual meeting and ensured that women graduate students in attendance were included in the important informal social networks central to professional meetings.

Finally, in this second phase of its development, under the leadership of Carol Bleser and others, the SAWH committed itself to a major fundraising effort to establish two prizes for scholarship by and about southern women. The endowments currently enable SAWH to award two prizes of $750 each. The Julia Cherry Spruill Prize, named in honor of the woman whose scholarship on southern women's history early in the twentieth century had inspired many members of the SAWH, is awarded for the best published book on southern women's history. The Willie Lee Rose Prize, named to honor the woman who had played a key role in improving the status of women historians, and whose serious illness prompted the creation of an award, is given for the best book on southern history authored by a woman. Now awarded annually, the prizes were initially given at the annual meeting only in odd-numbered years; the first prizes were awarded in 1987. Jacqueline Jones received the first Spruill prize for *Labor of Love, Labor of Sorrow: Black Women, Work, and the Family from Slavery to the Present,* and Anne C. Loveland received the Rose Prize for *Lillian Smith: A Southerner Confronting the South.*[17]

The first phase of the SAWH, between 1970 and 1975, was marked by a concentration on developing lines of communication and mutual support among southern women historians and on raising the consciousness of the profession in the region through documentation of the status and participation of southern women historians in teaching, publishing, presenting papers at conferences, and serving on committees. The work of the second phase of the organization, between 1975 and 1985, may best be characterized as consolidating its infrastructure. It then used that base both to participate in the political struggle in the South for adoption of the ERA, and to contribute to the development and growth of the field of southern women's history, among other things through presentation of distinguished lectures at SHA conferences, and the awarding of prizes

17. Jacqueline Jones, *Labor of Love, Labor of Sorrow: Black Women, Work, and the Family from Slavery to the Present* (New York: Basic Books, 1985); Anne C. Loveland, *Lillian Smith: A Southerner Confronting the South* (Baton Rouge: Louisiana State University Press, 1986).

for important scholarly work in the field. In the third phase of the organization's development, from 1985 to 1995, SAWH moved beyond its own borders and reached outside its own organizational structure to undertake several important new professional initiatives, which have transformed it into an organization with a national, even an international, identity and impact.

An important new initiative undertaken by the SAWH as a result of its 1985 structural reorganization was the establishment of an institutional home. During her 1985 presidency, Darlene Clark Hine articulated the need for additional staff to provide help with the expanded finances created by the fundraising and the administration of the prize funds. When Barbara Schnorrenberg resigned from her joint position of secretary-treasurer and *Newsletter* editor at the 1985 board meeting, the need became critical. Theda Perdue, SAWH president in 1986 and then on the faculty of Clemson University, working with Carol K. Bleser, president of the SAWH in 1980 and also a professor of history at Clemson University, persuaded their university to support the association with office space and a part-time staff person. Thus, in 1986, Rameth Owens, a part-time member of the Clemson history faculty, became the secretary-treasurer of SAWH, a position she held until 1992, when the office of SAWH moved to the University of Arkansas at Fayetteville, and Suzanne Maberry became its secretary-treasurer and *Newsletter* editor. Institutional support from the home institution(s) of the SAWH secretary-treasurer and *Newsletter* editor for preparing and mailing the *Newsletter*, assistance from students, and help with other crucial administrative tasks have subsequently come from Agnes Scott College in Atlanta, Georgia, Wake Forest University in Winston-Salem, North Carolina (Michele Gillespie), and Converse College in Spartanburg, South Carolina (Melissa Walker).

Institutional support became necessary in part because the growth in membership—over four hundred individuals by 1990—made it difficult for a single person operating without assistance to provide basic services to SAWH members. But institutional support also made it possible for the organization to undertake another initiative that moved the organization outward toward a growing scholarly audience interested in and contributing to the field of southern women's history. Planning began early in 1988 for the First Southern Conference on Women's History, to be held at Converse College in Spartanburg, South Carolina. Converse was celebrating its one hundredth anniversary as a college for women, and its administration welcomed the SAWH to the "sheltered gardens" of its campus as part of that event. The impetus for holding an SAWH-sponsored conference came in part from the example of the enormous success of the triennial Berkshire Conferences—the "Big Berks"—initiated in 1973, which in 1984 drew nearly two thousand participants to its Sixth Conference on the History of Women held at Smith College.[18] Several leaders of SAWH had participated in the Big Berks, but they were concerned that women faculty and graduate students at smaller colleges or regional universities within the South did not have the financial support to travel to New England. Moreover, a growing body of scholarship on southern women's history suggested the need for historians working in the field to exchange ideas.

That First Southern Conference on Women's History, held in June of 1988, succeeded far beyond the hopes of its organizers. Nearly four hundred women (and a few men) attended, ranging from graduate students participating in their first conference to the most senior scholars in the field. Discussions begun in formal sessions were continued in the dining halls and even late into the night in the hallways and lounges of the student dormitories housing participants. One such discussion, begun at a session on the difficulties of writing scholarly biographies of contemporary women, led to the immediate design, and the eventual publication, of a book entitled *The Challenge of Feminist Biography*, edited by Sara Alpern, Joyce Antler, Elisabeth Israels Perry, and Ingrid Winther Scobie for the University of Illinois Press in 1992. The success of that conference made its continuation a major thrust of SAWH planning and activities from then on. A second conference in 1991 at the University of North Carolina at Chapel Hill, a third at Rice University in 1994, a fourth at the College of Charleston in 1997, a fifth at the University of Richmond in 2000, and a sixth at the University of Georgia in 2003 testify to the growing vitality of scholarship on the history of southern women, and the important role SAWH has played in nourishing and promoting it.

From the conferences grew yet another initiative: the decision to edit and publish the best of the papers presented at conference sessions. The University of Missouri Press published the first of these volumes, *Southern Women: Histories and Identities*, in 1992 drawing on papers from the First Southern Conference on Women's History. To date, four more volumes of essays have appeared, all included in a Southern Women series, which was initiated by the press in cooperation with the SAWH.[19]

18. See the web site for the Berkshire Conference, http://www.berksconference.org (accessed May 6, 2004) for the history of both the "Little Berks" and the "Big Berks," as the conferences are known.

19. The following volumes are all in the Southern Women series of the University of Missouri Press: Virginia Bernhard, Betty Brandon, Elizabeth Fox-Genovese, and Theda Perdue, eds., *Southern Women: Histories and Identities*, 1992; Virginia Bernhard,

The maturing of scholarship in the field of southern women's history and recognition of the importance of the role of the SAWH as a major influence on it has brought women historians in and of the South, and all scholars of the history of southern women, whatever their gender or geographic location, into increased visibility at the SHA. The receptions organized by the SAWH local arrangements committees at the annual fall meeting of the SHA, often held at historic venues such as museums and historic houses, are now major social events with a large attendance. Indeed, several of the interviews in this volume express the conviction that the annual SAWH "party," begun on a small scale in Carol Bleser's hotel room in the early 1980s, should share equal billing with the scholarly address that precedes it for raising the visibility of the organization within the SHA. The scholarly addresses of the SAWH annual meeting have become major intellectual events, their contributions gathered together by editors Michele Gillespie and Catherine Clinton into a volume in the University of Missouri Press Southern Women series, *Taking off the White Gloves: Southern Women and Women Historians* (1998). In addition the SAWH created in 1989 the A. Elizabeth Taylor Prize, awarded annually for the best article published during the preceding year in the field of southern women's history. It was first awarded in 1992. A. Elizabeth Taylor's career was devoted to the history of the woman suffrage movement in the South, and her main contribution to this scholarship was via articles published in scholarly journals. To encourage and foster excellence among graduate students, the SAWH also established the Jacquelyn Dowd Hall Prize for the best papers submitted by a graduate student to the Southern Conference on Women's History. The SAWH recognized Hall at the University of North Carolina as an outstanding mentor and graduate advisor, hence she was honored by this prize, first awarded in 1992.

Finally, in this third phase of its history, the SAWH has become a much more inclusive organization, reaching out and encouraging women of color to become part of its membership base, to participate in its leadership, and to contribute to scholarship shared at its conferences. Darlene

---

Betty Brandon, Elizabeth Fox-Genovese, Theda Perdue, and Elizabeth H. Turner, eds., *Hidden Histories of Women in the New South*, 1994; Janet L. Coryell, Martha H. Swain, Sandra Gioia Treadway, and Elizabeth Hayes Turner, eds., *Beyond Image and Convention: Explorations in Southern Women's History*, 1998; Janet L. Coryell, Thomas H. Appleton, Jr., Anastatia Sims, and Sandra Gioia Treadway, eds., *Negotiating Boundaries of Southern Womanhood: Dealing with the Powers That Be*, 2000; Thomas H. Appleton, Jr., and Angela Boswell, eds., *Searching for Their Places: Women in the South across Four Centuries*, 2003.

Clark Hine became the first African American president in 1985, followed by Elsa Barkley Brown in 1993, and Jacqueline A. Rouse in 2001. This inclusiveness represents a welcomed change from the beginning decade of the organization. Many of the founders and early leaders had themselves been active in the civil rights movement in the South. When asked in their interviews specifically about the presence of African American women in the organization then, however, most remember both that there were few women of color either at the meetings of the SHA or of the early gatherings of the caucus of women historians and that recruiting them was not a high priority. That may have been in part a result of the paucity of black women historians. Whatever the cause, by the late 1980s, led by women like Hine and stimulated by a growing activism of African American women historians within the larger profession, the SAWH began consciously to address this problem, recognizing at the same time the justness of demands for more study of the history of African American women.

At its twenty-fifth anniversary celebration, the SAWH could look back with pride on the long journey its members had made within the historical profession as well as forward to a challenging future. A new generation of scholars, trained in southern women's history, moved into key leadership roles in the organization. Like their predecessors, whose thoughts are reflected in the interviews in the remainder of this book, the younger generation sees a continued need for the SAWH as a separate women's organization even as southern women historians achieve leadership roles in and are recognized for their scholarly distinction by major national organizations like the OAH, the AHA, and the SHA. The presidential leadership after 1995 of women like Catherine Clinton, who put enormous energy into promoting and expanding the publication efforts of the SAWH, or of Marjorie Spruill Wheeler, Drew Faust, and Jacqueline Rouse in expanding the role of graduate students, in cementing relations with the SHA, and expanding the presence of African American women in the organization, have all helped to ensure that the SAWH will continue to thrive as an organization of and for southern women historians, promoting the study of southern women's history.

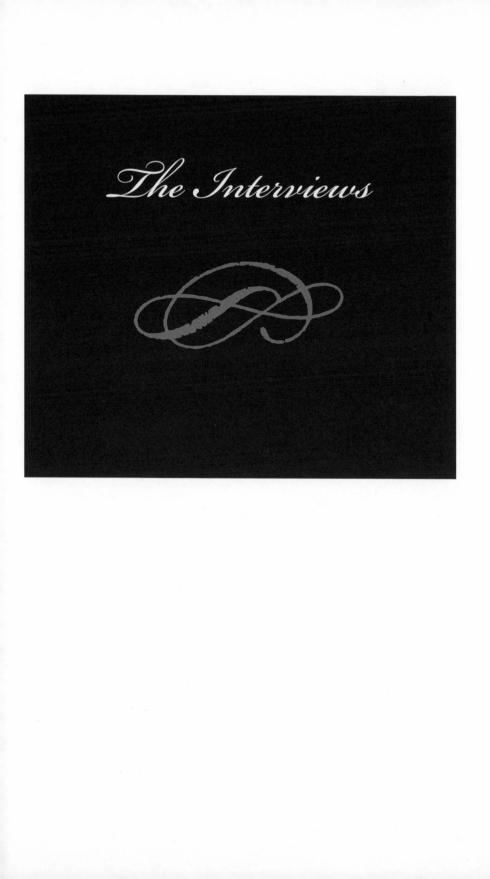

The Interviews

Pathfinders

Before 1970, women historians in the South could turn to few role models for professional guidance within the Southern Historical Association.[1] Two women had served as presidents of the SHA: Ella Lonn, a scholar of the Confederacy and Reconstruction, elected in 1945 to serve as the association's twelfth president; and Kathryn T. Abbey Hanna, the nineteenth president of the SHA, elected in 1953, who studied Confederate exiles in Venezuela. Other women had been chosen for leadership roles in the SHA, serving on program committees, on prize committees, and on the Executive Council, most notably A. Elizabeth Taylor and Mary Elizabeth Massey.

Taylor and Massey were scholars who had studied the lives of southern women. During the centennial of the Civil War, Massey contributed a volume on women's roles in the North and the South, *Bonnet Brigades*, published in 1966. She became the thirty-eighth president of the Southern in 1972. Taylor, as she relates below, made the study of southern suffragists

1. Scott, ed., *Unheard Voices*, provides in her introduction a detailed description of the lives and careers of a number of southern women historians, among them Julia Cherry Spruill. In 1970, these women and their scholarship were relatively unknown.

her life's work. Ironically, she insisted until the end of her life that she was not doing women's history at all, but a fuller version of American history that included women.

Anne Firor Scott, whose book *The Southern Lady: From Pedestal to Politics, 1830–1930* appeared in 1970, represented a new generation of scholars, a talented wave of historians who would create a new field of scholarship in southern women's history. She too had begun to play an active role in the major historical professional associations by 1970. Massey's death from cancer shortly after her presidential term, and Taylor's and Scott's increasing responsibilities in the SHA and other organizations, meant that while they supported the purposes of the new southern "caucus" of women historians, they did not take leadership roles in the early years.

In quite different ways, Taylor and Scott were "pathfinders" for the women who worked together to create an organization of women historians within the South. Both had benefited early in their careers from the advantages created for women scholars during the Second World War, receiving fellowships, taking advantage of opportunities that otherwise would have been offered to young men, in Taylor's case, or being thrust into the excitement of wartime Washington, in Scott's case. Both became important mentors for later generations of young women scholars. Of different scholarly generations themselves, the two women took different approaches to the ways in which the study of women in the South should be incorporated into the "canon" of historical scholarship and divergent pathways to success in the historical profession. The two women differed too in their personal circumstances, reflecting the variety of choices and experiences which still affect the lives of professional women. Readers will notice a common thread running through the interviews: choices made in the subjects' personal lives affect the contours of their professional lives. Some scholars, like Scott, married and raised children while pursuing their research and writing; others, like Taylor, remained single and devoted their lives to their universities and their students.

Younger readers of these two interviews will be amazed (and perhaps amused) at some of the experiences the women relate of carrying out research in the decades before the technological advances scholars enjoy today. As Taylor recalls, though microfilming had begun to make some sources more generally available, normally one had to travel to repositories in every state for the sources of women's history, and once there take extensive notes rather than make photocopies. Her tale of being allowed by one archivist to take documents home overnight reflects a time when manuscript curators were less security conscious than today.

A. Elizabeth Taylor

The late A. Elizabeth Taylor was the Minnie Stevens Piper Professor at Texas Woman's University, where she taught from 1943 until 1981. She earned her Ph.D. in American History from Vanderbilt University in 1943. She is the author of *The Woman Suffrage Movement in Tennessee* (1957) and of numerous articles, especially concerning woman suffrage in the South. From 1942 until 1980, she published in state and regional journals fourteen articles on the southern woman suffrage movements in Georgia, Tennessee, Texas, Arkansas, Florida, North Carolina, Mississippi, and South Carolina. At least four of her articles have been reprinted in anthologies. The SAWH has honored her by naming its award for the best article in southern women's history the A. Elizabeth Taylor Prize.

Interviewer: Pamela Dean
Transcriber: Toni N. Smart
The following interview took place November 5, 1992.

E. T.: My name is Antoinette Elizabeth Taylor. I was known as Elizabeth, and now my legal signature is A. Elizabeth Taylor. The other is a little too long. I was born in Columbus, Georgia, in 1917, the daughter of Angie Mae Miller Taylor and Thomas Earl Taylor. They were a young couple when I was born. My father was a merchant; he owned several businesses but settled down to a shoe store, a family style shoe store. My mother taught a year or so before she married. Housewives had so much to do in those days, there was little thought of any extra time. In time my father's business prospered, and we got a better house and all, but I never had any problems as a child in terms of my future. The marriage was stable, and I guess all my public schools were fortunate, but the high school in Columbus, Georgia, then the public high, was more like a private school today. Of course, times have changed a lot. And there were two there. One emphasized vocational things, and the other, college preparatory. It was always taken for granted that I would go to college, of course.

P. D.: Had your mother gone to college?

E. T.: Yes, she went to Valdosta, which was a two-year college. And my father did not go to college; he went into business. But they were always great believers in college, assumed that children would go to college. All around first cousins, the next generation, would go on to college. And so, just where would I go? Well, for no special good reasoning, except the availability, the University of Georgia. Women had been going there since World War I, but they were just beginning really to make it coed. Because I thought it was interesting, I decided on history but had no particular thoughts about women. And then I went to the University of North Carolina at Chapel Hill. I liked the idea of college teaching; I liked subject matter. And so it was that phase of college teaching that attracted me especially. I went on from University of Georgia to Chapel Hill and got a master's.

P. D.: Who did you work with at Chapel Hill?

E. T.: Fletcher [M.] Green. And I didn't have a good dissertation idea. I thought of several things, but finally, I think it was really at his suggestion that I chose the convict lease system in Georgia. I wrote a master's thesis on that, which was published as two articles in the *Georgia Historical Quarterly.*

P. D.: When was this, precisely? When did you finish your master's?

E. T.: I finished my bachelor's in 1938; and I finished the master's January 1, 1940. I was ready for a job on the college level; of course, I'd take any one I could get and be thankful, but as luck would have it, there was a vacancy at Judson College, a Baptist woman's college in Marion, Alabama. This is woman's stuff: the head of the department, Bessie Martin, her mother became ill, and she took a leave to take care of her mother. So I was asked to come over and just be there that semester. I was tickled to go, and meanwhile a high school job did open up for the next fall, but I was quite smitten, liked everything about college better than high school. Then Dr. Martin decided to extend her leave due to her mother's need. So I was asked to come back for the year. While there, quite by chance, I came across this six-volume history of woman suffrage. I had not known of that standard work. Five years of college, Phi Beta Kappa, and supposedly a good student, I was unaware of that.

P. D.: How did you come across it?

E. T.: Just happened to be browsing in the library at Judson, and I just picked that. Of course I'd heard of the woman suffrage movement, but that was about it. I just happened to start looking in there, and I thought, well, this is interesting; this is good material. I wonder what's been done? Maybe I should think about this for my dissertation. I found my subject quite by accident as if some divine power had guided me to that. But I was attracted to it, and so I thought, well, I'd like to do something in this. So I began. Well, would anybody tolerate it? I knew it would not be easily approved. As luck would have it, I got a fellowship at Vanderbilt University. Now, once again, World War II, and the men were being called. So that's the only reason they gave one to a woman. They admitted it; everybody admitted it. They said, "Oh, we think women are good students, but you know, these go to men." That was the way the world was. Anyway, I went to Vanderbilt and had this idea of working on woman suffrage. The men there were a very gentlemanly-like faculty (and I imagine they still are) and agreed that I could work on it, and it's a wonder they did, because a lot of places just wouldn't accept a subject like that. You know, just didn't think it was worthwhile.

P. D.: Who was on your committee?

E. T.: William B. Hesseltine and Frank Owsley. He [Owsley] wasn't especially interested, but he was always very sympathetic, and Daniel Robison, who later became editor of the *Tennessee Historical Quarterly.* They were the three main ones. Henry Lee Swint was a young instructor there.

But anyway, they approved. I was going to do the South just as an idea. Oh, another thing that caught my eye—these maps, and they showed the states that did not ratify, the solid South, you might say. But, always, there's the ironic note in southern history. The one that completed ratification, the thirty-sixth state, was a southern state. You know, that seems to be true of the South all along. There's always the exception. So I started feeling my way along at Vanderbilt, working on the federal amendment just for a term paper. But then came World War II, and that meant that travel would be impossible. In those days, you almost had to go where the material was and stay for weeks and months. Maybe years. So after wondering what to do, they decided at Vanderbilt that there would probably be enough on Tennessee for me to do a dissertation. So I would just settle on Tennessee. Of course, they had a lot of Tennessee material there in the state archives. In fact, in the state archives they had a pretty good set of woman suffrage papers from Carrie Chapman Catt and people who worked in Tennessee. They hadn't done much in gathering the whole history, but they did have a pretty good manuscript collection for the time. So, I managed to get a dissertation on Tennessee, and while I was studying Tennessee, I found out more. I found out that the woman suffrage movement in Georgia started in Columbus, my hometown. I'd never heard that in all my years of being around. The sister of the woman who started it was still alive. I made a point of looking her up the next summer I was at home. She had a few things, and I scoured around town and found some information, and that was the basis for that article on the origins of the woman suffrage movement in Georgia.

Then a job opening came, but by then I wanted very much to continue to study woman suffrage. I said, "I wonder if it would hurt my job prospects." Jobs always could be a little scarce, but once again, World War II made a difference. They would take women in the absence of men. The head of the department at Texas Woman's University, then the Texas State College for Women, went into the army, so I was invited to come. I didn't take on the headship, but that's how I got the first job. It was a temporary job, but it became permanent after a year or so.

P. D.: Now they didn't hire you to teach women's history. What were you teaching?

E. T.: No, there was no women's history. I was teaching general U.S. history, political history. I never thought of what I did as women's history. I thought of it as U.S. history. I had no conception of women's history. I just thought it was a subject that had not been worked on much. I don't think anybody, until this new feminism, thought of it as a field in its own right. I still think of it more as just history, or recent American history, or twentieth-century history, if you want, with emphasis, with attention, to women.

Well, I began to inquire around about sending articles out for publication. Dr. Robison, who'd taken over the *Tennessee Historical Quarterly*, wanted an article on Tennessee. One of the first ones I submitted was some of my dissertation. I was told, "We think an article of this type is . . . better suited to the League of Women Voters' publication, or the AAUW." I finally did get it published in the *Georgia Historical Quarterly*. Then being on programs, the subject was also a handicap because I was told, "We don't have anything to pair yours with." In time, a few more women were entering the profession, and some women friends said, well, "I wouldn't want to be identified with a subject about women. That's just poison." They just thought I put myself at a disadvantage.

P. D.: To some degree were they right?

E. T.: Yes, they were right. I don't know if I'd have done any better, but they were right. I've never minded being a little bit off to myself. I kind of liked the idea that not so many people were interested in working on it. So, anyway, it built up, more and more.

Then I got the job in Texas, so I got an opportunity there. Of course, Texas had a good woman suffrage movement. They had some papers. Jane McCallum in Austin had a good collection, her papers and Minnie Fisher Cunningham's papers, and she let me work in those, and even let me bring them back to Denton. I made trips back and forth, because we couldn't just have the whole thing copied. Technology just wasn't that advanced. Now, Mrs. McCallum and Minnie Fisher Cunningham were active when the woman suffrage amendment was passed. And McCallum was later secretary of state for Texas. Cunningham ran for governor and for the U.S. Senate unsuccessfully, but where are their papers today? In public libraries; they should have been in university libraries. They were important papers, had a lot of things about the national and the Texas movement, too. As southern states went, that was about the best set I found. I talked to many suffragists through the years hoping they'd have fragments. When I worked over in Nashville, I tried to contact all kinds of people and did have quite a few interviews. Occasionally there would be a fragment, but I had to scurry around to get material. So it built up, and I published many articles.

P. D.: You were active in the Southern Historical Association.

E. T.: Yes, I was active in it from the very beginning and was on many committees, and offered the position of chairman, but often I would be the only woman. For a long time, I was the only woman on the Executive Council. They didn't have a quota; it just seemed to fall into that pattern. That's kind of the way it was, but then times changed and we got the Committee on Women in the SHA. So I, and Mollie Davis, and LaWanda Cox were the first ones. But we pointed out some things, and one of them was that there was a need for more than one woman on the SHA council, and that was sort of a breakthrough. After that we had lots of women on the council, but one at a time, you know. It wasn't consciously, we had just fallen into that pattern. I think that changing times more than anything else increased the number of women.

In the 1940s, we had no women's group, and I remember Ella Lonn saying, "Well, maybe we ought to have a women's breakfast." But the women weren't interested because many people felt that you shouldn't segregate yourself. So we didn't. Well nobody was too interested in having our membership; I believe she did make the suggestion, but nobody followed through on it.

We had a meeting in Houston, and I think some of us were going to try to get together. Martha Swain was in the group. It was before I knew her very well, and so we'd get together just informally. I think about five people did. That was about the time Mary Elizabeth Massey got to be president of the SHA. Mary Elizabeth Massey was a good friend of mine. She dressed beautifully, had a wonderful sense of humor, was an interesting person, a hard worker, and highly intelligent. She could get along with men in a way that I've never noticed another woman brought up in the South could get along with them quite as well. She knew what was going on, and would tell them, and tell them off, and do it in a way that they would take it or just laugh. She was strong for women, too, but she didn't believe in favoring women just because they're women. I don't believe in that either, but I certainly do want them to have a fair deal. And I want opportunities there for them.

P. D.: She didn't get involved with the SAWH, did she?

E. T.: She joined when she was president of the SHA. At that time her health was failing. She died a couple of years later. There were some doubts as to whether she was going to be able to deliver her presidential

address. So she came along too late. I don't know, this is really confiden-
tial, but she was slightly uneasy for fear they might do something that
would embarrass her as a woman and as SHA president. But she was
with the establishment; she was going along with the SAWH, but she
was a little bit worried. That was when women were having demonstra-
tions. That's so out of character, you know, for us women in the Southern
Historical Association, that she felt a slight uneasiness. But she joined,
and she would have supported it, and she would have told a lot of the
men off because she knew how to do it in a way that they would laugh
about but not forget. Her health was failing, and she did get through her
presidential address but had to sit down at the reception. Not a year or so
later, I guess it was, she died. Something I regret, that I could have done
something about or at least made a suggestion, was that the women didn't
do anything for her in honor of her presidency, like have a party. We gave
her no recognition as a woman president. I don't know that she was expecting it, but later some people said, "Well, did they do anything for the
woman president?" We just weren't well enough organized; we were just
kind of doing well to survive. Then in the old days we weren't always
sure what we were doing exactly, where we were going. She wasn't of-
fended, but I think she was slightly uneasy there might be a bra-burning
type that might want to make a scene or break up the business meeting,
or something, and she wanted things to go smoothly, naturally. And they
did, of course.

I wasn't present at the Louisville convention when this organization
was formed. But the next year, I remember Mollie Davis was really carrying the load, and I did go to the meeting of the SAWH, and about two
dozen of us met. Since then the SAWH has functioned well, and I'm just
astonished at the wonderful progress that it's made. And in time a new
generation came along because the older ones were retiring or ill or de-
ceased. The nature of it sort of changed when it moved up to Clemson
University. Then having these summer conferences, and now, the *Newsletter*. I'm delighted that we have the SAWH. I don't consider it a substi-
tute for the SHA, or hostile to the SHA. In fact, one thing that disturbs me
a little is the Willie Lee Rose Award. Only females are eligible. That worried me about men not having their rights. It disturbs me a little philo-
sophically, but I wouldn't argue about it. I don't know about this award
that's being given for the first time—you know, the Taylor Award—
whether that restriction is in it or not. As for women's history, I guess I've
never been a true disciple of women's history: just focus on U.S. history
with proper attention given to women and their role. I think women

have made enormous progress and do good work. I don't think men are as intimidated by women as they used to be. Now I don't think they hesitate to join a women's group.

P. D.: Let me ask you to think back, if you can, to when you first heard about the Southern Association for Women Historians. Did you think that it was a needed organization?

E. T.: Of course we've had several names along the way. I was interested enough to participate from the beginning. I didn't think it was an essential organization. I thought it was all right. I don't know that I would have been the motivator, and I didn't think we needed that for the role of women or that I needed it as a woman. I didn't think of that, but I guess I just thought that it would not be a bad idea. Rosemary Carroll was a strong supporter of this, and I know one time we worked on the constitution. I think she did a lot to help get that revised. But she and Barbara Schnorrenberg and Mollie Davis, they carried the ball. I became a life member way back, and now I make a donation when I see all they do, and wonder how they do it. I think it's almost a miracle that it has succeeded so well. It certainly has added to the prestige of women. I think it was Rosemary Carroll who wanted to call it the "Southern Association *for* Women Historians" instead of "*of* Women Historians." That is a slight but an important distinction. Well, I never dreamed when I attended my first SHA convention in 1940 in Charleston, South Carolina, that fifty-two years later I would still be attending and giving out an interview of this type. I never knew SAWH would endure, or whether it would increase. I didn't expect it to prosper as much as it has. It seemed to kind of branch out after that first summer conference in 1988 at Converse College in Spartanburg; I did go to that.

P. D.: Do you think the Southern Association for Women Historians has simply benefited from the changes; do you think that within the Southern Historical Association it has promoted the changing status of women?

E. T.: It has in some ways, like setting up these awards, and, of course, the SHA let them put the SAWH meeting on the program, and so I think both. It has helped nudge along the SHA Committee on Women. I think women are respected as historians in the SHA. This organization has helped that, and the women who have been in it have been women whom the men respected. Southern women have been more generally acceptable women, in manner and conduct, rather than sensational women.

Some people may think that was bad, that we ought to have some sensational ones, but the SAWH has been women who worked with, or to some extent within, the established order.

P. D.: They've behaved professionally.

E. T.: We have behaved professionally, and most of us have been well qualified, and a lot of people are definitely good scholars. So I think the SAWH has been a benefit to women. I think now it has professional standing. When I think how far we've come, I wonder why anybody still gets mad about things. I guess when you get older you know that you're never going to have perfection; you get something corrected and then something else comes along that you hadn't thought about, but that's another problem.

Anne Firor Scott

Anne Firor Scott is W. K. Boyd Professor of History Emerita of Duke University. She earned her Ph.D. in American History from Radcliffe College in 1958. Earlier she had worked as a research associate, congressional representative, and editor of the *National Voter* for the League of Women Voters. She is the author of three books, *The Southern Lady: From Pedestal to Politics, 1830–1930* (1970), *Making the Invisible Woman Visible* (1984), and *Natural Allies: Women's Associations in American History* (1991). She is co-author or editor of six books and has published over thirty articles and chapters in anthologies. She is the recipient of numerous fellowships, awards, and honorary doctorates. She has served on many boards, including the National Humanities Center. She is a senior editor for the Women in American History series for the University of Illinois Press and was a member of the President's Advisory Council on the Status of Women from 1964 to 1969. She was President of the Organization of American Historians from 1983 to 1984 and President of the Southern Historical Association from 1988 to 1989. She received the Organization of American Historians' Distinguished Service Award for 2002.

Interviewer: Constance B. Schulz
Transcriber: Barb Jardee
The following interview took place January 2, 2001.

C. S.: What we want to do in this interview is to look at issues of both the field of southern women's history and the growing sense of identity and power among women historians living in the South. You're a crucial person in understanding the development of both of those things.

A. S.: But, you know, most of the time I didn't know what I was doing.

C. S.: I think that's true of most of us; we take opportunities. So my first question really has to do with your sense of your southernness. Do you FEEL southern?

A. S.: Oh, I'm a southerner. I'm a dedicated, patriotic southerner who fights with people at the drop of a hat. I was furious with Harvard when people would say to me, "Oh, you don't *seem* like a southerner." It was meant to be a compliment. I didn't understand what being southern was all about until I got to Northwestern University, which is where I went first. However, there's one earlier interval that might be important. My mother had a younger sister. She and her sister both went to college, which in 1917 was not common. Mother went to Simmons and majored in home economics. Judith wanted to go to Wellesley, but she flunked the exam, or didn't make a good enough grade on the entrance exam, and so she went to Boston University and studied history and married her history professor, Ralph Volney Harlow.

When I was twelve, he'd gone to Syracuse [University]. He had taught at Simmons; he'd taught at Yale and was lured to Syracuse when they told him he could have exclusive use of the Gerrit Smith papers if he would come and join the faculty, so he did. They had a younger daughter, their middle child, who had had TB when she was very young and who was very thin and frail and didn't look healthy. And so the doctor kept saying, "Well, she never has time to build up in the summer enough to survive these long cold winters." And my mother and her sister, if you can believe this, traded children for a year. So I went to Syracuse when I was twelve, and my cousin was only eight.

C. S.: So you grew up in a household of historians in that sense.

A. S.: Yes, my father was always interested in history. He was an agricultural economist. My grandmother grew up in Virginia, was named Byrd Lee Hill. If you want to talk about a sense of being southern! The Hill family papers are in the Virginia Historical Society, and I was amazed when I went to read them. And she grew up in Richmond on West Grace Street. She had an Ellen Glasgow kind of childhood. She was born in 1873, I think, wanted to go to college. The family view was that Virginia ladies didn't go off to college, but they did let her go to the George Peabody School of Education in Nashville. She was a real intellectual, but she died when I was five. The short answer is I've always been very southern, I still am, and I wanted to come back to the South. Andy [husband, Andrew Scott] was not necessarily very keen on the idea, but we got back.

C. S.: So you arrived at Harvard in graduate school, "A" a woman, "B" a southerner, and "C" a student who had some experience of life out in the world before you got there. I understand that in graduate school you knew Oscar and Mary Handlin and did your dissertation under Oscar's direction. Was he interested in encouraging you to explore southern issues?

A. S.: Oh, very much. And he was flexible. He had seventy-three Ph.D.s who did their work with him, and they're all over the map. It's not like, say, Frederick Jackson Turner, whose students tended to work on the frontier. Or it's not like any number of people that you and I could list if we put our minds to it who have a "school." Not Handlin. If you wanted to write about anything he was ready to encourage you. My association with him became close only after I passed my generals, because I was supposed to be working with Ben[jamin F.] Wright, and the day after my oral exam, Wright took the job as president of Smith College, and he called me up and said, "I'm not going to be able to direct your dissertation, my dear. Would you like to come and teach at Smith?" He was a character! But I said, "No." I didn't think I wanted to go teach at Smith. And what am I going to do now? So I went around and said to Handlin, "I've got to write a dissertation. What should I write about?" I must have been really naïve. And I guess he asked me a few questions, and he said, "Well, there's only one person doing any good work in southern history at this moment. His name is [C. Vann] Woodward, and he's down at Johns Hopkins." He said, "I think I've read that there were some interesting Progressives in North Carolina and places in the South. Why don't you see what you can learn about them?"

C. S.: You talked about Handlin and Wright. Who else were your mentors at Harvard, and did they continue to be supporters?

A. S.: I had good relationships with different people. Howard Mumford Jones, who was a literary scholar, ran an evening seminar at his house for all the American civilization students.

C. S.: And you said that American civilization really allowed you to branch out and do anything.

A. S.: Well, you can also call it a smorgasbord approach to graduate work, because I took courses with [F. O.] Matthissen, whom I really admired tremendously, and with Perry Miller, which was tension filled. He wasn't terribly keen about me nor I about him, but I learned a lot. And I worked, as I said, with Wright, and with William Yandell Elliott. I still thought of myself as a political scientist until after the general exam. Then Wright left, and I sort of slid on into history. There were three women in the American civilization graduate group when I was coming along, and one dropped out, so there were two of us, and there were about thirty men. Having been out and working for the League of Women Voters, I just tried to run Jones's seminar, because the men didn't know how to do discussions. They believed in the "Great Man" talking, which is not a seminar. But I knew about discussion leading, and Bill [William L.] Hedges in English and I took it on ourselves to make that seminar really be a seminar.

C. S.: It seems to me, looking back, that the League of Women Voters really played a crucial role. It explains why you turned in the directions that you did. How did you first get the job at the League?

A. S.: The only thing I knew about the League was that my Aunt Judith had been a member. I had no idea what the League of Women Voters was or did. But there were six of us who lived together in an apartment in Washington, D.C., when I was an intern. When the internship ended I went back to Northwestern to finish my master's degree, because my father couldn't bear unfinished degrees, and one of my roommates got a job with the League.

C. S.: What was your internship?

A. S.: With the National Institute of Public Affairs. They were the pioneers.

They had the conviction that they were going to find the number one graduates of thirty colleges every year and bring them to Washington and turn them into future bureaucrats and change the world. It was mostly men until the war. And then women had a chance. And so, again, that was serendipity, because I went back to Syracuse right after I graduated from college by accident in December of 1940. I had not planned to graduate, but they told me, "Look, you've got enough credits right here; you have to leave. You can't keep on being an undergraduate any longer." So I went on a trip. I'd won fifty dollars in a contest, with Georgia Tech [Georgia Institute of Technology], and I picked up fifty dollars and went on a trip to New York. I bought a ticket for thirteen dollars. I don't know where I got the rest of the money; my dad must have helped some. I went with the art majors to New York City, and they introduced me to the Museum of Modern Art and the Metropolitan Museum of Art. Then I went back to Syracuse just to sort of check in with the friends I'd had when I was twelve. They were all in college by then. I got a job and stayed there from February until June, and I was working for IBM and sort of fiddling around with what I wanted to do when I got this letter from one of these people from Syracuse days. She was an intern, and she was raving about this program. I thought *that* was what I really wanted to do. So I wrote to my father and said, "Listen, what I really want to do is to go to this Washington program. But of course I've already graduated, and I don't know how to get nominated." And he said, "Leave it me." So I went to Washington as an intern the summer of 1943.

C. S.: It must have been a wonderful time to be in Washington.

A. S.: Oh, it was, but you wouldn't believe it to hear my dad talk even though he had helped me get the appointment. He was so worried because he thought there's not enough housing, and he didn't know what was going to happen to all these women in Washington in this wartime, and they're not getting chaperoned, and oh boy! I think probably, roughly speaking, there were thirty interns, of whom maybe twenty were women by that time, because so many men had been drafted and gone off to war. And also, to deal with wartime conditions, instead of having one class a year, they had two. So there was one group that had come in at the end of the first semester, and they were already in place when we got there. Some of the women in that group had a house. Six of us got an apartment. One of my roommates said when we had a reunion in 1991, "Well, I do think we were the cream of the crop." Modesty was not our strong point.

C. S.: Was that the connection that got you into the League of Women Voters?

A. S.: Right. In the spring of 1944 the League had just had a revolution, and the entire staff had resigned. Anna Lord Strauss had been nominated from the floor (she wasn't the Nominating Committee's choice) and became president. My roommate was working for the League and suggested me for the job in August 1944. I was interviewed by Anna Strauss. She took me to lunch at the "Y" and paid fifty-seven cents for my lunch. The League was notoriously frugal. When we traveled, for example, we usually stayed with the president of the local chapter of the League. It was OK if she had a guest room, but if you ended up, as I often did, on somebody's living room sofa, that was not good.

C. S.: Did you do a lot of traveling? You said that you wrote and gave talks. Did you have a specific job?

A. S.: My job was foreign policy. When I went back to Northwestern, finished my M.A., and pleased my dad, I quickly shifted into political science. I had written a master's thesis about international organization, but really, I didn't know much. But Anna had no staff. And had to find people quickly. The only person who hadn't resigned after the 1944 convention was my roommate; because she'd been hired so recently, she didn't have all these old loyalties to that group that had been defeated at the convention. Here was Anna Strauss, this wonderful, wonderful woman, coming in as president with no staff. And the board resigned too—all the old members of the board. So she had to build a board from scratch, and she had to build a staff from scratch. Three of us in our twenties were the program staff.

C. S.: You wrote the position papers?

A. S.: We wrote the pamphlets; we wrote the *National Voter*. It wasn't the *National Voter* then; it was called *Trends*. Now, we did have board members who were more mature who supervised us. We weren't totally on our own.

C. S.: Did the League hone your writing?

A. S.: Oh, you bet. There was a woman named Kathryn Stone who was the vice president, and she was a demon editor. She taught me to write without excess verbiage. I owe the League a lot.

C. S.: Did you travel then, give talks?

A. S.: I went out to do discussions. They sent me all over. I spent a month once in Minnesota.

C. S.: Did you get sent to the South? Did the League have an active presence in the South when you were working for them?

A. S.: It's fascinating and complicated. The answer is that they had some Leagues in the South, many of which had died of super partisanship. They had a wonderful League in Georgia that would have nothing to do with the national office. Anna's purpose was to bring them all "back into the union," so to speak. It's a complicated story, having to do with the structure of the League, but the long and the short of it was, yes, we were working in the South. I spent a month in Kentucky in the summer of 1946. I worked in both Kentucky and Tennessee that summer and went to the Tennessee convention.

C. S.: You mentioned that you knew some of the grand old dames of the suffrage movement. (I hope that's not an unflattering description.) When you were in the League, were you aware as a young person of the importance of some of these women?

A. S.: Oh, sure. Oh, you couldn't help it. The League was a child of the suffrage movement. Carrie Chapman Catt founded the League. And Maud Wood Park was the first president of the League.

C. S.: You said you would get letters from these people.

A. S.: Oh, from Carrie Chapman Catt. Catt had very strong ideas, and I remember Anna saying, "Another letter!" Now, a much more direct influence on me was Katharine Ludington, who was a remarkable woman. She was a mover and shaker in the Connecticut League. I'm confident she had been on the board at some point. I don't remember all the ins and outs or who resigned in 1944, but she had been a suffragist, she and her comrade Mary Foulke Morrison. They were both really grand dames in appearance. And Mary Morrison remained beautiful in her eighties. But Katharine Ludington would come to Washington and sit by my desk and tell me what I ought to be thinking about, having to do with current affairs.

C. S.: Do you think you picked up from that generation some of your ideas about how women ought to organize?

A. S.: Sure. Well, for one thing, I'd been at IBM, and I'd worked in two government agencies before I did my internship with Congressman [H. Jerry] Voorhis of California, and I knew how badly men ran meetings, and the League women knew how to run meetings. I was very impressed. On the other hand, in all honesty, I used to get very tired of board meetings, because they had to debate every issue down to the last dotted "i" and crossed "t." And I'm sure there are things in my journal where I say something about democracy is the worst form of government except any other, because it took forever to reach a conclusion. But the board members were very encouraging, extremely well informed, and as staff people we had to be there every minute.

C. S.: Despite the political disruption, Catt and Ludington continued to be listened to and heard.

A. S.: Miss Ludington, in particular, I think, because of her interest in foreign policy. She was a power in Connecticut.

C. S.: So when you went back to the South, did you go because of your husband's job?

A. S.: Yes, he had a job. Absolutely. We came back here in 1958. I got the degree in 1958, I guess, when Rebecca was eight, David four, and Donald three. I got my degree three children later. Oscar [Handlin] used to say that I had a baby every chapter. Wasn't quite true. I had five pregnancies in that period.

C. S.: Were you writing as you were doing this?

A. S.: Off and on—mostly off, until we went to Dartmouth College in Hanover, New Hampshire. Hanover was such a cold place, there's nothing to do but sit in the house and write. And it was such a male-dominated society too. They didn't stop me from going to the library, but they didn't invite me to a lot of things. I'd been in Washington; I was wheeling and dealing. I came off of having tea with Walter Lippmann to being told that this is a stag party. I called myself a feminist in 1954.

C. S.: You did use that word.

A. S.: I have the documentary evidence, because when David was born, I shared the room with a woman who had just had her fifth girl, and everybody kept coming in and saying, "Oh, another girl!" And I wrote my father and said, "This is disgusting. I am a moderately militant feminist."

C. S.: But you did wind up back in the South?

A. S.: Yes. When I wrote my dissertation about southern Progressives, I found a lot of women, which nobody ever mentioned. Arthur S. Link never heard of women Progressives. So I found some. I had about four or five pages in my dissertation about them. When I got down here, I was told that the University of North Carolina had never hired a woman in the history department, and never would. Fletcher [M.] Green, who was chairman of the department, drove to Washington for the AHA. He went to Oscar Handlin, and he said, "Could you send me a young man to teach American history next year?" Oscar said, "I've already sent someone to Chapel Hill for you, Fletcher." Oscar had nothing to do with our coming to Chapel Hill, but that was Oscar. So Fletcher Green came back to Chapel Hill and called on the telephone and offered me a job. Such is the power of Harvard. It was part-time. They paid me $4,000 to teach four sections of the introductory course. In the first class I went to, Fletcher Green's twins were sitting on the front row. It was a great beginning!

C. S.: So they were reporting back, whether you were doing OK.

A. S.: That is right. Then they dropped the course, and Fletcher called me in and said, "Please, I don't want you to be upset. It was a matter of schedules." I never knew whether he was just being polite.

Anyway, the history department had a custom of having faculty seminars every spring, and they were very courteous to each other. It was a great southern gentleman department. And here was I. They didn't even give me an office. George Taylor, the historian of France, took pity on me, and said, "There are two desks in my office, Anne, if you need a place to sit." Oh! It was bad; it was bad. But some of the guys were really welcoming—Frank Klingberg was welcoming. So, in fact, were most of the men. Peter [F.] Walker had just been hired, and they shoved off on him the scutwork of planning this faculty seminar. Peter, as a way of thumbing his nose at his elders, asked me to give the first paper. So I thought, "What in the world am I going to do?" Then I thought, "Here was the southern historical section of the library; maybe I should go and do something about those women that I'd found." So I went off and started looking to see what was in the catalog, and I found Julia Cherry Spruill [*Women's Life and Work in the Southern Colonies*] and read it with great interest, because it was a great book. And then I went out to dinner somewhere, and there were the Spruills. I said, "Ah! I just read your book, and I just love it!" And Julia, who by that time had completely given up being a historian because of all the discouragement, immediately invited me to tea. I started having tea with her quite regularly.

C. S.: Was she helpful and a good respondent to your interest in Progressive women?

A. S.: Wonderful. Well, that was what she meant to write about, but then she found that there was no preliminary work, and that's the reason she did early southern women. And then she didn't get a job. She was just great! And then I began to find out about these other elderly women. I interviewed Adéle Clark in Virginia. I had met her through the League of Women Voters, actually much earlier. She had been part of the Virginia League. But before, when she had been a suffragist, she had had to develop the agenda, which the newly enfranchised women presented to the Virginia legislature. When I went to see her; she was in her nineties. She was living with an ancient cousin in a house that hadn't been dusted in at least ten years. No furnishings. She smoked like a chimney.

C. S.: Everything that a southern lady was not supposed to be!

A. S.: And her cousin, who came from New Orleans, was very quirky, and she said, yes, that she had grown up in New Orleans, and she had been visiting in Richmond when she discovered she was pregnant, and her family wanted her to come home at once, because they didn't want to have a child born up North. So they talked to me for one whole day, and I was exhausted. They were eighty-nine and ninety-two, and they were still going strong. Adele's papers were in chaos, so I persuaded two of my young students to go and spend the summer with them and organize those papers.

C. S.: Were you still teaching at Chapel Hill?

A. S.: No, I had gone to Duke. And I arranged for Duke to buy the papers because I knew she needed money. In the end, she gave them to the

Virginia Commonwealth because she couldn't bear to have them leave the state of Virginia. And I had Duke all lined up to buy them. Anyhow, I interviewed her at great length. And I talked to Kate Burr Johnson, the first director of welfare in North Carolina after suffrage. She would answer questions, but she wouldn't volunteer anything. So it got to be more and more painful. I felt as if I were pulling teeth. It was a cold and miserable January day. I got up to leave, we opened the door, the cold wind coming in, and then she started talking. Just incredible, standing there in this cold wind!

C. S.: So really, in some ways, Julia Cherry Spruill's connections, and interest, helped you.

A. S.: Her material was invaluable, but the other people I found pretty much through the League. I had an interesting relationship with A. Elizabeth Taylor. Elizabeth Taylor grew up in Georgia, and I went to college with her sister. I found her work on southern suffrage. Of course, that was the only other thing that existed. Julia Spruill and Elizabeth Taylor were the only things. Later I discovered the work of Guion Griffis Johnson, Marjorie Mendenhall, Virginia Gray, and Eleanor Boatwright. But I found, with Elizabeth Taylor—what should I say? Oh, it was indispensable but ever so boring, because she didn't have an analytical mind. And I didn't have sense enough to realize that I should only think about the strong point, which was her excellent research, and I should forget the fact that she didn't, by my lights, interpret her material. Then I'm afraid there were a couple of panels on which I was really hard on her, which I now regret. I was young and full of beans, and she was older and deserved more respect. She was the only person doing southern women's history at that point. The others had given up, though I knew three of them. Actually Guion Johnson went back to history from time to time, but her major work was in voluntary associations.

C. S.: You were in some ways not simply a teacher, but you were, from early on, also what would now be called a public historian, in the sense that as a historian, you served on commissions; you've served on boards. Would you agree with that? How important is that? You were asked by the governor [Terry Sanford] to chair the North Carolina Commission on the Status of Women.

A. S.: In 1963, I had no idea where he got my name, or how he chose me to do the job. I also had my hands full. I had no idea how to run a commission. I had to learn everything from the ground up.

C. S.: So through this commission you were organizing politically in the state of North Carolina, probably in the steps of the League of Women Voters and the suffragists before that.

A. S.: Right. And as a result we had the best commission report in the whole country, and the reason was that Terry Sanford gave us money.

C. S.: [Reading title from Scott's copy of the report] *The Many Lives of North Carolina Women, 1964: Report of the Governor's Commission on the Status of Women.* What were your goals for that? And did that become part of what you taught?

A. S.: I had no idea what a commission on the status of women was supposed to do, and I took it because I thought it would be great fun to work with the governor. And then I had the national commission as a model, and the issues which they had identified I'd been conscious of because various people that I knew in Washington were very much involved with the national commission, the one that Kennedy appointed. Our goal, which we probably arrived at jointly, was to identify the major issues as far as North Carolina was concerned. We worked with committees; all were committee reports. Some were better than others. And Guion Griffis Johnson's committee report is a classic, really a wonderful piece of work. Again, it took me a while to realize just how good it was. We published 10,000 copies of that, and the governor provided the money, and we distributed them free across the state.

C. S.: Where were you when you were on this commission, when you said you began to look into the seminar "Southern Progressive Women"?

A. S.: I did the seminar in 1959 or 1960. So I'd done that, and George [B.] Tindall had invited me to give a paper at the Southern. Possibly Elizabeth Taylor had given a paper. I'm not sure, but otherwise I think it would be the first paper on southern women's history ever given at the Southern. And I looked back to see what was said about it. You know how in the *Journal of Southern History* they always write up the history of the program? They said that Mrs. Scott represented her material with wit. They didn't say anything about the marvelous research.

C. S.: You said in an earlier interview that you first taught a course in women's history not at North Carolina, but when you were in Washington State. Did they have a program in Washington to teach southern women's history?

A. S.: Well, Mary [Aickin] Rothschild was a grad student at the University of Washington, and she was writing about the civil rights movement, and I guess she'd read *The Southern Lady;* it was just out. Anyway, my husband was invited to teach summer school at the University of Washington. And I was just going to go along for the ride. Mary heard that Andy was coming, and she said she went storming into the chairman of the history department and said, "Do you know that Anne Scott is going to be here this summer, and we haven't invited her to teach?!" And he said, "Who is Anne Scott?" And so Mary—she's very, very articulate—she's definitely an outspoken female—let him have it, but he said, "We really don't have any money."

C. S.: She was a graduate student?!

A. S.: Oh, yes. She was a pregnant graduate student. She went down to the dean's office. They had a special program in liberal arts, and the dean was a close friend of hers. So she got the money from him, and the chairman of the history department was authorized to offer me a summer job. Well, I didn't know any of this; I never heard any of it. I didn't know anything about it. I went to the OAH, and I gave a comment on two papers. There were three men giving papers, on subjects having to do with women. And they were all, by my lights, awful. I used to be very mean. I'm not so mean anymore. Anyway, I worked on this thing very hard, and it was a devastating comment. One of the guys wouldn't speak to me for five years. And the other one never has spoken to me again. So I finished this comment, and the chairman of the University of Washington history department came up and said, "Would you like to come to teach with us this summer?" And I thought, wow, I really got through to him. It wasn't until I got out there that I met Mary and I got the whole story. That rather deflated me.

C. S.: Had you been incorporating women's history into your teaching before that?

A. S.: At Haverford I had people writing papers. All my women students at Duke read *The Feminine Mystique* when it came out. They also wrote papers on women's history topics. One did a paper on the North Carolina Federation of Women's Clubs, which years later I used in writing *Natural Allies.* So sure, I'd been doing it but had never taught a course that said "Social History of American Women."

C. S.: What I wanted to make sure we had a chance to talk about was your sense of the field of southern women's history and your entry into it. Lots of other people were beginning to turn in those directions, but the publication of *The Southern Lady* was one of the key moments in terms of creating the field.

A. S.: There were all kinds of people—graduate students in particular—looking for subjects at that time. And so I started out in 1970, which is when *The Southern Lady* was published. The only existing book on women's history in general—contemporary book—was Eleanor Flexner's *Century of Struggle.* But Carroll Smith-Rosenberg published *Religion and the Rise of the American City: The New York City Mission Movement, 1812–1870,* which is really women's history. And Ann Douglas was publishing some very postmodern literary stuff, but as far as history goes.

C. S.: But had Gerda Lerner published at that point?

A. S.: She published the *Grimké Sisters.* But actually, you know, really, no one had understood the southern stuff very well. It's just not what someone born and raised in Vienna who has spent her life in New York can get a grip on very well. But she's fascinated by Sarah Grimké, and she's revised her own past work on Sarah Grimké.

C. S.: And as you said, Elizabeth Taylor had been doing the history of southern women.

A. S.: And she kept on, you know. Elizabeth Taylor had published one thing after another, article after article. In the end, she had done either a book or an article about every southern state, on the suffrage movement, I think. She certainly did a lot of them. I think the next stage was launched with Jacquelyn Dowd Hall's *Revolt against Chivalry.* And then after that, there were so many I can't keep track of them. It just boomed!

C. S.: When did the inclusion of African American women begin? Did you include them from the beginning?

A. S.: No; in the new edition of *The Southern Lady* I did an epilogue, you know, along that line, and I said, "This is the big vacancy in this book." I think it began to happen—and it's still not as prevalent as it should be—but I think now with people like Darlene Clark Hine pressing us this is good, and Elsa Barkley Brown, who deals with southern women. Darlene's interests are wide. Her first book, of course, was about Texas, but it was about white primaries; it wasn't about women. I would say, I couldn't put a date on it, but certainly after the civil rights movement, people had to pay attention. And Kathleen Berkeley did include African Americans in that early article about Memphis.

C. S.: I want to talk, in addition, about the importance, for you, obviously, of organizations. You began your involvement with organizations with the League of Women Voters. In some ways that's one of the real continuous themes, both in your scholarship and in your connections. Do you think that the women's professional organizations that have emerged across the board have been important for women?

A. S.: Well, I certainly think that the Berkshire Conference and the SAWH have been very important to scholarship. My focus has been on the board of the Southern or the OAH. So I was on both those boards to try to educate some very self-satisfied male historians. We will not name names, but there were some who were immovable. And a very distinguished historian assured me that Woodrow Wilson was responsible for the suffrage amendment. Woodrow Wilson had fought it tooth and nail for years. Then, of course, the OAH had a Committee on the Status of Women early on, in 1978, and we went to the board.

C. S.: And you were chair of that committee, right?

A. S.: And I went to the board with this detailed report about what was not in the textbooks. And bless his heart, Vann Woodward, my old dear friend, sat there and said, "Anne are you trying to censor us?"

C. S.: Putting things in is censorship?

A. S.: Not censorship—expansion. Expansion is what we're after. So I would say it was through that effort that I got really involved in the OAH. David Potter asked me to chair that committee, and I had known him through the Southern Historical Association.

C. S.: So from your point of view, organizations and professional associations have been crucial.

A. S.: I also think that both the OAH presidency and the Southern presidency gave me a lot of visibility, and therefore gave the idea of women's history visibility, and a certain kind of respectability that we were needing in those days. I think now that we're totally respectable, but there were years and years and years when male historians kept saying, "It's a passing fad," or "Oh, it's political, it had nothing to do with history." They were so sweet, so generous, so southern gentlemanly, and so impervious. They truly treated individual people with great courtesy and always acted as if you were just absolutely wonderful, but they wouldn't read what you wrote.

C. S.: Were you able, through that, to get women historians on key committees?

A. S.: The answer is yes. One of the more ironical moments in my professional life is when, after I was president of the SHA I guess, I was told that when the committee of the Southern was considering nominating me, someone said, "When she was president of OAH, she didn't pay much attention to women." Nothing could have been further from the truth, but people form their impressions. I don't know who the person was. There may have been somebody that person thought ought to have been on a committee. My Program Committee chairs for the OAH were a man and a woman. But in any event, I think that I was able in those organizations to make some critical advances as far as the respectability of the field was concerned. When I was president of the Southern, I hope I had an influence on the way they ran board meetings.

C. S.: Again, the League of Women Voters!

A. S.: That's right. I got the reputation of being the fastest gavel in the South. Because I didn't let them just go on and on.

C. S.: You have said in other circumstances that you really thought it was important for women to have an active presence in these major organizations. And you were in a position to do that. You were very supportive of and not reluctant to join and respect the women's organizations that emerged, but you were in a position to have an influence in the major nongendered organizations.

A. S.: I'm not sure I thought of it that carefully, but my instinct, my intuition, was that there were dedicated people who were doing CCWHP [Coordinating Committee on Women in the Historical Profession], who were doing the SAWH, and that what I was doing was what I was in a position to do. And therefore, in effect, they didn't need me. But I never failed to go. I never missed a meeting. I missed one Berkshire meeting in my whole life, and that time I sent my daughter and paid for her to go.

C. S.: To my mind a lot of the exciting scholarship is in southern history, and specifically in southern women's history.

A. S.: Right, and that comes out of SAWH meetings.

C. S.: Do you remember going to the first one at Converse College in 1988?

A. S.: I remember it as being very exciting to see all these people doing what they were doing. It also launched a book, which came out from the University of Illinois Press on writing women's biography. Sara Alpern and Joyce Antler gave the press the idea for [*The Challenge of Feminist Biography: Writing the Lives of Modern American Women*]. Then the next one would have been at Carolina. All my former students now had two- and three- and four-year-olds, and they wanted to talk about it, and at the most recent one, they all wanted to talk about teenagers.

C. S.: And they all wanted to talk about it?

A. S.: I give sage advice. Of course now they're way ahead of me. I became aware very early how much talent there is, and it's much more useful to encourage the Glenda Gilmores and the Kathleen Berkeleys and people like Suzanne [Lebsock]. Suzanne would look at every single document before she made a generalization. I started encouraging her when she was a grad student. Last year I sent her this huge file of letters that I'd written to her about what she was doing. I really think that if St. Peter asked me to justify myself that students are the justification, not the scholarship. It was helpful, but it won't be here forever. But students will have students will have students forever.

C. S.: And the links keep following: Carrie Chapman Catt up to Glenda Gilmore.

A. S.: Right, exactly. Gerda Lerner and I once figured we could work our way back to Mary Wollstonecraft. I know we just made link after link because Elizabeth Cady Stanton and Susan B. Anthony were very aware of the Grimkés and Sarah Grimké's book, *Letters on the Equality of the Sexes*.

C. S.: But it seems to me, from what you're saying, that professional organizations like the SAWH have transformed intellectual inference into personal networks.

A. S.: I really believe that encouraging young people is the thing to do. My father did that, and he trained practically everybody in the state of Georgia who desired to be an agricultural economist. And it showed in the state for years and years and years. Thirty years after he died, a great many of those people made contributions to a scholarship at the University of Georgia. That was my model. We had students in our house all the time. I stay in touch with a lot of my undergraduates.

C. S.: Your role as a teacher continues on, in these professional organizations.

A. S.: One of the things I did was to keep a list of people by my telephone so that when people call and say, "Could you come to North Dakota and give a talk on so-and-so?" I could say, "No, but So-and-So would be a good person for it." Nancy Hewitt would say right now that this is what got her started. You see you get them started, and they take off without any help from anybody. But just that little initial push is sometimes helpful.

Founders

The women who attended the "caucus" in the Kentucky Hotel in Louisville at the November 1970 meeting of the Southern Historical Association did not know they were founders of anything. They only knew that there was a need to call attention to their presence in the profession, and they sought the company and the encouragement of women like themselves. Most of them were new, young scholars, not yet established in the mainline professional organizations, beginning their careers as teachers and scholars. The impetus for their gathering came from the determination of the newly formed caucus of women who had gathered at the American Historical Association meeting in Washington, D.C., in December 1969 to reach out to women in various regions of the country. Berenice Carroll came to Louisville to help organize a southern arm of what became the CCWHP. Mollie Davis, Charlotte Davis, Rosemary Carroll, and others who had been in Washington were among the perhaps thirty women who gathered in the basement room of the hotel, having heard by word of mouth when and where the meeting would be held.

After that first gathering, a small group, determined to keep the movement alive, took on the task of arranging for meetings of the Caucus of Women in History (CWH) at subsequent SHA meetings. Mollie Davis

and Charlotte Davis served as cochairs until 1973, although personal circumstances led Charlotte Davis gradually to withdraw from the organization. They saw themselves initially as involved in establishment of a
regional branch of the CCWHP rather than of a separate independent organization. They communicated with other interested women by creating a mailing list and a newsletter and collected token dues to cover the
costs of mailing it.

At the 1972 meeting of the SHA in Florida, one of the founders not present at the 1970 gathering, Barbara Schnorrenberg, volunteered to take
over some of the responsibilities that Charlotte Davis was no longer able
to fulfill, becoming the first secretary-treasurer of the group, a post she
held from 1972 to 1986. Her long tenure in the office brought needed stability to the organization, and her status as a historian of eighteenth-
century Britain, and after 1976 as an independent scholar, brought
diversity of interest. Although she was born in the South and has lived
there most of her adult life, Schnorrenberg spent her formative undergraduate years in the North, at a women's college.

Mollie Davis was probably the most essential of the women who had
been in Louisville. She invested enormous amounts of time and energy
organizing meetings at the SHA annual meeting, keeping and adding to
lists of interested women, getting the *Newsletter* out to those on the list,
passing the hat at gatherings. Her correspondence from those years forms
the bulk of the organization's earliest records at the Southern Historical
Collection. Davis was born in Georgia. The daughter of a Democratic
member of the House of Representatives, she was raised partially in Washington, D.C., at the end of the New Deal and the beginning of World War II.
Active in the civil rights movement in her hometown of Atlanta during
the 1960s, Mollie brought her activist zeal to the task of raising the consciousness of other women historians in the South. When Connie Myers
and Charlotte Davis, who functioned with Mollie as the organizing committee in the first years, dropped out for personal reasons, Mollie kept
going, writing requests to Bennett Wall for meeting rooms for the CWH
at the Southern, organizing scholarly panels, keeping open the lines of
communication with the CCWPH.

Arnita Jones in 1975 and Rosemary Carroll in 1976 both served terms
as SAWH presidents. Each was present at the Louisville organizational
meeting of SAWH in 1970. Jones had been active in the SHA while still in
graduate school at Emory and was then living in Louisville with her husband, a political scientist. Like Schnorrenberg, she decided to marry and
to move to Louisville, where her husband had an academic position but
where there were few career opportunities for her. That decision had a

profound effect on the trajectory of her professional life. Jones eventually became an early leader in the development of the field of public history during the late 1970s. Though she was born and educated in the South, she has spent much of her professional career outside of the South. This experience lends an interesting perspective to her recollections of the ways in which southern male scholars perceived and mentored talented young women graduate students.

Like Jones, Rosemary Carroll has spent most of her professional career outside the South. Born in Rhode Island, educated at Brown University and at Rutgers University, and since 1971 on the faculty at Coe College in Iowa, she was first introduced to the SHA by Martha Swain in the late 1960s. She has been a faithful member and attendee of the SHA and the SAWH ever since. Like Mollie Davis, she first became involved with the women historians organizing to pursue goals of equity in the profession at the CCWPH meeting in Washington in 1969.

Barbara Brandon Schnorrenberg

Barbara Brandon Schnorrenberg has been an independent scholar since 1976, first in Birmingham, Alabama, and now in Alexandria, Virginia. She earned her Ph.D. from Duke University in 1958 specializing in British History. She was a Fulbright Scholar from 1955 to 1956 and has received numerous grants, including a National Endowment for the Humanities summer stipend. Her work deals with eighteenth-century British women's history and the history of Episcopal women in Alabama. She is the author of over fifteen articles in various journals and anthologies, numerous encyclopedia entries, and histories of two Birmingham Episcopal parishes. She taught at the Woman's College of the University of North Carolina, now the University of North Carolina at Greensboro, the University of North Carolina at Chapel Hill, and the University of Alabama, Tuscaloosa. She has been a member of the executive boards of the American Society for Eighteenth-Century Studies (Treasurer, 1985–1995), the Southeastern American Society for Eighteenth Century Studies (President, 1978–1979), the Southern Conference on British Studies (President, 1987–1989), the Episcopal Women's History Project (President, 1998–2002), and served on the Executive Council of the Southern Historical Association

(1987–1989). She served as SAWH Secretary-Treasurer and editor of the *Newsletter* from 1972 to 1986.

Interviewer: Toni N. Smart
Transcriber: Toni N. Smart
The following interview took place May 24, 1995.

B. S.: Well, I'm from the South. My mother was from North Carolina, and my father was from Georgia. He went to graduate school in Chapel Hill and decided to become a North Carolinian. I was born in North Carolina, but we lived around over the South. My father commanded Civilian Conservation Corps camps, and then he was called back into the army during the Second World War, but we never got north of Virginia. So I went to public schools in North Carolina and Georgia and graduated from high school in Virginia.

Both my parents had been to graduate school—neither of them finished the Ph.D. because they were finishing in 1929 and got married in 1930, which is not a good date, and then I came along fairly quickly. He was teaching in college when I was born, and my mother had taught at Winthrop College in the year before they were married. And they were both historians, political scientists, and then he worked as an historian with the National Park Service. Obviously they were both interested in education, and I was an only child for ten years so that I was basically brought up by both of them and guided. So, when my mother had gone to what is now the University of North Carolina at Greensboro, then the North Carolina College for Women, she had been influenced by several women who were active in the suffrage movement. She went to the University of North Carolina and got her master's there; that was where they met in the mid- or late twenties. And then she had the first of the fellowships for southern history people going from Carolina or Duke. And so there was a very strong woman "doing things" background there, and my father was equally pushed in that way. There was never any question you wouldn't go to college. My father said the only limitation on where I wanted to go to college was my brains and his pocketbook. And so I applied to various places and got into and got a scholarship to Wellesley College.

So I went there, and it was a wonderful experience. It was this community of women and lots of women teachers. I was tall; I was very young and not socially very mature, so it was all together a great experience. At any rate, I came from the position really that women do things, and you do what you can. My major was history, obviously, and my mother, who was teaching, said I ought to try something else, so I did. I tried economics and hated it. I wanted to go to graduate school, and I didn't because there wasn't any money, so I taught for a year in a prep school in Connecticut. Then I got a small scholarship from Wellesley. The cheapest place I could go was to Chapel Hill. I went there, and then I went to Duke and finished my doctorate at Duke. *

Now I'm not an American historian; I'm an English historian. I grew up with American history, and, in fact, though I was read other history by my father, as a child I was brought up with his books that all ended in 1870. But I remember deciding early on that I didn't want to do American history because there weren't any interesting women, whereas there was Queen Elizabeth and people like that. Now obviously, as I've become a women's historian, I don't do royalty but still do British history. When I was in graduate school, one did political history, and social history really didn't exist. It was intellectual history, reading texts written by white men, and you just accepted these limits. So I did diplomatic history, though I was always interested in the other thing. When I was at Duke you had to have an out-of-department minor, and I suggested I would like to do mine in English because I was interested in what the people were reading. But I was told that one couldn't do that because it wasn't history. You could do your out-of-department minor in political science, church history—because of the divinity school at Duke—or economics. Things have changed, fortunately, for the better. So I did political theory, which is all right; I have no regrets about the courses I took because when I teach now, I am glad I have a sound grounding in that.

So then I had a Fulbright from Duke to do research for my dissertation, and I was in Germany because I was doing it on the Hanoverian connection, and it was easier to get a Fulbright to Germany than it was to England. So though I didn't really speak German, I learned to speak German, at least enough to get by. I got the offer of a job; well actually I had one before I found out about the Fulbright, from a women's college. They wanted a woman to teach British history, and I turned it down. I was sure I was going to get the Fulbright, you know. I wanted to finish anyway. And then the same college offered the job again to me while I was in Germany, which I heard about after the fact. I got a letter from my advisor who said that he had talked to my father, and they had decided that I didn't want it. And they were right, but I was furious. It was pretty incredible. But then in spring of the year that I was in Germany, I had to go to England to do most of my research. I was going to go back to England and have a little free time and travel. And I got this letter; this time it was clearly felt back home that I ought to take this job from what was by then the Women's College of the University of North Carolina.

T. S.: Where your mother had gone.

B. S.: Where my mother had gone. They offered me this job because they wanted a woman to teach English history. But, of course, there was no advertising, and the chair at WC had called up somebody at Duke and said, "I'm looking for a woman to teach history. Do you have anybody?" And they said, "Yes." You know if you were in the right time, the right place, you can get a job, but it was accidental. So I went to teaching in Greensboro, was there for six years, and finished my dissertation while I was there.

T. S.: How many women were on the faculty?

B. S.: Well, it was pretty good. It wasn't as good as Wellesley. Wellesley is the only college in the country that has always had more that 50 percent of the faculty women. Greensboro wasn't quite that high. The history department was about half. I replaced a woman that taught my mother. One of the people in the department was a class or so behind my mother there, and another woman had known her. But there were many women my age in the English department. Several young women had been hired. This was in the mid-1950s; most of the older faculty women had only the M.A. Some had the Ph.D., but many of them had only the M.A. As those people retired, they were being replaced with people with Ph.D.s, and so I was part of that change over. I was the young one; some more people came in after I was there, but I must have been probably [number] thirty-two of the women coming in.

Then I got married. My husband and I met in graduate school in Chapel Hill, and I didn't want to commute sixty miles. And so I wrote to Duke, and I wrote to Chapel Hill saying did they have any jobs, and I got the answer back from Chapel Hill saying yes. And so I went to Chapel Hill. I was not as politically savvy then; I was nice and sweet and southern. My experience at Chapel Hill changed this, and there were no women in the department. Anne Scott had been there. So I went without tenure and lived to regret it. When two other women were hired, we were all shoveled into a single slot of an office. The first black member of the department said to us, with a smile, they would never dare do that to a black, which is true. At one point all three of us went down to complain about scheduling. Why were we still teaching four courses when everybody else had three, you know? And this was in the glory days in history departments when you had 120 people in the survey of English history in the late 1960s. The chairman said that he never regarded any of us as permanent. He had a wife with a Ph.D. in history; she's never taught. She did publish her dissertation finally. But otherwise she did volunteer work. And so, you know, that was the sort of atmosphere we were in.

By the late 1960s, early 1970s, things began to get tighter. There began to be more restrictions, not that we cared much, rank did not seem to be particularly important. I was allowed to teach graduate courses occasionally, and then those began to tighten up, and new people came. You know one of the things that has been lost in many ways is civility. That begins to go as the old cutthroat problems begin. So that was that side of the coin, and the other was that in the late 1960s, early 1970s, women's history was getting started, and I realized that was what I really wanted to do. So I went down to this charming chairman—we were at that time having undergraduate seminars—and said that I wanted to do one in women's history and he said, "OK." He said, "It's not here to stay; I don't regard it or black history as anything that will last."

T. S.: He thought it was a fad.

B. S.: He thought it was a passing fad. But it couldn't hurt much if I did it; so I taught the first women's history course at Chapel Hill.

T. S.: And how did it go over?

B. S.: It went over quite well. You know it was small; I think enrollment was limited maybe to twelve, and I had that.

T. S.: Were they all women?

B. S.: No, interestingly, they weren't. I even had one or two men. And I did that a couple of years. And then they hired Joan Scott. So she took over. And so that was basically where I was when the SAWH got started. I was not at the first meeting in Louisville where it was founded.

T. S.: How did you come to hear about the SAWH?

B. S.: I got a mailing from Mollie Davis that spring, and she said, "Would you be interested?" I was then teaching this course for the first time, and it was really experimental. I had a graduate assistant, and so I sent him down to the library just to go to the card catalog and find out what there was available. And so this mimeographed flyer said, "We want to have a meeting and talk about the problems of teaching women's history and how to do it and exchange bibliographies and course outlines." And so, if you were interested, write back. So I did respond.

T. S.: Were you a member of SHA at this time?

B. S.: Yes, I had been taken by the hand my second year at Duke, which was my last year in residence. My advisor really was a nice man, though prejudiced. He would make these remarks like one time in Greensboro I said to him I had a very good student, and Duke admitted her, but they didn't give her any money, and I saw him and I said to him, "Why didn't you give 'X' any money?" And he said, "We don't want to pay to educate somebody's cook." Well, I had the largest graduate assistantship in the department for the two years that I was there, so you know personally I never felt this. But I went that second year to the SHA meeting in Columbia. And William B. Hamilton said to me, "Are you going to the Southern Historical?" And I said I hadn't planned to because I was not on the job market, and I was determined I was going to finish my dissertation if possible before I got a job. And he said, "Well, you better go. You can ride down with me." And I said, "Yes, sir." And I'm glad I did; it was fun. This again is what good people ought to do; they take you into the future and tell you what you ought to join. So I had joined, and I had been at the Southern in Durham one year. I was in Greensboro, so I would go to that, but you know I didn't make a big thing about it because in those days—it's bad enough now if you're in British history, but in those days—it was one section on anything non-American. So there was no real reason for me to go. But I wasn't at that Louisville meeting. So I went to Houston and was on the program. Mollie Davis called me up recently sometime in the fall, and she had found some old papers, and did I remember who else was on that panel in Houston? And I said, "No, I had no recollection at all." And it was Newt Gingrich. So that was my introduction.

T. S.: You became active in the SAWH from the very beginning.

B. S.: Yes, the next year really. The next year the meeting was in Miami, and I organized, I think, the panel for that. Now I was trying to get some Europeanists to get a more cross-cultural history, and so Mollie and Charlotte Davis had basically been organizing the SAWH from the Atlanta area. But Charlotte was in the process of disappearing, and Connie

Myers volunteered for being president, and so I volunteered to be secretary.

T. S.: And you held that position for a very long time.

B. S.: Thirteen years. Until after we moved to Birmingham.

T. S.: I would think that with your mother's influence and going to Wellesley, an all-women's college, that there would be heavy strains of feminism.

B. S.: Very much. Very much. So that was one of the reasons I was willing to take this on, because I wanted to do something. I had certainly, in the first parts of my academic career, had enemies and problems. I practically started the women's faculty organization at the University of North Carolina at Chapel Hill, too. The first meeting we had somebody was running it, and you couldn't hear it, couldn't project, couldn't be heard in a very large room. I always felt that I ought to do it.

T. S.: Do you think that this feminism spurred the beginning of the SAWH? I think a lot of people were afraid that it was radical or that it was going to get out of hand.

B. S.: Sure. I don't know why they thought that because most of the people who were involved in it were good southern girls, and in my generation we were brought up in the old ways. Just this spring I was at Tuscaloosa and teaching American women's history, and I talk about the sort of nineteenth-century views of the lady, and this is what I was brought up as.

T. S.: What did you expect to accomplish with the founding of the SAWH?

B. S.: Two things: One was to encourage interest and panels and programs on women's history. So it was a mighty struggle the first few years. Behind the garbage cans we would be allowed to meet at some hour when nobody else was meeting; everybody else was drinking.

T. S.: Four o'clock.

B. S.: Four o'clock. That's right. The European section was by then beginning to get a little larger, and they were more open to panels than the

American people were. So that's how I got that panel on the program, I'm sure. But that was part of it, to get women's history panels, and that took four or five years before it became a matter of course; in fact, there would be somebody on the program to be responsible for women's history. And the other was to get more women onto committees and power positions of the SHA. Now it's almost embarrassing because I think in the last some years the SHA has been (behind the scenes, of course, it's a terribly undemocratic organization) run by the SAWH. We'd normally have two people on a three-person Nominating Committee, and that's real power. There are no contested elections in the SHA. The Nominating Committee nominates one person to each office, and that's it. So, the way you get office or [become a] member of a council in the SHA is to influence the Nominating Committee. I've been on the Executive Council of the SHA, and there's always one non-American council member. Betsy Jacoway was on the SHA Nominating Committee in 1986, the year that I was put up, and so we're certainly in the halls of power such as it is in the organization. She went on to chair the Nominating Committee beginning in 1987.

T. S.: But, still for the SAWH to start out in the 1970s, and now it's so influential.

B. S.: I would say others think the breaking point was the year that we raised protest over meeting in a non-ERA state.

T. S.: When was this?

B. S.: In 1976; we were supposed to go to Washington, D.C. I'm sure the ERA had limited-time ratification, and we had kept an eagle eye out. The SHA actually was not scheduled to meet in a nonratified place as it happened, and we were supposed to go to D.C., and those chintzy men—it is the cheapest organization that I know of—decided it cost too much to go to Washington, and they decided to move it back to Atlanta. Judy Gentry was president of SAWH and was on the SHA Program Committee, and when she heard about it, we started writing. We naturally didn't get them to change their minds, but we caused an uproar. At this point Anne Scott was on the SHA Executive Council, and this was great getting her to support us. In 1981 they grudgingly agreed to appoint a Committee on the Status of Women in the SHA. And I think that was probably the breakthrough. Obviously we didn't get it changed, but that did happen. And it's no longer an ad hoc committee; it's a standing committee.

[Editors' note: The Executive Council of the SHA in November 1981 created an ad hoc Committee on the Status of Women Historians in the Southern Historical Association. By 1987 the name had changed to Committee on Women in the SHA.]

T. S.: What do you think about the progress the SAWH has made over its twenty-five years?

B. S.: Remarkable, but I think maybe it needs to have some kind of, "Where do you go from here?" I don't think it should disband, but do we need to do something else? Do we just hold the line? This may be the answer. We've talked about it, and there have been some new, younger faces. I think the Southern Women's History Conference is certainly taking off.

T. S.: But you do see it as having a future?

B. S.: Yes, I hope so. It's interesting. I have a number of women friends that I met through the SAWH, but some of my other women friends don't do women's organizations. I don't see any point in separating. Integration; I think it can go on, and maybe if we're not, there will be backsliding. I think it's a real problem—it needs to find an adequate home, and one of the problems probably with it is with finances. It takes money to support an organization. Until we moved here in 1976, the money had lived in my bank account, because you can't have an account with less than one hundred dollars in it. We never had that much money; we barely had enough money to put out the *Newsletter.* And the newsletters brought in just about enough to pay for the next one. But this may be another question that needs to be raised and particularly now. We started, of course, with terribly minimal dues. We worked up to five dollars. And this is because many women were so badly paid. I got a Social Security statement the other day, and I looked with some horror at how little I was paid. I know that's why we wanted to make it open and available to everybody. And this is the question that all organizations of this sort have to face.

Mollie C. Davis

Mollie C. Davis is currently Professor of History Emerita from Queens College, Charlotte, North Carolina. In 1972 she earned her Ph.D. in American History from the University of Georgia, where she studied under Willard B. Gatewood. She is the author of numerous articles, including a chapter of her own life entitled "Two Catalysts in My Life: Voter Registration Drives and CCWHP," for the volume *Voices of Women Historians: The Personal, the Political, the Professional* (1999). She has served as chair of the Department of History, Queens College, and as Program Officer and Humanist Administrator for the NEH. As an academic activist, she has served on Gov. James B. Hunt's Mecklenburg County State Executive Committee; as Vice President of the Mecklenburg County Democratic Women's Club; as cofounder of the Coalition for Pro-Choice, Charlotte; and as a member of the Charlotte Historic District Commission. She served on the SHA Executive Council from 1992 to 1994 and was President of the CCWHP from 1982 until 1985. She was one of the organizing founders of the southern Caucus of Women in History in 1970 (which later became the SAWH), and served as its President from 1971 to 1973.

Interviewer: Pamela Dean
Transcriber: Toni N. Smart
The following interview took place November 6, 1992.

M. D.: My name is Mollie C. Davis. The middle initial stands for Camp. I was born and reared in Newnan, Georgia. My father [A. Sidney Camp, Democratic representative from Georgia, 1939–1954] was a congressman, elected in 1939, but he had been assistant district attorney in Atlanta, I think, almost since my birth. My birth required a new job for him. He had worked in the early New Deal campaign for Franklin Delano Roosevelt. By the way, Warm Springs was in our district, or the then district my father represented. I grew up, I guess, at the footsteps of politicians and New Deal enthusiasts. There was a great deal of difference in the first and second New Deal insofar as I remember even as a little girl. So, the excitement of activism was always in our household. My mother is a cousin of the former governor, Ellis Gibbs Arnall, who was a bit to the left, perhaps, of my father, but who did away with the balls and chains of the convicts who passed daily to the work quarries in our county. And so, I think that there was a bit of social justice, or social consciousness, or, if you will, social gospel.

My grandmother owned a house until she lost it, and we bought it from her. It had been a rooming house as well as where she and our family lived. It was a Victorian-type house, and so there was a great deal of feeling for working women in the home. Those kinds of jobs never get recorded—those who run boardinghouses and those who are widowed at age forty, and who aren't, under Georgia law, permitted to write a check. So she tells me, "Never forget to vote, whatever the boys are in there doing," and they were always in there arguing. Her other daughters married; one married an East Tennessee Republican, the other one married a World War I veteran who had been a victim of mustard gas attacks and became judge of whatever circuit was the western part of Tennessee. They're ardent Democrats. So they always argued religion— none of them were the same religion—and politics. And she let them. She called them her boys. And they argued. So we grew up allowed to debate and argue if we wished to. It's been a hard lesson my brother and I have had to learn. If we wish to say what we saw as a flaw, we felt free to do it. And society doesn't permit that, particularly from a woman growing up in the thirties and in World War II.

My father filled an unexpired term in Congress in 1939 and then went on serving until his death. We spent a goodly portion of the year in

Washington and a good portion of the year in Georgia. My mother was an invalid, and this was a difficulty, so my grandmother tended to us, but my father put me in the Library of Congress. I had free run of the stacks, which people don't have anymore, and Archibald MacLeish read Uncle Wiggly to me. MacLeish, the Librarian of Congress [1939–1944] permitted me to use a room near him and to read Peter Rabbit, and later books on the Bobsey twins, and wonderful things of that nature. I thought that you were supposed to be in the stacks of the library, and to be an activist. I tell you this to say that when my husband had a complete mental breakdown, and I had to find some way to make ends meet other than to stay home with the children, I thought of books. I had to work, and there was a great difficulty, because I had had polio and couldn't lift things; there was nothing I really thought I could do except use my mind. This was a time that grants, fortunately, were there, and the Ford Foundation wanted you to go back into the teaching field. So in the back door I got a Ford grant.

P. D.: When was this?

M. D.: This was 1962 or 1963, and an unwritten part of that Ford Foundation grant was to help integrate the Atlanta school system. Nobody ever talked about it, but that's what it was all about, I really think. And we went back to teach Johnny how to read and write—those of us who had no education courses—and immediately I saw I wasn't fit to teach second grade, and I went into the secondary school program. The first M.A.T. program failed. We all know it failed; it was the equivalent of two master's. And I worked with history and with education.

P. D.: Now where were you going to school?

M. D.: Emory University. And I was there in those wonderful months and summers when Emory opened its dorms and cafeterias to the freedom riders and others, and where Jimmy [James W.] Silver came up. He had been thrown out of Mississippi, so to speak, and this was before he went to Notre Dame. We had the free lectures for people who were in the cafeterias, and I had little children at home but just was so enthralled with the free lectures. It was 1963, 1964, and 1965; I was slow getting the master's, and then I got my first job in 1965 at West Georgia College (now the State University of West Georgia). They wanted you. They called you up and said, "We have a job, would you like this job?" It was that kind of market. They said, "You can't be a member of the NAACP or the ACLU."

You had to sign this contract that you aren't and no one else kin to you is. Several of us from Emory were hired but were upset over the loyalty oath, and a number of us, incognito, took class action, or whatever it was. And so immediately after we were hired we worked on the loyalty oath case and got that taken out of the state of Georgia.

I wanted to go back to get my doctorate but there was a problem. Emory University said that I didn't have the best GREs, but they also said, "You'll never pass the language requirement." Finally they accepted me into the Ph.D. program with no money. But I was able to turn them down because some of my father's former political friends decided the University of Georgia board of regents needed to give its first grant to a woman from West Georgia. There had been males who had received grants at West Georgia prior to mine, but no females. And so I got that to go to the University of Georgia. I went there in 1967.

I'd been very active in the meantime. I had worked for Ellis Arnall, a write-in candidate for governor in 1966, and had worked to ensure adherence to the Voter Registration Act, and was a founding member of the ACLU chapter at West Georgia College. So there was a lot of activity going on. The Voting Rights Act of 1965 was being contested in my county, and we tried to make a great lawsuit out of it but failed completely.

I went to the University of Georgia in 1967–1969 in the heart of all this to see that Georgia had not integrated its YMCA. I couldn't believe some of the things I did, but I think that I dressed like a lady with the white gloves, and I was over there, and I was watching, and I had wonderful friends there, and I was working towards my degree, but I saw what was going on in the higher echelons.

I got mad at Emory. They later made wonderful amends, but I saw what had happened with some of my friends. Back in 1965, we had offered to teach at the Atlanta University complex. It was part of the Ford Foundation grant, and I was doing my practice teaching. You had to do an internship back in 1965. This is really what got to me: I was teaching at Walter George High School, and they gave me the first group of people because I was in this Ford Foundation program. I had a little homeroom of seventh graders, some of whom were from the heart of the black community near Atlanta University who had well-educated parents, and there was a group of children in the room with them who had KKK backgrounds in their families. The whites who came into the school at this particular time, at least in my class, based on a little survey I took, had no newspaper, nor were there magazines, and yet their fathers were making an ample amount of money to have a dictionary in·the home. It was a great contrast with the ones handpicked to be integrated in that school. I tell you this, I was sort of bitten by the activism bug of wanting to do something about it. And at Georgia I was permitted to.

You had to go back and teach a year if the regents funded you a year toward the doctorate. So I had to go back and teach at West Georgia in 1969–1970. I had the fall and winter quarters off, but I had to sign a contract for the academic year. When I went back, they told me they didn't want to raise my salary. Nixon had frozen wages, but a change of status permitted an exemption. They had always raised people who were ABD [all but dissertation]; even my salary with the master's pay was $1,200 under what my male colleague from Emory was getting. We had compared, which you're not supposed to do, but we had compared. I was furious in 1969 that the Equal Pay Act did not include professional people. I demanded that they give me a leave before I even came back and that they fund me to maybe get my dissertation completed.

Thus I went to Washington, D.C., to do the research, and, of course, while I was sitting up in the Library of Congress in 1969 there also was a great antiwar effort, and I was doing my chapter on pacifism. I got very, very active in the peace movement, and we formed what we called the "White Glove Peace March" to show Spiro Agnew that we were not all wicked. We had people in limousines and so forth. And so a good deal of the time that I should have been writing my dissertation was spent in doing other things. My ten-year-old son came up to help me write. So it's that kind of background that I had in 1969. I think I got fifteen dollars a week from my husband, and I stayed in a home very close to where the new Senate office building is. I was not planning to go to the American Historical Association meeting that December in Washington, but I did. I came a day late and didn't get to the very first meeting of CCWHP and its formation. But the next day they had a big sign-up for those interested in the CCWHP, and I signed with Professor Gerda Lerner of the New York–area historians and others. There were a number of wonderful people whom I met, and we decided we would all come back the following year with great gusto and do great things. Constance Myers from Augusta told me about it, as did some others whom I met.

In the meantime, the southern people were to keep in touch with Connie Myers, and we were to form an arm of the CCWHP, just as did the western people. Dorothy Sexter was to form a West Coast association of women. And we were to speak with unity within the AHA, and we wanted to demand a rewritten constitution, which of course they did. Our aim was to complement the overall aim of the CCWHP, which was the same as the West Coast association, the same as the southern association was to be. There was also the Berkshire Conference, which adopted these as very worthwhile aims. They were founded in the thirties as a response to another whole set of questions that came in the twenties. Many of the older founders were still alive, though, and this activism was a real iffy kind of thing. That was the reason they couldn't feel free to be an arm of CCWHP, and yet they were an arm, and we worked in tandem. We worked very, very closely with these wonderful women. We were all in the same boat.

By 1970 my husband was in Augusta in a mental hospital. I'd not applied for divorce, and I was writing my dissertation and teaching and trying to look for a job other than the one I had at West Georgia. Auburn was going to put up a Ph.D. program, and they were getting ready to solicit, and they needed people. I could virtually commute to Auburn from Newnan, eighty or ninety miles, but it would have been very difficult, and I was told not even to bother because you had to live in the state of Alabama to get a state check. If you lived in Georgia you were stuck. A female's residence was that of her husband. And I thought, what, what, what? There were many archaic things, and so I began to write to somebody named Martha Griffiths, who was new in the House of Representatives.

Anyway, I was always political about things. I wrote letters all the time to people. But I began to write them on behalf of women. And on behalf of people like myself. How fortunate I was, you know, to be able to go back to school, to have a mother who picked up the cost of a housekeeper, and to have a Ford Foundation grant. I never finished that part of the story. I'd like to black this out: when I was teaching high school in my internship in 1965, I was also doing some other kind of small civil rights activities about which we don't need to talk. But I was active in the civil rights movement. And the Klan blew up my car. Riding home I knew something was funny with the car, and I turned in the first filling station and hopped out, and the car blew up. And it scared me so, I hate to admit what a chicken I was. Now that I look back, I certainly should have been more careful about things. And working in the voter registration drives, some of us should have been more careful. And so my husband, who was not sick at this time, said to me, "Try something easier, like teaching in a college." So, that's why I went to the West Georgia job.

So there I am mad as a wet hen in 1969–1970 that I'm not getting a raise, and then in the following year Nixon is talking about freezing the salaries, and always these men. There were eighty men in the division of social sciences at West Georgia, and they had not yet divided off into economics and sociology and all these departments. The student body went from twelve hundred to about five thousand in the late 1960s. It was too much of a gain. I think women in particular weren't taught by their mentors or anyone how to make a contract, how to deal with this, and everything was so secret, and we were all mad. Those people who met in 1969 in Washington at the first CCWHP meeting were furious; and those people who met the following year at the Southern in Louisville were furious. It was a consciousness-raising type of thing in those days to hear that there was someone else who felt put upon. And we voiced great anger and frustration.

P. D.: Tell me about some of the other people that were at the 1970 Louisville meeting.

M. D.: Well, first of all, I have to tell you that Connie Myers had gone with her husband to California. Her husband took a job, and her school where she had taught was to forward the mail, and they never did. So I had no way to reach them, and I finally saw that a woman named Berenice Carroll was doing the regional organizing for CCWHP, and she at that time was at the University of Illinois, Urbana, where she stayed a long number of years. She was a political scientist. But at any rate, Berenice was to come to the SHA meeting to show us what we needed to do because we had to be the arm of the CCWHP in the South, and I think she brought someone with her; I think it could have been Hilda L. Smith, who now is a professor of history at the University of Cincinnati. She's in British history.

Anyway, some newsletter, maybe it was the CCWHP one, said that those who wished to contact Berenice could contact her, and this is what we did, because Connie's letters had not yet been answered. Berenice had nothing to do with the Southern except that she came as a representative of the CCWHP to help us organize and tell us best how to handle things. I really don't know exactly what happened, but we were there, and I had a feeling that they had had much correspondence and perhaps phone calls with a rather large group of about eight people who were from New Orleans. There was a contingent from New Orleans who wanted to have New Orleans as its [the CCWHP's] southern arm headquarters. Well, New Orleans is Gulf Coast, and some of us felt that Atlanta would be reachable from Mississippi, Alabama, and Tennessee as the gateway to the South. And although we were not in a group and had never known each other before, we decided that maybe the best way we could do it was to have a regional meeting in Atlanta. This was their original intent down in the New Orleans area. And that then they would draw from Texas and other states of course. But the South was such a large and amorphous geographic region. We had envisioned that we would probably hold our meetings at the SHA because it went to Texas and New Orleans and Atlanta. And at each place it would puff up our little membership from that region. We were also thinking in terms of having an annual meeting in the spring along with the fall meeting in conjunction with the Southern Historical Association.

So when we met in Louisville in 1970, Ben Wall had evidently had a problem with Berenice and vice versa, and we had a room sort of in a terrible location. There had been a mix-up. I'm sure there were words spoken between the two of them, but I must tell you that there's never ever, ever, in all the many years I've been going to the Southern Historical Association, well over twenty-five, there never ever was such a meeting as the Louisville meeting. You waited three hours just to get into the hotel. They evidently had lost all the reservations. It was just an unreal meeting. So poor Ben Wall was in orbit. And just one more thing to make him in orbit was, you might say, an aggressive female. And he, of course, has difficulty. He's a wonderful person in many ways, but also "anti" any of the feminist kinds of things in those days.

P. D.: He wasn't prepared to cope with that.

M. D.: Could not cope with that. And he and Berenice had these ill feelings. I had had a course at Emory with him and was very fond of Ben when Ben and Neva first married. I'd been very friendly with Ben Wall; he had taught me at Emory one summer and introduced me to Jimmy Silver and all these kinds of wonderful things. I felt that he had a great influence on my life. He's the one who signed my graduate student application for the Southern. He recommended me for jobs such as this, and so I had told him that they were having this meeting, and that I wanted his support for a room for us to have it in. For some reason we didn't know the ropes. I thought that the Southern would have to OK it. This is what you call real green. High school people know more now. And he said, "Oh, we have nothing to do with that. It's not a part of the Southern." And I said, "Well, let's make it a part of the Southern." And that was not the right thing to say. We had lots of words about this, but I went to the meeting in Louisville, and we did get another room for a meeting in Houston for the 1971 meeting.

Charlotte Davis (later Kinch), no kin to me, an ABD was there from Clark College, a traditionally black institution. Part of the efforts of the civil rights movement was to integrate, and sort of the backdoor way to integrate was to swap students or faculty; white and black people swapped places. Emory had a wonderful system of swapping its single graduate students and its people. It was very good under Bell Irvin Wiley and others. And these Emory people were my friends. I kept up with my Emory people because I lived down in Newnan, Georgia. Harvey Young is an Emory professor I particularly remember. He was probably my mentor. But, at any rate, Charlotte Davis was one of my Emory friends. There was also an elderly black woman who came from Alcorn Agricultural and Mechanical College, a traditionally black institution, with her latest "daughter," as she called her—Louise Spears of the University of Michigan. Her name was Melerson Guy Dunham. She and her husband had worked in the civil rights movement, and they had no children, but they sent people through, very quietly. They helped to send them through the best schools, and the current one was going to University of Michigan for a Ph.D. Melerson was an influential activist who later wrote the history of Alcorn A & M. She was a friend of Fannie Lou Hamer and other civil rights activists. Louise and Melerson knew Mary Frances Berry and told me that if I would call her we would set up appointments and she would introduce me to people who might help our little association. And it was very clear to me that this CCWHP, sweet as it was, was lily-white at that time. And as a southerner, I particularly felt that this was a movement for human rights and not just female rights. That I wanted my rights, there's no question, but Melerson wanted hers too, and she felt we could make some partnerships in this regard. Melerson said that Mississippi was not so far from Georgia that she could not get to Atlanta, and Atlanta would be eminently better for her than New Orleans. So we agreed to meet in Atlanta in the spring, apart from any history conferences.

So I have to tell you that we thought (and here again, it's such a joke when you think back) that there would be more respectability if we had it in Atlanta and tried to keep it a bit more professional and that we would always welcome our own. We could even have black theater at our meetings and so forth in the spring as we envisioned it. We would divide. One arm would be the status arm, and one arm would be the research history arm. We wanted women's history rather than women's studies.

But we did think that if we were going to have to meet at the Southern Historical Association that we would want to work through the ropes at that point. Rosemary Carroll, who was at Coe College in Iowa, was at that 1970 meeting. Marsha Kass Marks was at that meeting, a young Jewish woman who had taught briefly at Georgia State University. Marsha and Henry Marks came, and a young woman named Joy Dickinson from the College of William and Mary, and none of us really had our degrees. I'm not certain, maybe A. Elizabeth Taylor dropped by that time. It had not been in the SHA Program, as Berenice had so desired. When we finally did get the room, they moved us from one room to another where we had to put handmade signs in the lobby saying the first room and then go back and say move to another room. We were supposed to be meeting in the middle of the day, and it was 4:30 in the afternoon. And that's why we still have our meetings at 4:30, in memory of our strife. We were even offered a part on the regular program; we said, "No." But anyway, however it was, it was an ill-fated sort of thing. We passed the hat. Willie Lee Rose came very late. When we were passing the hat, I think she gave a nice amount.

Anyway we just said we would meet and organize it. Those of us who were living close to each other would meet, and I took some money out of some account I had from somewhere, and we were to meet here in this area [i.e., in Atlanta]. I was still at West Georgia College, and Charlotte Davis at Clark College. Ed Sweat was the department chair over at Clark College, and I think he permitted us to use what little room at Clark College in the dead of the winter that we could find. And Melerson rode over all the way from Mississippi, and Marsha came up from Huntsville, Alabama, to see her mother, and Henry came with her and hung around. Anyway, we sort of organized the beginning of a newsletter. We just took it over; there was no vote. We did get the first vote that we would put Charlotte Davis in as president, and that this would be, what we in those days called, temporary president until we could organize. And she had the affiliation at Clark; I had the affiliation at West Georgia College, and my college had a small phone budget as well, which you could use for things of a professional nature. And so I could use a WATS line, which we had all across the Deep South in those days. But I could take the *Newsletter* if Charlotte would type it. She was an excellent typist, and I could get it either mimeographed or I could get it Xeroxed. We had a photocopier, and those were not that easy to come by. And also there was a small departmental mail budget; they would rate the mailing as supportive even though they weren't supportive of women. There came a time when I mailed the newsletters ten a day for several days running, and so I don't know exactly how many people have done that before or since, but I think that's what we did. We wanted to make this thing work, and Charlotte would visit me for a period of time, and we together would put the little raggedy-tail *Newsletter* out. We would copy from the CCWHP, and we sent it to every single person who appeared in any capacity on any program. We didn't know that if you looked in the

Southern Program for 1970, that that would have been maybe the year prior's Program Committee. We didn't know any of these things, but we wrote to every single person or called, just brazenly picked up the phone and called Anne Firor Scott and the women who were written down in the *Program*.

Willie Lee Rose gave us marvelous advice. That Christmas, Charlotte and I went to the American Historical Association in 1970 for Willie Rose to deliver her famous report. I was elected as southern representative of the CCWHP and worked at that time to promote southern region women who were not active in the SHA. We counted noses in every catalog. We were doing this out of my living room on the weekends. We tried to get the New Orleans people to work, and one or two did. But a number of us, Arnita Jones from Indiana University Southeast, for example, was very, very active. We counted in a stupid fashion, but we also began just to write letters, "Won't you join; it's only five dollars, and here's what we want to do." [Editors' note: The dues collected at that time were two dollars.]

We passed the hat at each meeting to raise money, and at that first Louisville meeting we had had a sizeable amount of money; we weren't sure, but we saw people write checks. I know what I gave, and at that time it was a lot. And there were others who passed the hat and put cash in it. And the list went with a person who was not in the Atlanta area, and no one ever saw or heard from her, except for Charlotte Davis who tracked her down, and some horrible story went with tracking her down. And Charlotte said it's better to leave the rock on top of it rather than fool with it. So whatever little amount of money we had went probably for a good cause. Somebody was going to be our secretary-treasurer who then ran into some problems. Of course, all of us were women with problems, right? And she ran into an even greater problem. And evidently the money was so little she couldn't remember, she'd lost the list and we'll just forget it.

P. D.: It's one of those telling little details about how hard it is to get these kinds of things going.

M. D.: But we lost the list. Gerda Lerner and I talked about this one time much later, and please don't think I'm paranoid, but it is the truth. We later found out that there were people involved in the women's movement and the civil rights movement in 1968, 1969, and 1970, who automatically got on a list. And there was always a mole in there. And we have laughed and tried to figure out for years who was the mole in CCWHP. Gerda thinks she knows. And I have often laughed and wondered, because the one thing that you read about was how the Nixon administration—and this was in the beginning of the Nixon administration—undid a lot of the progress that these movements were making by losing their lists, losing their money, and then writing their letters. So there was all of this, and why bother, was Charlotte's attitude. She was at Clark and frantically trying to figure out where she could go. She felt she needed to leave Atlanta and went into the Washington, D.C., area.

By this time we were very involved, and we had written people, and people had sent us little checks, and we were keeping a list of the members on three-by-five cards, some of which are in Chapel Hill at the Southern Historical Collection. At every meeting we decided whoever was going to meetings would take our list. We did this at the SHA, the OAH, and the AHA for several years. We had a sign that identified us as the "Caucus of Women in History," and we claimed to be loosely associated with the SHA, as we had our meetings at the annual SHA meeting. A woman from California, who at that time was organizing the Women's Archives at Berkeley, would rent or spend a little money to get a table on the outside of the book exhibit, and so she told me one night that anytime we wanted to use one corner of the table that she had paid for we could use it. So we would sit there in between H. L. Mitchell and the Southern Tenant Farmers' Union, which made us appear more radical. Mitchell lived in Alabama, and he always came to the SHA meetings. You had a number of organizations that now have become mainstream whose materials were just on top of the table saying come do this, do that. And there was always the gay group and the Radical Historians, and we went to each and every one of both fringe and mainstream kinds of things with our list and built our little list up.

And then Charlotte went to Washington. The CCWHP, with southern women's help, was lobbying the American Historical Association to hire a staff assistant for women's issues. The first AHA staff assistant for women was Dorothy Ross, who now is a professor at Johns Hopkins University. Dorothy Ross ran a little employment information bulletin. You called the AHA office, if you were a woman, and this person, whose sole responsibility was to help women get jobs, told women where there were places, and it was our answer to the "old boys" network. Dorothy Ross told me that there was a good job for $13,500 at Queens College. By this time I had my divorce, and my dissertation, and my salary at West Georgia was frozen at some ungodly $7,200. No kidding. She said that when my children got of the right age they could go to Duke or any place Queens had a swapping agreement. I just figured if I got stuck there, the kids would be educated. (Of course, they took that benefit away immediately.) But Dorothy also had me on hold for a job somewhere else for three years thereafter. So it was a very useful thing. Women would benefit greatly if they had that now. If you needed a mentor on a project, you could get one. A number of us got mentors. I didn't follow through with mine as I should have, but it was thought that perhaps you might need a female mentor to guide you through. It's hard to believe we sat around on the floor, and they would tell you, "This is what you need to do with your dissertation; you need to do this." I didn't do these things correctly.

P. D.: There weren't too many people around who could serve as mentors, were there?

M. D.: No, but there were a lot of men who also felt that the time had come. For example, I was told that Carl Degler had a special love for the underdog (his book *Out of Our Past* and other books, were very popular at that time) and that if you thought you needed his help, you should go to him. Clarke Chambers of Minnesota was one who would help. They identified men who would help.

P. D.: They would not tell you that as a woman, or as someone writing on a women's topic, that you were not hopelessly marginal?

M. D.: Right. There were people in the South who would also help women like that, and we were to pass this kind of survival technique on. We really wanted to get higher education activists, and we used to utilize people and let them see that it was needed. This is back in 1970. George Tindall of UNC–Chapel Hill and Mary Elizabeth Massey of Winthrop College were helpful in advice later on.

Some of our mentors told us that back at Louisville in the fall we should have had somebody up there that was knowledgeable enough to tell us that just counting the people in the SHA *Program* was not the answer, you have to keep lobbying to put women scholars on the program giving papers. But in December 1970, when we met at the AHA meeting in Boston with the Willie Lee Rose Report, there was great hoopla, and we met more and more women who came. These were people who had long had their Ph.D.s, and they were trying to make the SHA put them on sessions. Remember the SHA Program for 1971 has already been set by December of 1970; it's solid, but we don't know these things. We are not in the loop. And they were getting zilch, nowhere. So Willie Lee Rose said, "I know people on the Program Committee; sometimes things work out. Try to get on the program, I will help you." I got back home, and I just picked up the phone. I'm working up this session, and I called A. Elizabeth Taylor to ask would she work to get us on the program. We put together this session, and we asked A. Elizabeth Taylor to chair it, which is not the way the Southern does. You don't send in the name of a chair. So as a result Elizabeth Taylor thinks I'm on the Program Committee calling to ask her, and she says, "Yes." It was kind of funny. Then evidently the Program Committee didn't exactly know what to do about this, but since Taylor was so well respected we ended up being on the program.

Well SHA was to be at Houston in 1971, and I called Ben Wall and I said, "Now I want to cash my chips in. You're a great friend and all, but we want a meeting room for minorities and others." This was to be our business meeting, complete with a program. And he gave us a room at 4:30, in an awful place. But then I picked up the phone, and I called Edgar A. Toppin from Virginia State College in Petersburg. I bet it's one of the few times an African American ever had been program chairman, right? I said, "I hope your program is not set in stone; I have committed a program for the southern women's 'caucus,'" and he said, "I'll get you on that program." He wrote back and said, "Now we're going to let you have not only a 4:30 room to have your CWH [Caucus of Women in History] program, but you can have a 4:30 room at another time and have the session that you might want." They had bumped the session with A. Elizabeth Taylor to the following year, but we could get up another, you might say, consciousness-raising session. Toppin's wife appeared for that. She was, I think, born in the Caribbean, and she had something she wanted to present. And you may be interested in knowing this: an opportunist at my school, at West Georgia College, named Newt Gingrich, said that he wanted to come and that he had always favored African American history and women's history, and he thought it would be beneficial if he came to Houston, and he had the piece that he could talk about the Belgian Congo. And he came and did a nice job at the first CWH program.

Just getting the simplest thing like getting on the program was hard, and we thought that not just about the Southern Historical Association, but that southern people and southern members who were doing research and wanted to go forward with that research, should make a little pressure on the OAH and other organizations about getting themselves on the program. We demanded that there be a woman on the Nominating Committee. It's so tacky to always have to demand, but we had to demand that there be not just a token, but that there be some kind of open-mindedness. We would make great strides, and then we would lose everything the next year, depending on who was president. And we had struggles, we still have struggles. You know, I figured I'd never be a big scholar and this was one thing that I could bring to the South that maybe would be a little quicker than if they had to wait. It would have come, but. . . .

P. D.: But it took somebody to pull it together and keep hammering at it.

M. D.: Right. And I do think that there have been people hammering.

Arnita A. Jones

Arnita A. Jones is currently Executive Director of the American Historical Association, following a term as Executive Director of the OAH from 1988 to 1999. She earned her Ph.D. in modern European History from Emory University in 1968. She has also served as Director of the National Coordinating Committee for the Promotion of History of the American Historical Association from 1977 to 1979, as Program Officer for Planning and Assessment Studies for the National Endowment for the Humanities from 1979 to 1984; and as Senior Historian for History Associates, Incorporated, from 1984 to 1989. She has published numerous articles in the field of public history and has served on many boards and committees, among them the American Council of Learned Societies, CCWHP, and the Mellon Foundation. She served as President of the SAWH from 1974 to 1975.

Interviewer: Constance B. Schulz
Transcriber: Victoria Kalemaris
The following interview took place October 11, 1995.

A. J.: I went to undergraduate school at Vanderbilt University. I graduated in 1962 with a bachelor's degree in history. I never really considered doing anything other than history because I loved doing it so much. However, I really did agonize about what to do with it once I got to graduate school. I guess I should add, I ended up in graduate school because I got a Woodrow Wilson Fellowship. That's a bit of an interesting story.

C. S.: Was that unusual for a woman to get a Woodrow Wilson Fellowship?

A. J.: Yes, when I was nominated they told me that they had a very specific ratio beyond which they would not take women in that program. I've forgotten what it was, but they were very clear about it. The chances of getting a Wilson if you were female were much less. But one of my clearest memories of that whole process is going for the interview for the Woodrow Wilson Fellowship, which was held locally in Nashville, but the people participating in it were not people I knew. They may or may not have been Vanderbilt faculty. But there was one other woman who was being interviewed that day. Her interview was right before mine, and she came out of it crying hysterically. I've never known why, but I was curious to see whether she received a fellowship, which needless to say she did not. But in any case, it was very clear there was room for a few women but a very few. And in those days, of course, I thought that was an interesting challenge. I really wasn't thinking as much about the system as the challenge at that point. So anyway, I did get one, which meant of course I needed to go on to graduate school, and I was scared of stopping because I saw too many women getting mired down in marriage and families and not ever going back to an education. But I really was distressed by the notion that if you went on to graduate school in a field like history, you were going to be a college professor, and that wasn't necessarily what I wanted to do, but I didn't know what I wanted to do.

C. S.: So in a sense you were already thinking along the lines that led you eventually to a public history career.

A. J.: Oh, yes, absolutely. It never really all came together until I found public history. But I did go, and I did sort of accept the socialization. I went to Emory, which was a new graduate school, more or less. It certainly was beginning to expand dramatically at the time, although I've always been grateful that it never expanded that much as so many programs did during those years. I mean this is, after all, 1962 when I started, and a number of institutions started turning out literally hundreds of Ph.D.s in history. So it was more a handcrafted kind of situation at Emory, and I found that really congenial.

C. S.: Did the fellowship last through your entire graduate career?

A. J.: You got a fellowship for the first year, the way the Woodrow Wilson worked. Then the institution was supposed to support you the second year, although there was not a legal obligation to do so, and presumably on through graduate school. There was not in those years any notion of dissertation fellowships because one finished prelims and one went on out to a good tenure-track teaching job because that's what the market was like. Interesting to remember those days. So they did, in fact, support me with a good fellowship the next year and the next, after which I was supposed to be finished with prelims, and I was. What I did then was get married. That actually accelerated my process of finishing the degree because I moved. The move didn't accelerate it, but I did, in fact, move to Waynesburg College where my husband, who had just finished a Ph.D. in political science at Emory, was in his first job. I didn't work, I just worked on the dissertation. I taught maybe a couple of courses, but I just spent about two years working pretty hard on that.

C. S.: Was there anything either in your undergraduate or in your graduate training that prepared you to think about the history of women or made you aware of women in the historical profession?

A. J.: A couple of things happened during the graduate process. One thing I left out that is relevant here in terms of applying to graduate school. I sort of ended up at Emory as a second choice. Where I wanted to go was Johns Hopkins because, of course, that's where graduate study in the U.S. started, and I thought that was a neat idea and really didn't think too much about alternatives. Got a letter back from them saying, well, it's nice that you have a Wilson Fellowship, but we really can't accept you because if we did, we'd have to support you the next year. The way we would do that is by a teaching assistantship, and we couldn't have you teaching our male undergraduates. I kept that letter for years, but I don't still have it. It's a wonderful document though. It was just so clear.

C. S.: Very much a document of its time.

A. J.: Absolutely. At Emory, which had been a male undergraduate school too until probably only four or five years before I went there as a graduate student, there were members of the faculty who made it very clear that one was an interloper. Some of them later made their peace with it and turned around. It is one of the clear memories I have from those years too; there's almost an innocence about the discrimination that's just so fascinating.

C. S.: It's so open and so assumed.

A. J.: That's right. I had done what all graduate school students did after they'd been there three years. I looked for a job, had a placement file put together, and asked the people I'd worked with to write letters for me in the Emory placement office. Several years after that, maybe even as much as ten years after that, a job came up that I really thought I might want to apply for. I've even forgotten what the job was now. It was a real hurry-up thing; I didn't see it until it was about to close. I remember talking to my husband and saying, "Gee it's too bad. I can't possibly get letters of recommendation in this time." And he said, "Well, call the Emory placement office and see if they have something they could ship out really fast." I said, "But oh it's been so long; it's been years." "Why don't you give them a call," he says. So I did, and this wonderful woman answered the phone, and she said, "Well let me look up your file, and I'll read you what's there." She meant it. She read me the letters in the file. I would never have asked her. I almost said, "Oh, no, don't; you're not supposed to." But she's on the other end of the phone saying, "Wow. This is fascinating!" And they were letters by these men at Emory; trying, because they thought I was a good student and they liked me, to do the best they could for me. One comment I remember was something like "Miss Ament seems really quite normal, and I think would fit in easily." I mean literally stuff like that; it was just wonderful. And I wanted to cry after I listened to it because these guys were trying to help me.

C. S.: They were being mentors and being supportive.

A. J.: Yes, they were, but the language was awful—a lot of language about appearance, a lot. I mean I don't think there was a letter that didn't describe how I looked.

C. S.: And this would have been what came out of the placement file or was put in the placement file as you were finishing your degree and beginning to seek jobs, roughly 1967 or 1968?

A. J.: Yes, maybe even a little earlier, I'm not sure.

C. S.: Did you sense any of this same ambivalence as you were looking for jobs in the job interview process or in your assessment of how you were being evaluated when you were interviewed?

A. J.: That's not an easy question to answer. Basically I took what was around because I got into a situation of two careers in one city and small children. I never really went out on the job market. I can remember an interview, for a job I actually did take until we moved, with a small Catholic school in Louisville, and there was a wonderful dean there who was a priest, a Franciscan. Basically he bargained with me about how little I would take because obviously it was a second salary. It was just an interesting conversation. Once again a lot of innocence, I mean those were not times when there was the notion that you had the right to an equal salary or when people couldn't talk about family considerations. I was expecting another baby. "What are you going to do about the child?" I mean people felt free to talk about that stuff in those years.

C. S.: Had you been active in the Southern Historical Association before 1970? I'm aiming at a discussion of the very origins of the Southern Association for Women Historians.

A. J.: I had been a member of the Southern as a graduate student. During those years and for people like me, it was the primary organization. It was the first meeting I ever went to, and graduate students went every fall. You just piled in cars from Atlanta and you went.

C. S.: Was your sense then of the Southern that it was welcoming to you as a woman, either as a graduate student or later as a professional?

A. J.: Yes.

C. S.: Did you have any sense of frustration either professionally or personally that might have led you to participate in the early meetings of women that became the SAWH?

A. J.: Let's think about what we're talking about in terms of years. I want to try to be clear here. You say welcoming, and I did feel welcomed. It partly goes back to Emory, a small graduate school, and they didn't have that many graduate students who could be doing well. They didn't have that many Woodrow Wilson Fellowships. I was single. If there were any women who were going to be encouraged, I was. It makes you feel good not to be a sexist by saying, "Miss Ament will certainly be OK." Marriage was then a difficult hurdle. There is a lovely, lovely little story that tells you a lot about Emory in those days. I've already said I married another graduate student there. He was about four years ahead of me so we only overlapped a couple of years. He was in the political science department, which was run by a wonderfully autocratic southern gentleman. My advisor in the history department was a young man who had been brought into German history, and he was amused because he was of a much different generation and had a more liberal outlook on all of these things. But when Landis and I decided to get married and this was announced, his graduate advisor went to call on my graduate advisor as in the groom's parents calling on the bride's. They had this formal visit, and it was exactly like that. The guy I worked with was much, much amused. But it really was a very old-fashioned paternalism. Part of the visit was to find out whether I was going to be acceptable. From the bridegroom perspective, of course, getting an academic wife was fine because they could help. For my advisor, this might be the end of my career, so he was not so happy about it. That was sort of the way. But a couple of the guys at Emory had wives who had pursued writing careers—if out of secondary school teaching or private schools, but nonetheless had pursued historical research and writing. I mean they were not the least liberated folks in academia, but they were still writing those letters of recommendation. If you think back into those times, it was not an unsupportive context. The curmudgeons were so blatant that you could just kind of laugh at them.

C. S.: Your career has been initially, in the South, and then in Washington, D.C., and now in Indiana. Do you have a sense that the treatment you received was different in the South than it might have been in the North? We've had some of the interviewees suggest that there is a courtesy about southernness that has made it both more difficult and, paradoxically, more easy, personally.

A. J.: I think it's true. There is a toleration of eccentricity in the South, particularly in women. The crazy southern lady could take an academic form. So there was that side to it, at least as I've experienced it, which is after all not Deep South, growing up and then going to school in Atlanta and Nashville, which had already in those years become cities that had experienced dramatic change. But, nonetheless, there is not the premium placed on aggressiveness I think that there is still today. Insofar as men get socialized to be more aggressive and women don't, you're not as disadvantaged, I think, in southern culture in that way.

C. S.: I'd like to bring us back, based on some of the discussion, to why you went to that early meeting, if you even remember that as a conscious choice, and what your sense of the beginning of the SAWH as an organization was? Did you feel the need or did you have a sense of what the SAWH's purpose was and you agreed with it or was it just sort of accident that you wound up at the beginning?

A. J.: I think probably I'd lean more heavily on the accident that I happened to be there, and some people I knew drew me in. I don't feel that I was leading anything at that point. I certainly wouldn't describe myself as someone who saw a need for something to be organized and tried to make it happen. I've done that at other points in my career, but I wouldn't claim to have done it then. I have the feeling that other people were the primary movers.

C. S.: What makes you an interesting interview subject is that although you were there, you were not one of the leaders and so your perceptions of what the organization was about have an important perspective. Do you have any sense or any memory of what they intended or whether they even did intend anything?

A. J.: If I had to characterize what that was about, it probably was about getting a fair shake for women in the profession. By this time it really was clear that there was discrimination—something that obviously I had experienced with the antinepotism rules. I could not teach at the University of Louisville, which was where my husband went to take a job. I had to look at other institutions because it was not possible at that point. There were things like that that people were beginning not to settle for.

C. S.: And did you have a sense that either the SAWH or the SHA was willing to take on those issues?

A. J.: Maybe the SAWH in a limited degree. I don't think I had illusions that they were going to be able to effect a lot of change.

C. S.: You in your career went on to become very active both in the AHA and then the OAH. Can you talk a little bit about your relationship to those organizations and again connect it back to your beginnings in the Southern Historical Association and the SAWH?

A. J.: Well, it was probably in the Southern Historical Association and the SAWH that I realized how easy in a sense and how useful organizations could be, and that other women could be a good support group. This had not really been my experience at Emory because there weren't very many other women. There were some, but some were pretty badly marginalized. There weren't that many mainstreamed, you know, who were supposed to really go on and have careers. It was in those organizations that I began to find a network and to realize the possibilities of making some differences.

C. S.: Did you see, yourself, or did others in your position begin to see those networks as radical or in the process of radicalizing those organizations?

A. J.: I don't think I would have looked at it that way. In fact, I probably still don't. Insofar as one encourages them to be true to their own goals, I don't think of it as radical.

C. S.: And those organizations didn't always articulate what their goals were back then.

A. J.: Right, but you know, if it's promoting history, and all of a sudden we've discovered that women's history is out there, then why shouldn't they promote that? I can go on to some later issues like the boycott of the AHA over the Equal Rights Amendment, which was a tactic I was not enthusiastic about and which I might have seen as more radical, but the basics of it—equal opportunity for jobs, for access to graduate education, for fellowships, and that sort of thing. Those organizations should have been supportive of those goals; I don't think it was all that radical. I think there was some innocence on my part and maybe some of the other women involved. I don't know; it was a very different world. I'm much more cynical than I was thirty, forty years ago.

C. S.: You went on to become very active as a public historian and were one of the founders of the National Council on Public History. Did you feel that the public history community was more welcoming or more accommodating to the needs and professional interests of women or women's history?

A. J.: I just never have thought that was a difficult issue. Public historians needed to be organized, and I was very activist in doing that, both for the federal historians and for the National Council on Public History. They felt discriminated against and marginalized professionally, but most of those people didn't work in women's history. A number of them were women, but actually more were not.

C. S.: And particularly for history in the federal government.

A. J.: Exactly, I was going to say that. I think most of the people that I worked with on those efforts were fairly relaxed about women becoming professional historians or functioning as professional historians. There is an interesting aspect, however, and somewhere I did an article about this, maybe fifteen years ago. Women historians I think were much more timid about venturing into public history. I do believe it has changed for women, particularly for those who had gone back into degree programs and established careers as historians after they had been homemakers, and that's a lot of women, whether that homemaking phase that absorbed them was relatively brief or whether it was a decade or more. An awful lot of women, particularly women my age, went through that phase rather than having always tried to combine them.

C. S.: Or if they did combine them, they combined them with the professional career being very part-time.

A. J.: That's right and to some degree I did a little of that but very, very little. My point is that the academic career then, of graduate school, which may have taken longer, then part-time teaching, was a very hard one in terms of personal identity. For people like me and a lot of younger people, it came fairly easily. You get a fellowship, you go to graduate school, you do well, everything is going fine until you begin to have trouble juggling. It's a big complaint. But if you do the family thing first, and then you go in, then you gradually get yourself back at great cost to you personally. It's hard to give up that self-image and go work a forty-hour week in a government office; that isn't what you sacrificed for. It's not why you did it.

C. S.: So it was difficult for women to see themselves in that public history role, which was primarily one of federal employment.

A. J.: Yes, or a business, heaven forbid. You know some of these jobs weren't that high level. So here you were fighting for professional status, and you're going to work in an office. This is not what you do that for. Obviously, some women did make those choices, but a lot were unwilling to. There's some numbers on this, and in that article I did, I looked at some of this. [Arnita Jones, "Humanities Labor Force: Women Historians as a Special Case," *History Teacher* 15 (May 1982).] The numbers suggested in those years that women tended to go into part-time teaching rather than public history. And I think that was true for that time. I don't know that it is true anymore or that it was true maybe even for the last decade. But when you have that big glut on the market, people had to face the choice. First of all, women could do part-time, usually because that generation was not totally dependent on earnings, but also it was a way of keeping a self-image that had been difficult to create.

C. S.: I'd like to get back and talk about the SAWH. Do you remember any particular issues or concerns at the time you were an officer and more active that you might tell us about?

A. J.: I have to tell you that the real reason I ended up being president was because D'Ann Campbell recruited me.

C. S.: But again networks.

A. J.: It's that simple. It wasn't something that I sought, and frankly I don't think it was something that was particularly contested. The number of people involved in this was still pretty small I think in 1974.

C. S.: What was the function of the organization at that point?

A. J.: It was a kind of women's caucus within the Southern. It was to try to get the Southern to do the right thing in those areas where it did things: women on programs, that sort of thing. And, I really think it probably was a matter largely of giving women some visibility at those annual SHA meetings.

C. S.: How important was Ben Wall or, in fact, Neva Wall, his wife, in those years in terms of encouraging women? Or did they have any attitudes or activities that you remember vis-à-vis the SAWH?

A. J.: Ben seemed to be the personification of the organization.

C. S.: I remember that even ten years later!

A. J.: More than any historical organization I've known, the Southern was Ben Wall and Ben Wall was the Southern. So it was a matter of whether you could convince him to do what you wanted him to do. And my memory is that he was fairly accommodating.

C. S.: There are two interests that have surfaced that are actually sort of ahistorical in that they're reading back into the past issues that have arisen today. One of them has to do with the recognition or the presence or recruiting of African Americans. Do you remember African American women in the Southern? Or were there any that were involved even in the first decade of the Southern Association for Women Historians? And can you expand that to include the Southern as well?

A. J.: I don't remember any. I think the first Southern meeting that I went to was probably in Asheville, and the fellow from Mississippi, whose name was James W. Silver, spoke about his experiences. He was president of the Southern in 1962, and even that was an act of defiance because he had been very controversial. I have the memory that the Southern Historical Association was opposed to segregation and was opposed to a kind of tough stand on behalf of state's rights, as they called it during those years, and certainly supportive of efforts on the part of blacks to get voting rights, civil rights, all that sort of thing. I don't remember African Americans at those meetings. I certainly don't remember any African American women from those years. Now, my husband has clear memories. I don't know why we were talking about this the other day; it was a totally different context. But we were speaking of the Southern Political Science Association always meeting in Gatlinburg, Tennessee, because it was the only place that you could have an integrated meeting, driving from Atlanta to Gatlinburg with colleagues, other faculty, graduate students. He taught as full-time faculty at Emory and as a graduate student, going to those meetings and driving with blacks and not being able to eat until you got to Gatlinburg because they couldn't eat, and you weren't going to go in and eat without them.

C. S.: The other area that we have been curious about is outreach as historians to those teaching in the secondary schools and particular an interest in sharing the new scholarship on the history of women or the history of African Americans. Do you remember the Southern Association for Women Historians either being concerned about that or did you yourself play a role in bringing women's history into either the Indiana or the Kentucky communities where you taught?

A. J.: No. I don't remember ever having thought about it in those years.

This goes back a little bit to what women are escaping from, and it was teaching in high schools. Think about it. It was more difficult, I think, psychologically to make those connections. I now know that in the 1960s there were some people around the country who were involved in doing things with the schools, but I don't remember that any of the associations were. This would be individuals and departments, for instance at Indiana University. But certainly I don't think it was an issue for women historians at that point to try to make an impact on what was being taught in the high schools. It's a matter of what you're talking about in terms of timing. Probably it was the first AHA that I went to, I remember hearing Gerda Lerner do a session on women's history. That was a revelation. There was a session on women's history at one of the meetings, and it was just so exciting and so wonderful. Clearly a lot of people were beginning to do some work but this was early, even mid-1970s. Could you go out and put together a long bibliography? No. So the idea that there was a corpus of printed work to get into the high schools was not really possible, I think. By the time you get to 1980, it would be a different story, but if you're talking about 1970, it wasn't there. It just wasn't there.

Rosemary F. Carroll

Rosemary F. Carroll is currently the Henry and Margaret Hagge Distinguished Professor Emerita of History of Coe College. She earned her Ph.D. in American History from Rutgers University in 1968 and her J.D. from the College of Law, University of Iowa in 1983. She is the author of several articles and has written extensively on Lou Henry Hoover. She has received numerous awards and travel grants, including a National Endowment for the Humanities travel grant and a Hoover grant from the Hoover Presidential Library Association. She served as chair of the Department of History at Coe College from 1988 until her retirement in 2001, and as Affirmative Action Officer and as Prelaw Advisor for Coe College. She was President of the SAWH from 1975 to 1976.

Interviewer: Constance B. Schulz
Transcriber: Victoria Kalemaris
The following interview took place October 26, 1995.

R. C.: Let's begin with my educational background. I hold a bachelor of arts degree from Brown University in the field of American civilization. I hold a master of arts from Wesleyan University in Connecticut in the field of political science and history, and I hold a Ph.D. degree from Rutgers University in intellectual and cultural history, and a law degree from the College of Law, University of Iowa. I began my academic career by teaching at a small college in New York City, on Staten Island, Notre Dame College, where I was for two years from 1968 to 1970. I then went as a visiting assistant professor for a year to Denison University in Granville, Ohio. Subsequently, in 1971, I went as an assistant professor to Coe College in Cedar Rapids, Iowa. I have worked as an assistant, associate, and full professor, and since 1988 have chaired the Department of History. When I took my appointment at Coe, a couple of years after I came here, I was asked to be the college's affirmative action officer and equal employment opportunity officer, which subsequently led me to go to the College of Law at the University of Iowa and receive a Juris Doctor degree. I have been since 1983 a licensed attorney in the state of Iowa.

Also in the early 1970s, I think it was about 1973, the president of Coe asked me to begin a program of continuing education for women in the greater Cedar Rapids area. The women either had never been to college or had gone to college for a short time and interrupted it to raise a family and then were coming back. When I began the program, there was nothing in the way of a women's movement outside of a very small nucleus of the National Organization for Women (NOW) in Cedar Rapids. I am very happy to say that the program has grown and flourished. I personally ran the program for five years, did all of the recruiting and counseling, and actually taught an introductory course for these people because many of these women were so nervous about going back to school in the January term. Coe was on a four-one-four calendar, and January was the only time I could be released from my offerings in the history department. By 1978, it was becoming very clear that these women could easily funnel directly into college-level courses. At that time the college also was thinking about expanding the program to include men as well as women, which was all very fine, but by this point my responsibilities in the Department of History were so great that I said, I guess this is where I need to get off.

In any case, I no longer was directing that program, but I was very much interested in the history of American women. I came to realize more and more in dealing with these women the importance of it. This was at the time, of course, in the early to mid-1970s, when women's history as a field was really just beginning to develop. I think about people like Gerda Lerner and Anne Firor Scott, who were early on very much interested in women's history. I went to many sessions at either the OAH or the AHA meetings where they had sessions about women or were beginning to form a women's caucus. I was at the meeting in 1969 where the CCWHP was formed in Washington.

C. S.: So you really were present at many foundings.

R. C.: Yes, at that one, and then the next year Mollie Davis and Barbara Schnorrenberg, Arnita Jones, and others of us went to the Southern meeting in Louisville. I notice from looking back on my notes on my association with the Southern Association for Women Historians that the hotels where we had met are now no longer in existence. They seem to have been demolished. We were at the Kentucky Hotel in 1970 in Louisville; that was the place where there was the concern about would we be able to get a space for a meeting. Well, as others have doubtless told you, we did get space. It happened to be in the basement next to the boiler room. There were perhaps fifteen, twenty people there at the time; we were calling ourselves at that time the women's caucus. It was an informal kind of group, and the strategy at that time was how can we be certain to get a more suitable room next year and to get the message—because it was largely word of mouth—out to others that we would be having a meeting of the group. This informal structure went on from that 1970 meeting until by 1973, 1974, but particularly by 1974, we were more organized and we began to think about having officers. One of the major things in those very early years was recruitment—to get members. There were efforts made with the various southern colleges and universities. We were trying to get persons from a variety of schools in the South and also get people, like myself, who were in other parts of the United States.

C. S.: Was that to attend the SHA and come to the meeting of the caucus?

R. C.: Yes, and come to the women's caucus. Barbara Schnorrenberg was beginning to put out little announcements for us. I would say that it was in certainly 1973 or 1974 but more probably 1974 that we had officers as such. I remember Charlotte Davis and Mollie Davis worked as cochairs, and then I believe the next person in line was Constance Myers, and then Arnita Jones. By this point, I had been asked if I would chair a committee on bylaws. I was asked by Mollie Davis to chair a bylaws committee to set a more formal structure for what has been an ongoing women's caucus in the SHA since 1970. I suspect I had been asked to do this since I had been at every meeting of the caucus since its founding in Louisville in 1970 and was one of the quote, unquote, "originals" at the founding of the CCWHP in 1969. Since our group in the SHA was neither large nor very formal in structure, I drafted a very simple set of bylaws, which I sent to Mollie Davis. What she said was that they added a statement that the group is interested in the serious study and advancement of historical knowledge. I had sent them also to two other people chosen at the recent Dallas meeting, A. Elizabeth Taylor and Martha Swain, both of Texas Woman's University. From what Mollie had written to me, it seemed apparent that the women's caucus of SHA should ask for independent affiliated status so that it could continue to hold its meeting annually at the SHA in the event that the SHA followed the path of the AHA on this subject.

It was after the more formal structure was formed that I was president of the organization in 1975–1976, and it was at that meeting in 1975 that we formally adopted the bylaws and also a different name, the Southern Association for Women Historians. I just was looking at a letter that I had, dated December 16, 1976, from A. Elizabeth Taylor in which she said, "I want to congratulate you on this splendid job that you did with the women's association. I think you've put it on a sound base and it is now on its way towards becoming a lasting influence among Southern Women Historians. The new name is quite an improvement over Women's Caucus." And, of course, A. Elizabeth Taylor was really kind of a founding grandmother along with us. She was right there with us from the very outset.

C. S.: I wanted to ask a question about that Louisville meeting and that was, did that meeting occur because people who knew they would be at the SHA meeting planned it in advance and made arrangements beforehand?

R. C.: Right. It was out of that CCWHP meeting in Washington the year before. I believe it was at the OAH meeting in spring 1970, that we planned that at the next Southern meeting in fall 1970 we would meet as a women's group.

C. S.: So it was preplanned, and you were able to get that room that you were concerned about in advance and to make an announcement that it would occur?

R. C.: Well, I was not in on the room-arrangement business, but I should think that Mollie Davis and others were in touch with Ben Wall about securing a place. And whether or not the actual location was known prior to their arrival in Louisville or just when they arrived in Louisville, I don't know. But there was nothing in the *Program*. As I say, so much of this was word of mouth. I can remember that much of the strategy of those first couple of years of the meeting was how best to approach the officers of the SHA about getting an announcement in the *Program*.

C. S.: Is your memory that they were really resistant and didn't want you to get a room or have an announcement?

R. C.: We just didn't know. We just didn't know how they were going to react to it, and I remember that D'Ann Campbell was also with us, and as it turned out, I think, we were perhaps needlessly concerned. We were unduly fretful about the most gracious way to get on the program. Should we call? Should we write about being published in the *Program*? It turned out that it was as easy as could be because Ben Wall was quite cooperative and said, "Sure that could be put in." Then we were so delighted that in 1971 we had graduated to the first floor. The next step was that not only were we going to meet but we got a definite room, and we were always in much more commodious settings. And the interesting thing was that when I spoke to the group at the meeting in the fall of 1976, which was during the time of my presidency and presiding over that meeting, we were quite delighted that our membership had grown to ninety-three.

Initially we were about twenty people, maybe thirty, and then by that point we were ninety-three. The dues were $2, and then we had to go up to $2.50, and then we went to $3.50 but $2.50 for students. All of this was engendered by the fact that postage rates were climbing, and we wanted to remain solvent. It's a great delight to me that we not only remained solvent but also that we have literally flourished. And we've also made that determination by 1975 or 1976 that we would have men in the organization, it would not be exclusively for women. Anybody working in the field of women's history was welcome.

C. S.: Were there men interested before 1975 and 1976 in being part of your group or involved in encouraging you to form a separate group?

R. C.: There were different people who were interested. Of course, Mollie Davis's mentor at the University of Georgia, Willard B. Gatewood was interested. He was always very supportive and other people who were interested in women's history like Bill Chafe at Duke, and there were others. They were really very supportive. Once we got the organization and we felt we were on a kind of solid footing, our next concern was beginning to get women on the program and to get women on the various councils.

C. S.: When you say the next concern, does that mean perhaps next in importance but in the same meetings of 1971, and 1972, or do you mean later chronologically in time?

R. C.: Chronologically later. For example, I might just read this to you. This is the *Newsletter* from Barbara that was published in January 1977, which was reporting on the meeting in November of 1976 at the SHA, which was held in Atlanta at the now-defunct Sheraton-Biltmore Hotel. "At the meeting we heard a very informative talk by Mary Elizabeth Murdock on the Sophia Smith Collection at Smith College. Helena Lewis, who was at Appalachian State College and was vice-president, reported on the Berkshire Conference held in June, and we heard from Judy Gentry, who was another early member on the SHA Program Committee. Linda Piper, University of Georgia, told us about a successful local women's group in Athens. President Rosemary Carroll, Coe College, introduced several matters of business. All members are urged to join both CCWHP and the Southern Historical Association."

C. S.: So from the beginning you were really also promoting membership in the Southern, and this was clearly an organization that was to remain part of the Southern. Is that part of your memory?

R. C.: Right. This was the women's organization, like CCWHP was in the AHA. The whole idea of this was to make a kind of counterpart in the Southern. Initially, in those early years we were using the term *Women's Caucus,* and by that 1976 meeting, it was formally accepted that we would be the Southern Association for Women Historians and even had stationery printed with that name on it. The meeting considered the question of formal association with the CCWHP, which was supported by several members. A motion to make formal affiliation was passed unanimously. And then Barbara made the report that our number of dues-paying members tripled in 1976. This means, of course, more money but even better, active and increasing interest and support of SAWH. Though our treasury is larger now than it ever has been, expenses are rising also. One way that we have been able to increase our membership is by mailing out increasing numbers of *Newsletter*s. Therefore, it was moved and passed that the section of the bylaws which fixed the dues at two dollars be changed to read, "Dues are fixed by the annual meeting of the Association and may be subject to periodic increase." The meeting also changed the membership provision of the bylaws to read, "Membership in the association is open to all interested historians and graduate students in history." Elections for 1976–1977 were held, and the following person after me was Helena Lewis at Appalachian State University, the vice president chosen was A. Elizabeth Taylor, and Barbara Schnorrenberg remained secretary-treasurer. [Editors' note: In its early years the SAWH organizational structure was informal, and presidents chose their successors; Martha Swain remembers that Taylor refused to serve and insisted that Swain be chosen in her place as 1977 vice president and, thus, 1978 president.]

C. S.: Do you have some particular impressions stemming from what you're reminded of by that *Newsletter* that are not in the *Newsletter* that would be valuable for this purpose?

R. C.: I'm just looking at my own notes when I was president. These pertained to the annual meeting of the association, my agenda for the meeting that was on November 11, 1976, at 4:30 p.m. in the Biltmore Hotel in Atlanta. This was the seventh annual meeting of SAWH, and we had nearly one hundred members, really ninety-three, and the speaker. There was much talk about the dues because of the postage problem; we addressed CCWHP resolutions, and then we were talking about regional centers, and that was what Linda Piper reported from Georgia. Then we discussed the need for paper proposals for the spring and how we were encouraging people to send in paper proposals to get on the program. I have a section in my notes called "future directions": Send in names of candidates for committee position, work to get women on committees and on the Executive Council of the SHA. That was what we were much interested in doing, that and updating the bylaws. The SAWH Executive Council tended to meet informally at the spring OAH meeting to set the agenda for the fall.

Then we began to look into the matter of grants for the organization and also asking those in the regional groups if they would send information. Just after I had been made the president, there were certain things that I wrote to both Barbara and the vice president. For example [reading from her notes]: "We will need to have an annual business meeting, which I think should be on Thursday at 4:30 for which we should perhaps have an announced agenda by way of a newsletter in order to attract more than a handful of people. . . . I would like to settle on a time for the meeting so that we can be sure to have it printed in the *Program*." We wanted a definite room assignment. I wrote that "perhaps we should have the business meeting in conjunction with a cash bar cocktail hour or coffee hour if the former is not feasible in terms of cost. Secondly, we should contact Edwin A. Miles, University of Houston, chair of the Program Committee, offering a list of women who could serve as commentators or chairpersons. Thirdly, about having someone in the Atlanta area to be in charge of local arrangements. At the breakfast meeting we had in Washington, the name of Rosemary Begemann of Georgia State College–Milledgeville, was suggested. Fourthly, that we invite local people in Atlanta to come to the meeting. Fifth, I would appreciate your suggestions on a proposed agenda for the business meeting if you think that is a good idea."

The idea was that this information would go out in an early fall mailing. These were suggestions that I made to the other officers in December of 1975 looking forward to the meeting the following year. And then, as I say, there were the bylaws.

Then another thing we were very much interested in was feminine survival and advancement in the historical profession. At the 1975 SAWH meeting, Jane DeHart Matthews, of the University of North Carolina at Greensboro, gave a talk on "Women Attend Graduate School: Emotional, Financial and Peer Group Support." Then D'Ann Campbell, UNC–Chapel Hill, spoke on "Women Enter the Historical Profession: Discrimination, Masculine Backlash, and Job Prices"; Eleanor F. Straub, assistant executive director for the American Historical Association, "Past, Present and Future Prospects for Women in the Historical Profession."

C. S.: Was this a session on the program?

R. C.: Yes, this was at our annual meeting, and that meeting was at the Shoreham-Americana Hotel in Washington, D.C., in November 1975. Helena Lewis spoke also on "Women in the Historical Profession and the Role of Affirmative Action." And then I also talked on the subject of affirmative action because, as I say, I have been the affirmative action officer at the college since 1973.

C. S.: As you were speaking, it struck me that for you professionally the OAH had been a very important predecessor to your becoming involved and active in SAWH. And I just wanted to go back and clarify, were you active in the SHA or the OAH, and was SAWH something that was added on to that? Or did you really become involved in SAWH because you were not able to be active or have an active role in those other organizations?

R. C.: I would say this. In the very early part of my career, my Ph.D. is 1968, we would go to these meetings, and there would not be many women. For instance, if you went to a general session, many of the women were either like myself, new, or they were on the edge of retirement. When I secured my degree, I immediately joined the OAH, and I joined the AHA. Then Martha Swain was a longtime friend of mine; we had taught together in a National Endowment for the Humanities Summer Institute in 1965. She said she wanted me to join the Southern, so it was at her instigation that I joined the Southern. I guess I must have joined it in 1969 or 1970, something like that. We women who would go to the OAH or AHA and go to the Southern became a kind of a coterie that kept reappearing year after year. We would always get together and talk. It was out of that, particularly I think the impetus of Gerda Lerner coming to talk at one of the OAH meetings, that I was adamant about the importance of forming the SAWH.

C. S.: For the Southern.

R. C.: In the Southern that's where Mollie Davis and Connie Myers and Judy Gentry and all of these other people, Jody Carrigan—people like myself decided that now was the time, and so we started in a kind of timorous and groping way in 1970. We were really feeling very good by 1975, 1976; we had nearly one hundred members; we had bylaws and a structure; and we had our name in the *Program* and a definite room. Now we were moving into getting women on the program, even if it was just a woman, a session. We were really regularized and flourishing by the end of the seventies. As you well know, in the eighties we were able to actually have the Willie Lee Rose Prize and the Julia Cherry Spruill Prize developed so that SAWH became a very major organization. One of the questions you people kindly sent to me was about the radicalization of feminism. That clearly was not in any way an issue in the early 1970s. What our concern was at that time was very much equal employment opportunity.

C. S.: Which might have been a radical idea.

R. C.: The problem was the old-boy network in terms of employment.

C. S.: Did you feel that you had difficulty after graduating with a degree from Rutgers in terms of finding the first position?

R. C.: My Rutgers degree was not the impediment. You know in graduate school you do not have a class, but there is a group of you who enters together and there were ten in the group. Of the ten that entered in the fall of 1964, myself and Claudia Koonz, who is now at Duke in German history, were among that group. Alice Kessler-Harris had entered before us, but I remember she was in one of my seminars. She was ahead of me, but she was in one of the Warren Susman seminars with me. In any case, I was at Rutgers four years, 1964 to 1968. I had a teaching assistantship and a research assistantship and then was very fortunate to get one of the eleven university fellowships. And then in my last year, when I was writing the dissertation, I did have a job offer, because Rutgers had someone going on leave in the department. I had a minor field in Latin American history. I taught the Latin American survey, a tutorial in U.S. history for some honors students, and an American studies seminar with a senior professor in the English department. I was the first woman to hold the rank of instructor at Rutgers College, which was the men's college. For the year, they were very good; they blocked my classes so they were on Tuesdays and Thursdays so I would have time to do my writing of the dissertation, which I did during that year of 1967 and 1968 and finished the degree. But here is what happened while I was writing the dissertation. One of the professors said to me, "You are no question our best graduate student, but we don't know what we're going to do about placing you." So there we were. It just was a matter of record that I had had all of these fellowships, and I had a straight-A record in the program. The interesting thing of how I secured the first job was that there was a notice on the bulletin board that there was this opening for an assistant professor at Notre Dame College, which was a small Catholic college, now defunct, on Staten Island. The notice gave the name of the academic dean. I simply called, because at this point I was so tired, Connie, of sending out letters and either getting no response or getting them back. One response was outrageous, "It is the policy of this department not to hire women." I just picked up the telephone and called this academic dean at Notre Dame College, and he and I, just one of those happy, fortuitous events, had a cordial conversation. Well, in our conversation, he invited me to the campus for an interview.

C. S.: Was your dissertation advisor supportive of you and helpful in trying to find jobs?

R. C.: He was supportive and actually was one of the ones in the department who first began to take on women graduate students.

C. S.: Who was this?

R. C.: That was Warren Susman. He would begin looking at, shopping around, talking to different people, and so on. And he would come up with ideas about places.

It was really like trying to find a diamond in a haystack. I remember a young man who had had some difficulty in the first round of his orals. I spent a great deal of time prepping him for when he had to retake them. He just couldn't seem to comprehend American Puritanism, and that had been his downfall. Interestingly enough, when he went to a meeting to have a job interview at the AHA meeting in Toronto, he met a man in the airport who was going there from a particular school. They struck up a conversation, and this fellow arranged for my graduate student friend to have an interview. Lo and behold, he got the job right away at a very fine school. So the joke among us women used to be, "Don't go to the meetings, go to the airport." It was really very, very tough going. We were young and looking to the future of our careers; we were looking for tenure-track appointments; we weren't interested in part-time jobs.

C. S.: Was there an assumption that that's all you ought to have?

R. C.: I think that there was a general assumption initially that you just wouldn't have anything, frankly, and then, I don't know. It was kind of like this was a new phenomenon. Who are these women, what are we supposed to do with them? They were beginning, some of them, to love to have them as students, but I don't know that they all felt terribly a sense of responsibility to make strong efforts in placing them once they got through their work.

C. S.: I'm curious, in those early years between 1970 and 1975 do you remember from those meetings were there many African American women or even African American men and was that ever part of the initial concern of the SAWH to be inclusive in terms of race?

R. C.: That was very much a concern and we did have a few Afro-American women who would appear and reappear. Their numbers were always small, but we were very, very interested in getting them integrated with the organization and joining with us women. One of the things of course, as you know historically, with the African American women, was that race was a more predominant concern than sex, certainly at the time, but they did come to the meetings, and we were always very welcoming and certainly wanted to have them with us.

C. S.: I'm curious, at that point there was neither a Women's Committee in the AHA nor a Women's Committee in the Southern?

R. C.: The AHA Committee on the Status of Women of which Willie Lee Rose was the chair was in 1970. That was the one that did the big report—"Rose Report"—and found out that a major university had never had a woman historian in the department. For example, when I was at Rutgers, that was a department of somewhere from eighteen to twenty; there were no women who were technically on the history faculty at Rutgers.

C. S.: Have you actually taught women's history courses, or has there been pressure on you to do so if you didn't, either at Coe College or earlier on Staten Island?

R. C.: My teaching of women's history developed out of my own interest. My first sabbatical at Coe was in 1976, and I spent that at the Sophia Smith Collection and at the Schlesinger Library at Radcliffe because, as you can well appreciate, when I went through undergraduate college and the graduate Ph.D. program, there was no such thing as a course in women's history. I came back to Coe in the fall of 1976 and offered a seminar on women's history; it went extraordinarily well. I developed the course further to be a regular history course offering. Initially, the men in the department agreed that I would offer it as an occasional course and that meant I offered it in alternate years, always in the fall. Then a few years later I said, "Gentlemen, this course is getting very fine enrollment; I'd really like to keep up the momentum," so I was able to offer it annually. "Women in America" was the first catalog course at Coe in the field of women, dealing with women exclusively and in women's history. So ever since 1983 it has been a regular course offered every fall and it's become a foundation course in what has developed in the college, a program, just started a year ago, in gender studies.

C. S.: Do you think that it was your involvement in women's issues as a professional historian that led you to an interest in the history of women? I'm looking for a relationship between the two.

R. C.: I think it went all the way back to my undergraduate days. I took a course at Brown University on social and intellectual history in America; I was junior at Brown.

C. S.: Were you actually at Brown or were you enrolled in Pembroke at that point?

R. C.: It was called Pembroke College in Brown University.

C. S.: So women were in Brown as such?

R. C.: Right, they'd been there since the 1890s. I always said I was a Brown University graduate even before the official merger in 1969 for this reason, when you received your degree, it said Brown University, not a word about Pembroke, and all your classes were integrated, as were the library facilities. The only classes that weren't integrated were a physical education requirement and a course in speech. Now why the speech course wasn't integrated, I have no idea. Really what the Pembroke campus essentially meant was that we had our own exclusively women's dormitories and we had our own student government and student activities; the *Pembroke Record* was the newspaper, this sort of thing. In terms of the actual academic courses, they were always integrated from the very beginning.

In this particular course on social and intellectual history of the United States, we were to do an original research paper. My home city is Newport, Rhode Island. Located there is the very fine Redwood Library, begun in 1747 by Abraham Redwood; it's the oldest private, ongoing library in the United States. My parents always encouraged me. My mother was an elementary school principal and was always very interested in my education. Mother had been a successful professional woman; my father was extremely supportive, and he had had a successful professional career. Their attitude towards their daughter (I was an only child) was you do whatever you wish in terms of your capabilities and do the best of which you're capable. I thought it would be kind of interesting to do something about women. I said I'm interested in this woman, Margaret Fuller. I had taken several books out of what was then the main library at Brown, the John Hay Library; Mother went to the Redwood, and, Connie, what a treasure trove she found for me! She kindly went to the Redwood Library during the weekend and found these first editions. So of course I had a stellar paper for that course. Margaret Fuller was more on the back burner in those days.

C. S.: No one had heard of her.

R. C.: Exactly. Here this woman had done so many wonderful things and been associated with and had her conversation classes with Melville, Hawthorne, Thoreau, and Emerson in the mid-nineteenth century. That had been an interest of mine. Cultural and intellectual history has always been my major interest, and I think that kind of flowed nicely with American civilization. My interest in women's history came from that background. My first published article was for a course in the history of the American South that Eugene Genovese gave at Rutgers. He said to us graduate students, "I want you to write a quality paper that is of the publishable type." I took him at his word. I went to the archives at Rutgers, which had just accessioned the William Elliot Griffis papers because Griffis was an 1869 graduate of Rutgers. Among the collection was his sister's diaries, Margaret Clark Griffis, who served as a plantation teacher in three different plantations in the South, in Tennessee and in Virginia, and was there at the opening of the Civil War. The first article was on her diaries from 1859 to 1861, which I published in the *Tennessee Historical Quarterly*; that came out my last year at Rutgers, in 1969.

C. S.: So you were able to do women's history research and publish in women's history, and that may have led you to being aware of the need for women activism.

R. C.: Right. We were all very interested, and I think there was some sort of sense of security to the way we sort of hung together, sat together, had meals together. We were upset about that fact that you'd get these programs and nary a woman was on a committee or nary a woman was in any kind of office or even on the program so our focus was to change that. In other words, we wanted to make our invisible selves visible.

Builders

By 1976, the caucus of southern women historians had begun to function as a separate organization, independent of the SHA. The group of women whose interviews make up this section became the "builders" who took a loosely structured ad hoc gathering of like-minded women historians and created an organization. Working with those who had founded the organization and kept it going, they gave it a new name—the Southern Association for Women Historians. They wrote a set of bylaws, organized a Membership Committee, and began the SAWH tradition of making their annual gathering at the SHA meeting a scholarly as well as a social occasion by inviting distinguished scholars to give an address to those attending. Martha Swain served as president in 1978, Judith Gentry in 1979, Carol Bleser in 1980, Elizabeth Jacoway in 1981, Jo Anne Carrigan in 1982, and Betty Brandon in 1983.

By the late 1970s, the SAWH found itself concerned with a number of issues on which its leaders took sometimes contradictory positions. The final push to adopt an Equal Rights Amendment, guaranteeing women a constitutional basis for equal treatment under the law, faced opposition in many southern states. The SAWH adopted a position in support of an initial SHA decision to boycott those states that had not ratified the amendment, but not all SAWH leaders were comfortable with transforming their organization into an advocacy group. Within the membership a younger cohort of scholars, trained in doctoral programs where the study of the history of women had emerged as part of the "new social history," began to stress the need for the organization to play a role in the development of the new scholarly field of women's history. Others insisted that women's organizations like the SAWH needed to keep clearly focused on the continued need to fight for women's equity within the profession.

Martha Swain has spent most of her life and all of her professional career in the Deep South. Almost alone among the women interviewed for this project, she is a role model for the late-twentieth-century phenomenon of women who came to universities as "returning students," for she began her doctorate in history at Vanderbilt after having already had a sixteen-year career as a public school teacher. Her Vanderbilt education gave her an important link to its alumni, notably A. Elizabeth Taylor, and provided the basis for her initial involvement in the SHA and eventually the SAWH. Like her mentor, Taylor, her own research has consistently focused on the history of southern women. Swain, however, insists that women historians must lead the way in the inclusion of women within the larger study of American history rather than on creation of separate courses in women's history. That emphasis may be in part because she spent most of her university teaching career at Texas Woman's University. Swain played an important role in expanding the membership of the SAWH in a critical period, drawing on the community of other women scholars so crucial to her own professional development, and organizing an effective letter-writing promotional campaign to recruit others into the organization.

Judith Gentry came into the presidency of the SAWH just as the fight for passage of the ERA became an urgent issue for professional women, and as her interview relates, she used her office to encourage the SHA to support boycott of non-ERA southern states in planning the annual SHA meeting. Like a number of others interviewed for this project, her lifelong association with the University of Southwestern Louisiana began as a "spousal hire," when she followed her husband to the community where he had an academic position. Gentry's doctoral field of study, the fiscal and economic history of the Civil War, has made her a builder of the SAWH financial stability, an area that became increasingly important as the organization grew. During her presidency, she worked with Treasurer Barbara Schnorrenberg to manage the growing budget of a maturing organization, and subsequently served for some time as chair of the

Finance Committee as it took on the responsibility of monitoring the major investments that secure the endowments for the SAWH prizes. Born and raised in the Upper South, educated at the University of Maryland and at Rice University in Houston, Texas, Gentry provides thoughtful comment on two themes that are constant, though sometimes implicit, throughout the interviews: the mentoring support that her generation of women scholars received from the "old school" tradition of "southern gentlemen"; and the impact of the liberal and activist context of the times on her and on the women with whom she worked in the SAWH.

If Swain's and Gentry's tenures can be characterized as strengthening the infrastructure of the growing SAWH organization, Carol Bleser's role in the leadership was important for insisting on reaching out to make it and the work of its members more visible. A southerner by birth, she credits her entry into serious study of history to the influence of her undergraduate education at Converse College, a southern women's college, but for more than twenty years she studied the South and its history from the North, completing her Ph.D. at Columbia University and then teaching in northern universities until appointed to a distinguished professorship at Clemson University. Like others, she was influenced in the location of her teaching career by her marriage after graduate school. Eventually, she and her husband accommodated their dual careers by maintaining more than one residence. She observes perceptively that women historians in the North in the 1930s rarely married. As SAWH president in 1980, she was a leader in the movement to initiate and raise money for the organization's two prizes, particularly the Willie Lee Rose Prize, which she insisted must go to a woman scholar. Before her presidency, the parties SAWH leaders held in their rooms after the annual business meeting at the Southern provided an important social component; Bleser made sure that leaders of the SHA were invited to the party held in her suite, and she characterizes the social visibility that resulted as part of a wise political strategy increasingly followed by women determined to play a larger role in mainstream professional organizations.

For southern women historians who began their professional careers in the second half of the twentieth century, the backdrop of their own education was the civil rights movement; race and gender issues were often intertwined. Elizabeth Jacoway, like Mollie Davis, was raised in a prominent, privileged family, and she was profoundly influenced by that movement. The choices she has made in her own career as a writer and historian to be also a traditional wife and mother have given her story a somewhat different character. An independent scholar by necessity of geographic location as well as by choice, Jacoway brought to her presidency of the

SAWH in 1981 experience as a woman community leader. She insisted that the amount of money awarded in the Spruill and Rose prizes should be substantial to validate in yet another way the importance of that scholarship by and about southern women.

Jody Carrigan, whose career as a historian began in the South with her education in Louisiana, has a foot strongly in the Midwest with her long teaching career at the University of Nebraska in Omaha. She recalls that her own awakening to the key role of women's history in expanding an understanding of the past came when she was asked to teach a course in women's history in 1973 and observes that increasingly what she believed was only common sense in pursuing inclusiveness in the historical enterprise has been labeled by male historians as radical. Like the other women "builders" of the organization, she became president in 1981 through an informal system that brought rising women scholars into the SAWH by inviting them to take leadership roles. As president, she helped to create the compromise whereby the SAWH awarded two prizes, one for scholarship by a woman, and one for scholarship about southern women. During her presidency, the SHA finally instituted a permanent Committee on the Status of Women, in which she played a persuasive role.

Betty Brandon thus came to her role as SAWH president in November of 1982 when much had been accomplished: though the first prizes would not be awarded until 1987, the process of establishing and raising funds to support them was well under way. The SHA appointed A. Elizabeth Taylor as chair of the Committee on the Status of Women. Brandon had been a member of the SHA since 1964; she had been in Louisville in 1970 and "present at the creation" of the southern women's caucus there; she had initiated courses in the history of women at the University of South Alabama, where she has taught since 1969. In her interview, therefore, she stresses the importance of cooperation, of pushing steadily for gradual change.

By the end of 1983 the builders could look back on thirteen prosperous years of growth and change. Perhaps symptomatic of the changes brought by growth were the shifts in the constitution adopted that year: a change of the organization's name, originally the Caucus of Women Historians, changed in 1975 to the Southern Association *of* Women Historians, and since 1983, the Southern Association *for* Women Historians.

Martha Swain

Martha Swain is Cornaro Professor of History Emerita of Texas Woman's University and is concurrently Professor of History at Mississippi State University. She earned her Ph.D. from Vanderbilt University in 1975 and is the author of two books: *Pat Harrison: The New Deal Years* (1978); and *Ellen S. Woodward: New Deal Advocate for Women* (1995). She has authored over twenty articles and encyclopedia entries and has been awarded numerous grants, fellowships, and prizes, including the Eudora Welty Prize from the Mississippi University for Women for her manuscript on Ellen Woodward. She has served on the Board of Editors for the *Journal of Southern History* and the *Journal of Mississippi History.* She also has served on numerous organizational advisory boards and review committees, including the National Endowment for the Humanities. She was President of the SAWH from 1977 to 1978.

Interviewer: Victoria Kalemaris
Transcriber: Victoria Kalemaris
The following interview took place November 10, 1995.

M. S.: I grew up in Northeast Mississippi, went to schools there, graduated from Starkville High, and then went across the street from where I lived to go to Mississippi State University, and I graduated with a social sciences major in 1950. I wanted to be a social studies teacher. I did that a couple years, and then I got my master's at Vanderbilt, and I went to teach in Natchez, Mississippi. Then I taught in Pensacola. After teaching those sixteen years in the public schools, I decided that I was unfulfilled without a Ph.D. So at age forty, I went to Vanderbilt to begin the Ph.D. and was able to stay there until I had the dissertation written and left there in 1974 and went to teach at Texas Woman's University. My mentors—the persons who were really responsible for my getting the job there—were Vanderbilt graduates, particularly A. Elizabeth Taylor, who, of course, is a name that everybody can recognize. I taught there twenty-one years, and I just retired last May. Now I have a part-time appointment as professor of history at Mississippi State University.

V. K.: Did you face any discrimination or find any difficulties in terms of the fact that you were a woman getting your Ph.D. in history?

M. S.: No, I don't know what the other experiences of women at Vanderbilt have been, but I was treated with a great deal of respect. But then you see it was different; I was older than many of my professors, and I also had gone to Vanderbilt and gotten my master's. I'd been out and had sort of proven myself, so they were helpful to me, very cordial to me, and I experienced no discrimination whatsoever. I was there at a time when there was no one teaching women's history, and so I had no women's history. I didn't think of myself as being a women's historian, and I still don't. I went there to do New Deal history, and my research and writing have all been in the Roosevelt and the Truman era, but I have gotten very interested in women, particularly Mississippi women, and the work that I am doing is now women's history. It's called that, but to me it's still Roosevelt and Truman era.

V. K.: You got your master's degree in history as well?

M. S.: My master's was in history, and I'd written my thesis on ten years of Senator Pat Harrison of Mississippi. Then when I went back sixteen years later, the topic was still there, and so I did the New Deal Years of Pat Harrison. It did get published in 1978.

V. K.: Again you didn't face any sort of problems when you were getting your master's degree at Vanderbilt?

M. S.: No, I'd say there were five or six women students getting their master's degrees at Vanderbilt.

V. K.: And were there any women professors there at that point?

M. S.: No, there were no women professors there. There had been though. Blanche Henry Clark Weaver had taught at Vanderbilt at an earlier time. Her husband, Herbert Weaver, taught us all, and she was very, very loving and very cordial, and we knew that she was a name historian. She was certainly someone to look to. There were other women around Vanderbilt. There was a Nora C. Chaffin, who had gotten her Ph.D. and had taught at Vanderbilt and over at Peabody.

V. K.: Were there women professors in the history department when you were getting your Ph.D.?

M. S.: No, there were no women history professors there.

V. K.: When you were looking for your job, you said that previous Vanderbilt graduates such as A. Elizabeth Taylor had been very helpful.

M. S.: Yes, this was before you had to have national searches. In fact, I didn't even have to go for an interview at TWU. A vacancy came up in the summer, and my major professor, Dewey Grantham, had circulated my name. He probably wrote thirty-five departments putting my name out. TWU was one of them, and A. Elizabeth Taylor picked up on that. Also Wilmon Droze, who had gotten his doctorate from Vanderbilt under Dr. Grantham, was in the department there and also in administration. It was really the good-old-boy network, and good-old-girl in this case. Of course those things don't happen anymore.

V. K.: A lot of people have said they had experiences of universities writing back and saying, "You're very qualified, but we're sorry, our department won't hire women."

M. S.: No, I didn't have that. There was a department that had what they call the seed-catalog of graduate students, and they wrote Dr. Grantham, who called me in and said this department says they must have or want a woman and therefore they are interested in you. I said, "Forget it. I cannot go to anyplace where they're just interested in me because I am a woman." It was really a heartbreak because it was a desperate time to get jobs, and that may have turned out to be a good one but that just really repulsed me that anyone would be given a job or have some interest expressed because of sex or race. Thus I ended up at a woman's school.

V. K.: Was the faculty there predominantly women?

M. S.: Predominantly women, primarily because it has nursing and health science, and they are overwhelmingly women, and so the whole faculty was probably 75 percent women. It was nice; it was very nice because they were friends. There were lots of parties and dinners and teas and lots of unmarried faculty, so there was just a good social group to fall into, and so it was really a very pleasant place to be.

By that time, I knew about the culture of a woman's school, and I liked that. In fact, I had always thought, until we moved across the street from Mississippi State, that I would go to Mississippi State College for Women. It never entered my mind that I would go anywhere else because my older sister had gone there, done well, and been a history major. I thought that was just what I wanted. I used to hang around in the high school library looking at yearbooks of women's schools. They had one of Sullins, Hollins, Virginia Intermont, Brenau, and Belhaven colleges, and it just never occurred to me that there was anywhere to go but to a woman's school if you really wanted to be a scholar and keep your mind on your books. I was a nerdy little thing, and I thought I wanted to go to the "W," and it was really disappointing that for financial reasons, with a twin to be sent at the same time, that I should go to Mississippi State, but it turned out to be a very supporting faculty there. I have gone back there, and, of course, I love it, and it's home so I really have no regrets about that.

V. K.: You said you were a social sciences major?

M. S.: Yes, because I wanted to be a history teacher, and they had broad field social studies, you know that's what it's called. I ended up taking every elective in social science, which was a mistake. I should have done more language and science and math, but I took seventy-eight hours in the social sciences, I had thirty-six hours in history. I had the equivalent of a history major, but the degree says social sciences.

V. K.: Were there a lot of women in your undergraduate program?

M. S.: No, probably only about 10 percent women. I was a day student, you see, and probably most of the women on campus were day students, or commuters, we would call them now.

V. K.: Did it just turn out that way or was there a shortage of housing for the women students?

M. S.: No, Mississippi State had been predominantly male. It was a land-grant college. Women coeds had not been permitted back in until about 1930, and most women, girls, that's what we were then, girls, in the state who wanted to go to a coed school would go to Ole Miss. Mostly veterans were coming back by then, and so there were some veterans' wives, but there was only one small dormitory for women students. It was nice because we knew everybody, we all knew each other, and there were two sororities, and most girls were in one or the other, if they wanted to be in a sorority at all. So that was fine.

V. K.: Why don't we talk a little bit about your public school teaching experience. Were there many women social studies teachers?

M. S.: Oh, yes, women and coaches. That's the split, primarily.

V. K.: Were you at the founding meeting of the SAWH?

M. S.: I was a first-year graduate student in 1969–1970, and so I think I was at the Louisville SHA meeting. I really was not even aware of it, and then I gradually became aware that there was a group that had formed, and by then I had begun to hear about the CCWHP and the various other committees within the professions. But I was a graduate student. Since then, of course, the SAWH, and the other groups, too, have done very well by graduate students, but then there just wasn't that component. It was older women who had been in the profession, well not so much older; some of them were probably younger than I was. But they were removed from me; they were established historians, and I just didn't think of myself as being in that group, that category.

V. K.: Do you remember how you heard about it?

M. S.: I began to hear about it, and the group was very interested in Elizabeth Taylor, with whom I taught by then, and so I think she may have gone to some of those early meetings that were more caucuses than they were meetings. I think she attended them as a sort of quiet member; she was not really active in that. I think she was sort of leery about what the group might be all about because she was so focused on women being scholars. We always came to SHA together, and so we began to attend the meetings, and I can remember going to a meeting in 1975 or

1976 and 1977, and then I was president at the 1978 meeting. By then they'd begun to shift away from being a caucus to being actually a session, and that's when my interest in it began to rise. I was teaching by then; I was faculty. [Editors' note: In those early days of the organization it was so informal that presidents chose their successors. Martha Swain recalled in a 2002 conversation that at the 1976 SAWH meeting A. Elizabeth Taylor, who was not present, was named to be the next vice president. Shortly thereafter, during the course of the SHA meeting, Taylor heard about being selected. She insistently refused, said she would not serve, and turned to Martha and said she should do it instead. That, says Martha, is how she came to be vice president in 1977 and then president of SAWH in 1978.]

V. K.: For you, your interest was more on their focus on women as scholars rather than the networking?

M. S.: As scholars and then the subject matter, yes. The networking part as such did not interest me. I wanted to meet other people, but networking was a word that I was uneasy about because I've seen so many people who say, "Oh, I'm networking," and they're being very manipulative; they're being very opportunistic; they're looking for the main chance. They're saying, "How can I meet this person because of what this person can do for me?" And there have been some things that have gone on by people who say, "I've got to network." That's not attractive behavior.

V. K.: Did you feel that the SAWH was doing any sort of manipulating?

M. S.: No. I think some of them called it networking, but to me it was just an association, just to go there and to meet other women who were interested in any kind of history. Maybe it was because I was out there in Texas, and that's a long way away, really. You get back over to where you could meet people from other schools because not very many people came through Texas. It was the associations and forming the friendships—I mean really good, good friendships that I appreciated getting through SAWH or just coming to SHA.

V. K.: What did you see as being their goals when you first started to hear about them and get involved in them, do you recall?

M. S.: I remember that women historians had some real concerns about the SHA, and there were legitimate concerns because you didn't see women on the program. You didn't see topics on women's history; you didn't see women on the Executive Council. I think certainly the SAWH has brought about a change in that. I think SAWH has been the reason for that. Then, of course, just all the growing number of women who have come into history as graduate students, just the number, the massive numbers. That's meant a lot.

V. K.: Can we talk about when you were president? You said that it was at that point that they were starting to focus a little bit more on sessions.

M. S.: Yes, I remember, I think it was Rosemary Carroll who had been president who had had the first program that I remember that dealt with what I'd call real history. I think it was a program that she had someone speak on the Sophia Smith Collection and on the Schlesinger Collection, and that attracted a large group. There were probably thirty-five or forty people who came to that, and I was very interested in that. And then when I became president, I thought, I want to have a real session. And I remember I got Betsy Jacoway to come, and she talked on the oral history that she was involved in with some Junior League women who had been involved in integration. But I remember that we went into this room that was probably about the size of this suite right here, and people just flooded in. What really meant a lot to me is that men came. George Tindall came. Of course, he came because she had been his student, but there were others, and I looked around, and I thought this kind of session is really going to get us recognition as being historians. From then on, every session has been a real session. Of course, you know how it is now. We had as many people come almost as come to hear the presidential addresses. It's just absolutely overwhelming. It's just the real calling card of the convention. Just major speakers, major scholarship. I think this is what has really put SAWH over, gotten it respect. It's become a showcase for women scholars.

V. K.: Were there men who were members at the time when you were president?

M. S.: Yes, there were some men who were members. I remember that one thing that we always talked about was that we needed to get more members. When I became president, I tried to work on membership. I think it helped a little because I decided that I was going to have a membership chair in each state. Of course this is what the AHA does and the OAH does and SHA does. I thought, we'll pattern that, so I designated someone in each state and got up, as far as I could, a list of women historians in the states. I used the college catalogs, and then these membership chairs in each state would do that, and they sent out their letters, and it brought about a little surge in membership. Then subsequent presidents would use that approach too. Membership began to pick up.

V. K.: In terms of the men who were in it, were they interested in women's history or were they people who were in the SHA and helped?

M. S.: Some of them had been major professors of the young women who were coming into SAWH. Some of them were men who actually taught women's history. Of course, we can look around today, and we can think of some very prominent men who are teaching women's history, who write women's history, but I don't know if they're members of the SAWH. They should be. The name, the Southern Association for Women Historians, may become the Southern Association for Women's History. You know the way that the CCWHP and the Conference Group on Women Historians have gone through this same thing. Of course you've got those who are interested in women's history no matter what sex. But then when you say, Southern Association for Women Historians that seems exclusive of men.

V. K.: Well the name changed from *of* Women Historians to *for* Women Historians.

M. S.: For Women Historians as in for historians of women and also women historians.

V. K.: When you were president did you find any sort of resistance or difficulty from the SHA?

M. S.: No, I really didn't. I know a lot of people have had experiences of one kind or another with Ben Wall, but he was always gracious to me, and I never felt any animosity there. Setting up arrangements was always fine. Now we didn't have the reception then. It was really a pretty simple thing, and, of course, Barbara Schnorrenberg just ran the *Newsletter* out of her workroom. It was really a much smaller organization.

V. K.: By the time you were president, it was being placed in the *Program*, right?

M. S.: Yes, it was getting in the *Program*.

V. K.: Were you involved in any of the other historical professional organizations like AHA and OAH?

M. S.: I haven't gone to very many AHA meetings. I was on a Program Committee for the AHA, and I was chair of the Congressional Fellowships Committee, so, yes, I've been involved; but I haven't often been to an AHA meeting. I've gone more often to the OAH, and when I go, I go to the women's breakfast. Of course, I read about the organizations. I've been a member all these years of the CCWHP, and then during those years in Texas, I joined the Western Association of Women Historians but was never able to go out to California during exam week, which is when they always seem to have their meetings, at least for us. I've kept up with what's been going on.

V. K.: And how did you feel that those organizations treated women? Was it different than the way women were treated in the SHA?

M. S.: I think that they were much more advocacy meetings. I think that when they have speakers at their breakfasts, or when they've had their caucus meetings, they have dealt with professional issues. They don't have a program spot, if you want to call it that, the way SAWH does. The AHA Committee on Women has its breakfast meeting, and the CCWHP or Conference Group on Women's History, has its breakfast meeting, but it doesn't have a scholarly session to my knowledge that focuses on some aspect of women's scholarship. I don't know whether they've not sought to do that or not thought that they should do that, but I think that's what's put SAWH where it is. I really do. I could go into one thing that came up when I was president in 1978. There was a group then within the SAWH that thought that the SHA should boycott the southern states that had not ratified the ERA. I was very much opposed to any kind of boycott, and I remember a business session where the matter came up, and I said my piece about it in presiding over the meeting. Later I was told that as the person presiding over the meeting, I should have been neutral and should not have entered into the discussion. But I just felt so strongly that it would work adversely, particularly against young women graduate students or high school teachers or anyone else if we did not have meetings in places where they could attend. There was that issue, and I remember in the 1:00 business session of the SHA, there would always be someone from the SAWH who wanted to have it brought to a vote on the Executive Council or at the business meeting that there would be a boycott. That was always defeated or averted somehow.

V. K.: For you, it was more an issue of fairness to high school teachers and women graduate students.

M. S.: The AHA had met at Dallas in the end of December 1977, and some of my students had gone there and gotten to work the locater file and done things because I had been on the Local Arrangements Committee. Dorothy DeMoss and I had these students, who were just thrilled to see the men, and some women too, who wrote books they'd heard about. It was a thrill, and I thought, if this thing has to go, if SHA has to go out of the South or even to the marginal states that had ratified the ERA, graduate students can't drive to the meetings, and young faculty, community college and high school teachers can't do this. I thought this just will not do. I thought we all should think more of the young women graduate school constituency of the SAWH instead of trying to deal with something which was pretty much a lost cause anyway.

V. K.: Were you concerned at all that by voting to boycott it would be seen as a sort of radical movement?

M. S.: It wasn't so much the radical part of it; I thought it just wasn't on balance. I can see the other side, but on balance, the greatest service to women graduate students and junior faculty, which I was just emerging out of being then (I would say I was still junior faculty then), was to keep the SHA where they and I could get to it, have a part, and do the things that you could involve the students in doing.

V. K.: Did you have any concern that if they had chosen to vote to boycott that that would somehow diminish SAWH's validity or role in the SHA?

M. S.: I think that it would have made the SAWH less acceptable. I think that it would have been viewed as being an advocacy group. Yes, I think that if the boycott had come about and it had been attributed to the SAWH, I think it would have been a bad thing for SAWH.

V. K.: Were you thinking about that or concerned about that at all, do you recall, or was it just the focus on the opportunity for graduate students?

M. S.: I think not, I think my focus was on keeping it in the South. I'm a real southerner at heart, and I just didn't want to have to see the SHA go out of the South or go back to Washington, where it had met before. I also was concerned about the women workers, the maids, the custodians, the waitresses and all, in these southern hotels who were losing their jobs, losing their tips and all because conventions weren't coming to their town. I thought when we take issues like boycotting to the higher plane, you forget that there are a lot of women who are really going to suffer for this on a day-to-day basis.

V. K.: We've talked a little bit about men in the SAWH. Do you recall the presence of minority women, or even minority, African American men or women in the SHA and the SAWH?

M. S.: I still can't think of any minority men who are in the SAWH. Minority women are certainly in the SAWH. I think the SAWH has always been very attentive to minority historians.

V. K.: From the very beginning?

M. S.: Particularly I'm talking about black women historians.

V. K.: You feel that from the seventies on that was a concern for the SAWH?

M. S.: I think they were always mindful of it, always attentive to and concerned about that. I never saw anything that was exclusionary regarding that.

V. K.: Do you recall in terms of the SHA itself whether there were a lot of black men and women involved in the seventies when the civil rights movement was starting to have its effect.

M. S.: They were certainly involved, and they were the name historians that we would know, and I would see them. I really do not know what percentage of faculty or graduate students were black males then. I always was very aware that black men and women were at the SHA. It's hard to know because I'm sure my perception of it would be different from theirs because they knew what their numbers were then. They knew what rejections there had been; they knew what tokenism they thought they were getting; which must have been offensive.

V. K.: It is hard because it's something that people weren't necessarily thinking about in the same way that they do now. Can we talk a little bit about teaching women's history? Was that something that you did when you were in Texas?

M. S.: No, I have never taught a course in women's history. Now, we all taught the survey because that was our bread and butter, and I taught the upper-level twentieth-century history classes, and I always included women. In fact, I would include so much that I wouldn't be able to get to the end of the course. I always had just a great deal. But you see, I didn't think of it particularly as women's history; it was just history. Then the research that I was doing, particularly on women in the twenties and the thirties, put me into finding out a great deal about what women were doing in the New Deal.

V. K.: I think that maybe part of it is that you were at a women's college.

M. S.: When we had an argument about whether we should have a women's studies curriculum or a women's studies emphasis, people would rise and say we are women's studies by nature. That is, the university in itself was women's studies. There were those that would argue, though, that women's studies is a discipline just as they argue that women's history is a discipline.

V. K.: Right, but was it your experience that the majority of the professors included women?

M. S.: No, I don't think they did. There again it's because their research had not pointed them in that direction. I'm just so hipped on the idea that you've got to do the research; you've got to write those papers before you're really going to be ready to get it into your courses—to really understand it and not just be doing this compensatory thing of dropping things in.

V. K.: So for you it was when you got involved in your research that you really started to include it.

M. S.: That's right; that's when I started to include it.

V. K.: Was there anything in particular that sparked your interest in doing research on women in the twenties and thirties?

M. S.: It was when I did the work on Pat Harrison and did the dissertation. I read ten years on microfilm of about five different newspapers, and I would see the articles on various women in the New Deal. Then when I got into the Pat Harrison papers, there was correspondence from and to Mississippi women who were interested in subjects. I began to index all of those things I wanted to go back to. Then when I did, I spent ten years the way we all do on something. I was by that time smothered in all this and just finding more and more and more and wanting to talk about it in class.

V. K.: Were the students receptive?

M. S.: They were receptive. I used to have some students who would come up and say I had too much on women's history because they wanted to get all the way past World War II and all the way to the present. Well, I got past World War II, but they would have rather had me push further chronologically with less emphasis on women. The thing about it is, there would be so many interesting newspaper articles and bits of correspondence that I could read to them that I'd found. I think that as long as you keep it interesting, it doesn't matter what it is. I just happen to have found so many goodies in the various correspondence and manuscripts I was reading, and I just had to put them in.

V. K.: Women were involved in the New Deal a lot from what you found?

M. S.: Good heavens, yes. Ellen Woodward lasted on through the Truman administration and one year of the Eisenhower administration. Her concerns were always social and economic issues for women. She had a lot of club memberships, particularly Business and Professional Women's Club (BPW). I've now gotten on to a good friend, her closest woman friend, Lucy Somerville Howorth, who is a hundred years old, still living. I have a stack of correspondence with her. She's in BPW and AAUW [the American Association of University Women].

V. K.: You really feel that the SAWH has helped women.

M. S.: Oh, yes. To me the thing that it's done that has been most valuable is the focus on women's history. You go through these programs that we have had, as I say, it's been a real showcase. It's been an opportunity for women historians. You look at the programs that have been presented, and then you look at the work that's been done by the graduate students. I'm repeating myself, but the SAWH has really tried to do well and has done well by graduate students. And then of course, its women's history conferences and all the publications that have come out of that. There's nothing else like it. The AHA and the OAH Women's Committees are caucuses, and they don't have books coming out, essays of proceedings. Besides that, the SAWH gives good parties. It has gotten to be that Thursday afternoon from 4:30 on at the SHA is just the high point of the convention, other than the presidential address and the presidential reception.

I know when I was in graduate school and coming along, there were some of the older, wiser heads who said to me, "Martha, make it as a scholar, and don't make it just because you've gotten in a movement." And I think that the SAWH has made it with their scholarship and not as a movement.

Judith F. Gentry

Judith F. Gentry is currently Professor of History at University of Louisiana at Lafayette. She earned her Ph.D. in American History in 1969 from Rice University, where she studied under Frank E. Vandiver. She has published numerous articles in the field of southern and Louisiana history and has been elected to the Company of Fellows of the Louisiana Historical Association for outstanding contributions to the history and culture of Louisiana. She has received several publication awards, a National Endowment for the Humanities Fellowship in quantitative history, a three-year NEH grant to fund "An Economic and Social History of Colonial Acadian Louisiana," and in 1994 she was awarded the Outstanding Teacher Award for the University of Southwestern Louisiana. She has served as President of the Louisiana Historical Association and as President of the Louisiana State Conference for AAUP. She served as President of the SAWH from 1978 to 1979.

Interviewer: Victoria Kalemaris
Transcriber: Victoria Kalemaris
The following interview took place November 10, 1995.

J. G.: I did my undergraduate bachelor's degree in history at the University of Maryland and then was able to earn an assistantship at Rice University in the history program there. I'm perhaps unusual in that I'm really not very aware of problems or obstacles that were put in my path either at the University of Maryland or at Rice University. At Rice University I decided to marry another graduate student there, so I became part of a two-career family, which might have made it very difficult to get a job. But this was 1969, which, as a matter of fact, was the last year in which it was relatively easy to get a job. My husband got a job at the university where I now teach, the University of Southwestern Louisiana, and when he inquired whether there might be anything for me, they replied that were looking for Europeanists or a Latin Americanist but not looking for an Americanist. At any rate, his was the only job that either of us got offered.

At the beginning of the year it had looked like there was going to be a good job market. At the end of the year we found out this was it. It had crashed. There was only one job. My husband asked if maybe there was something available for me, and they said, "Sure, probably, in the night school as an adjunct; what are her credentials?" When it turned out I actually had the Ph.D. in hand, I was welcomed with open arms; they created a position for me. Instead of hiring a Latin Americanist, they took me instead just because they were trying to build up the percentage of faculty that had Ph.D.s. So I really cannot complain in those terms. I also entered a department under the leadership of Amos Simpson. I am unaware of any obstacle placed in the way of my career there either. He was the person who hired me and ran the department for the first several years. I know now I'm an unusual specimen from the 1960s because I know there were problems that people encountered, I'm just unaware of any that were in my path.

V. K.: Are you a native southerner?

J. G.: I'm from Maryland, the northern Baltimore area. Maryland, of course, was a border state. My family background is actually Pennsylvania and German immigrants who arrived there in the 1850s. So I do not have a southern tradition. The foods I ate were not southern. I think that's a clue.

V. K.: When you were a graduate student, and when you first went to Southwestern Louisiana, were there a lot of women?

J. G.: No, I was one of very few. At Rice University, there had been one female Ph.D. prior to me. I believe that I was the third woman history Rice

Ph.D. Of course they had Katherine Drew on their faculty, who was well respected. We had some other women who entered the master's program at the time I did but stopped after the master's degree. So Rice had not had many female graduate students but was opening up to more women. Of course you have to understand that there were not many women who were teenagers in the 1950s who wanted Ph.D.s.

V. K.: Did you have many women professors at Maryland in the history department?

J. G.: No, I did not. There were one or two women professors there, but I don't think I had any women professors. I know Adrienne Koch was there soon thereafter. Two women were hired the year I was hired at the University of Louisiana at Lafayette. There had been a woman hired about five years earlier, so there were three of us, and the thing was, after hiring the group I was hired with—there were nine faculty members hired in 1969 and 1970—then we didn't hire for fifteen years. Out of those nine hired, there were two women, and there had already been one, and the three of us were it until quite recently. In the last six years or so we have added two more women faculty members. They replaced people who left, and now two of our women faculty members are about to retire so the issue is whether we'll continue to hire.

V. K.: Your research is U.S. history and according to the 1982 *Directory of American Scholars* economic history was your area of research.

J. G.: Well, yes. My research field is Civil War finance of the Confederacy. I've done two small things that may qualify as women's history, but I've done several other things that are more in the Civil War finance area. About when the interest in women's history began, my mentor, Frank Vandiver, was the 1976 president of the Southern Historical Association. The system then was the old-boy network, and I was a beneficiary of that. He appointed me to the Program Committee to find women's history sessions, so I had to become quickly interested in and aware of women's history. That was my first experience, and once I had begun to learn a little about it, I was an obvious person to respond to student demand. I can't remember when I began to teach a course called "Women in American History"; it was probably during the mid-seventies. But I never aspired to do a great deal of research in that area. I never shifted my research area. I developed a teaching field, "Women in America," and I wrote an article for a textbook in the 1980s on what would have happened if the Equal Rights Amendment had been a part of the original

Constitution. So I did a little bit, but mostly I've remained in the Civil War research area. I've prospered also and received respect within the Louisiana Historical Association and became president of the Louisiana Historical Association eventually, so I have good stories to tell.

V. K.: Why don't we start with your remembrances of your beginning in the SAWH?

J. G.: I was hired at the University of Louisiana in Lafayette in 1969, and the following year, 1970, I went to the Southern Historical Association meeting in Louisville. That is the year that SAWH was founded. I saw the signs posted around the hallways, and I went to the meeting. The meeting was in a room with one long table in it, and just enough room for the chairs to be pulled back to sit down. There were maybe, I don't know, twenty, twenty-five people who sat around the table. It was all brand-new to me. I did not at that time consider myself a feminist. I signed the roll and was present, but I did not become an active member at that time. It was four, five, or six years later, really when I was in a different place in terms of my understanding of what other people had encountered that I had not encountered. You see my background did not set me up to be immediately interested in this association, but as I became more aware, I began to be involved in the SAWH. At that time, it was still quite small and very informal. I was invited to be a candidate for the vice presidency and really entered into the SAWH at that level and became vice president, and then president in 1979, and then served on the Executive Committee. I had various roles which kept me involved with the Executive Committee of the SAWH from about 1975 to 1990. For about fifteen years, I attended those Wednesday meetings SAWH had at the SHA meeting. What I do remember is that when we met that first year, and then the year that I was president, the Executive Committee met in someone's hotel room each time, and five or six of us sat around on the beds and tried to decide in that informal fashion what we ought to do. In 1978, the year that I was moving up to president I decided (or maybe others put me up to it) that it was a shame that the SHA had never taken a stand on the Equal Rights Amendment. Prior to that time, the sort of things that the SAWH had been interested in were getting access for women to opportunities within the SHA. This was a little more controversial, getting the SHA to take a stand on a political issue.

We knew that the AHA was resisting taking a stand on the Equal Rights Amendment. We had never asked the SHA leadership, so we didn't know what they were going to do. We went out to dinner, and we talked about it, and we decided that we would press the SHA to take a stand. We developed a resolution to take before the business meeting of the SHA the next day. We thought that the wise and civil thing to do was to let the council know that we were going to do this. The business meeting of the SHA meeting is staid; nobody brings up anything, so we didn't want to just stand up and hit them all with shock. So we decided that I would go and tell Ben Wall, the secretary-treasurer of the SHA, that we were going to do this. I did so, and Ben was not too excited about that and took the position, as I remember it, that this was not an appropriate thing, that the SHA should focus on educational matters and scholarly matters rather than politics. He and I talked about an hour down in the lobby, and then I said, "Well I'm going to bring it up tomorrow at the business meeting." Surprisingly, I got a phone call shortly afterward and was invited to a special meeting of the Executive Council of the SHA. As far as I know, they had already finished their business, and they came back into session to talk to me, which was a surprise.

So I went, and I was all prepared to press the point that the SHA should endorse the Equal Rights Amendment. There were, as a matter of fact, three women on the SHA council at that time—probably the first time there were three women on the council. This was a shock of all shocks: when I got there, endorsement wasn't even the main issue on the agenda. Sure that was fine; they were ready to endorse the Equal Rights Amendment. At least some of the women who were already on the council of the SHA were pressing for the SHA to join the embargo—the boycott—so that the SHA would not have meetings in states that had not ratified the ERA. This was a difficult issue in the whole South, as there were very few places you could go for a meeting because most of the southern states were not ratifying the Equal Rights Amendment. It took me a few moments to perceive that I wasn't encountering what I expected to encounter. As a matter of fact, it was Anne Scott who was pressing extremely hard in the council. She was not involved with the SAWH at that time, but she was pressing the council for not only approval of what we were proposing, which was the ERA endorsement, but also for the boycott. It was going to be easy because it was already pretty much set up that they were already scheduled to meet in states that had ratified the ERA, or in Washington, D.C. So I supported her and said, "Yes, the SAWH also wants to join the boycott," and the council decided because it was easy to do it. That was kind of an odd thing that happened, that we got much more than what we wanted, and it's probably not so odd because there were some women on the council who weren't in our SAWH but were also working for it.

So the next day we got the support of the business meeting both for the endorsement of the ERA and to join the boycott of states that had not ratified the ERA. Unfortunately during that year, soon after that meeting, for practical reasons, the hotel in Washington, D.C., broke their contract or something like that, and in the effort to find another place, a quick emergency place to meet, Ben chose to go to Atlanta, which broke the boycott. Ben had the council's support to do that. So I engaged in a long correspondence with Ben, calling on him to reverse himself and to work harder to try to find a place for us to go that was not in a nonratifying state. I pointed out to them that the SHA had boycotted hotels in cities in the years past which would not allow our black members to stay in the hotel, and they had gone to great efforts and sacrifice. The association had sacrificed low hotel rates in order to be able to find a hotel to support our black members, and I urged that he make that same kind of sacrifice for the women of the association in this way. Well, it didn't work out, and we lost that battle. So my presidency was caught up in that process.

The SAWH was really still quite a small group in terms of membership and very informal in terms of our meetings, and we had two goals. One was a goal to achieve equity relating to the status of women in the profession, and our other goal was to promote women's history. Up until that time, paper-matching [finding compatible papers to present at conferences] and preparing session proposals had been the most effective at that. The association was working for equity by putting up for committee assignments the names of women who had done a lot for the SHA. We were trying to get women appointed to more committees, and as chairs of committees. The association had also been working toward creating a permanent SHA Committee on the Status of Women, so SAWH pressed for that.

We had done a lot in the equity area; to tell you the truth, I thought that what we also needed to achieve in the equity area was to become respectable. The members of the SHA who did not like what we were doing in setting up the SAWH claimed that we women didn't publish enough, and if we did, they'd have taken care of us. They had something. They had already had two women presidents of the SHA before SAWH ever formed, and they had had their third one in 1972. So their point was, you don't need this organization, just publish a lot, and we'll recognize you. So one thing that we ultimately did was to nominate women who published to be our vice president and president to gain respectability in that way. Another thing that we did was to establish a prize. As I remember it, I was one of the persons who first suggested that we establish a prize. The goal would be to reward and promote women's history and also pro-

mote scholarship, which would help the SAWH to become a more respectable organization.

The other kinds of things that we were doing at that time to try to get
the SHA more willing to do what we wanted them to do in support of
women is we began attending the business meeting regularly. The people who ran the SHA complained in general that not very many people
came to the business meeting, that nobody showed very much interest.
So we showed interest; we showed up in force regularly at the business
meetings. Another strategy that evolved soon after my presidency was to
throw some parties. I think Carol Bleser may have thrown the first, and
we started getting a suite and throwing parties and trying to bring men
to the party as well as the women so that they would realize we weren't
ogres. Having parties mattered.

I was appointed to chair the committee to establish a publishing prize.
It was Carol Bleser, Jody Carrigan, and myself, as I remember it. Carol
pressed for a prize on a book on any subject in southern history written
by a woman. I was still in that phase of not wanting to have a prize just
for a woman, and I pressed for a book prize written by anybody, a man
or a woman, on southern women's history. And Jody said, "Well, let's do
both." So that was the resolution of that. We decided to do both, and then
we needed to raise the money, and I chaired the committee that raised
the money. The truth is that Carol Bleser raised much of that money. We
decided to name the prize that she had wanted for Willie Lee Rose, and
Carol was very effective at approaching people throughout the association to honor Willie Lee Rose in this fashion. Anne Scott urged that we
name the other prize for Julia Cherry Spruill and worked also in raising
money. I kind of did the mass mailings to try to get anybody who was interested, also general publicity and recordkeeping, and we raised an endowment, which was sufficient at that time to pay a fairly substantial
prize. I've forgotten the amounts, but it looked pretty good at that time.
We later decided to raise some more. I wasn't involved in that. I think it's
a very successful thing, as I say. I give credit to others in terms of money-
raising; Carol was clearly the most important. That was a very important
first step, I think, for this association, which changed it dramatically from
what it had been before. When the prizes came into being, we didn't
know how many submissions we would get; in fact we received huge
numbers of them. The prizes have become very important to SAWH.

I then went on to manage the investments, which was not a particularly difficult job because we made a decision rightly or wrongly to in-
vest only in federally guaranteed funds, CDs, and treasury bonds, and
not to risk the principal. So I would be the one that would go down and

buy the CDs or whatever. I had an investment committee, an advisory committee to help me decide whether to go long or go short and all that sort of thing in terms of how long to buy those CDs for. We did a fairly good job of actually increasing the principal as well as raising enough to pay the costs of the award each two years—both of the awards each two years. I recommended immediately that we establish an audit committee because here I had $25,000, or whatever it was, which I could take and leave with, and you all wouldn't know. I was aware of an experience in another historical association where someone ran off with some of the money. So for the future, I knew I wasn't going to do anything, but I wanted to establish the principle that we would have an audit committee, and Kathleen Berkeley (who often served on audit committees) or whoever it was, would make certain that the money was still there. So that was all pretty good.

Another important step was to have a speaker at the annual SAWH meeting. In 1980 we decided to honor the three women presidents of the SHA, and we called upon senior women in the SHA at this time asking each one to do up a sketch honoring each woman. That was a panel presentation that time. We were still at that time being put in very small rooms. The SHA was giving us rooms, but they were extremely small and out of the way. This particular room was quite small; it may have seated twenty-five people, and there were huge pillars in the room that would block your view. Because we were honoring these women that the men in the SHA themselves honored, they came in droves, and there was standing room only for this presentation. I had not anticipated such a nice result. Thereafter we never had any trouble getting a bigger room. I thought that was an interesting way that things changed.

V. K.: Was that a conscious move on the part of SAWH to help increase its validity by having women do scholarly presentations at its annual meeting?

J. G.: I can't remember. I think that we went too far in that direction, and I'm engaged now in an effort to get an informal meeting restored so that our members can participate more, where we can actually have our members come together in a business meeting and talk about things that are important to women and maybe problems that they're encountering now. We lost that as a result of the move toward a more formal presentation, even though it was a good move at the time to support teaching and researching women's history by having a distinguished speaker. It got to where so many people who weren't members were coming to the meetings to hear the speakers that we no longer could really do our business there together. We lived with that for ten or fifteen years, I think to the detriment. We've lost touch with our roots, with our grassroots members. I just spoke with Marjorie Wheeler, and we're talking about having a second SAWH meeting at each annual SHA meeting, which will be a business meeting where members can talk about what's important to them. [Editors' note: The SAWH now holds a business meeting at the annual SHA meeting.]

As you know, there was a whole new generation of women entering the profession in the 1970s, and they were writing good history in women's history, in southern history, and in European history. Incidentally, European history members were, and probably are still, unhappy that they're not eligible for any of our prizes. At any rate, women were slowly accepted into membership on committees of the SHA and eventually chairs of committees on the SHA, and women also began to make significant numbers of appearances on the association program, one of the kinds of participation we always used as a benchmark. In 1984, 17 percent of the SHA membership was women; so we used that as a benchmark, saying, why aren't there 17 percent of women in these various categories? During the late 1980s and early 1990s, women became and then exceeded 17 percent of those positions, with the exception of the council, which was a harder nut to crack.

It was a requirement from the beginning that anybody who was on the Executive Committee of SAWH be an SHA member because we saw ourselves originally as a caucus of the SHA. You could be a member of the SAWH without being a member of the SHA, but we always encouraged SHA membership. The SHA was putting women on the programs through their normal processes. Some were SAWH members, and some were not. The SHA Program Committee probably didn't know which were which. Except for a few very visible people, they wouldn't really know if someone was a member of SAWH or not.

In 1982, the SHA created an ad hoc Committee on the Status of Women, and I was appointed to it in 1983. I served on that committee with Hans Schmitt and June K. Burton. June chaired the committee. We decided that we would do a serious statistical study of two things. One was women's participation in various elements of the SHA, and so we looked not only at articles in the *Journal of Southern History*, but also reviewers. You see, the editor has a lot more control over who reviews than over who submits articles. So we researched whether women were being asked to review books. With regard to membership on the council, we asked how many women presidents have there been, how many committee chairs, how many members of the committees. We asked whether women were just getting the hard work on the Membership Committee, or were we also getting positions on the other committees that made policy.

At the same time, we decided to do a study of women in the profession in the South. It was a statistical study of membership in history departments: and the percentage of history department members who were women; the percentage of history department chairs who were women; the percent of those who were tenured at each rank who were women. It was a very elaborate study which showed the great deficiencies on the part of southern colleges and universities in hiring and promoting women.

V. K.: Were any of the universities hesitant to participate in this?

J. G.: We didn't ask them; we used catalogs to do our study. We didn't do tenure, we did things you get from a catalog, like rank. We just did name recognition to identify women. We had a whole list of people whose first names we weren't sure of, and so to let the SHA know what we were doing, we circulated that. I wrote Ben Wall and other people and said, "Do you know these people? Are they men or women? We're doing this study and we need to know." We got it down to where we could pretty much identify the sex of virtually all of these people.

It became clear that women were hired more in the lesser schools and hired less in the big-name schools, and promotions were the same way. June suggested that on the front sheet of that whole study, we simply take the ten most recent presidents of the SHA and look at their schools' percentages, and boy it was terrible. They were among the worst. Seven of the ten schools that had provided presidents to the SHA had very poor records with regard to hiring and promoting women. I don't know how important that information was to the association at large or whether it was beneficial or harmful in terms of publishing that as part of our report, but we did. I hope that it embarrassed them into doing a better job.

The chair of the SHA Committee on the Status of Women reports every year to the SHA Executive Council. They would then carry back to the SAWH Executive Committee what the SHA council had said in response to the report, so there was a coordination. The person who chaired the SHA committee would also report as a matter of courtesy to the SAWH and keep us informed. June told me that there was a lot of interest in the report, a lot of respect for the work that had gone into preparing the report, but I'm not too excited about the long-term results of the report about the status of women employed in southern universities. There remains now still much work to do on that front. It turned out that 1984, the year in which the SHA Committee on the Status of Women did the study and delivered its report covering the years 1934–1983, SHA was fifty years old. The *Journal of Southern History* published the portion of our report which had studied the years when the SHA had relatively few women on their committees, their programs, or their council. As a historical study it showed improvements in the percentages of women that were involved in the SHA, but of course still not meeting the bench-marks.

Since the SHA committee on the status of women had become perma-nent and was functioning, the SAWH shifted its tone more and more. The equity-oriented aspects of the SAWH came to be deemphasized, and its focus came to be on promoting the history of women. I don't know that it was exclusive, but I see a shift that took place.

V. K.: You've talked about your role on the Executive Committee of SAWH and as president, and your role in establishing the prizes and then investing the prize money. What other sorts of things did you do? Was the investment of the prize money something that went on for sev-eral years?

J. G.: It was ten or more years before I passed it on to others. As a person who attended those Wednesday afternoon SAWH Executive Committee meetings, which had become more and more formal and longer and longer, I was on there a long time. People who were made president at that time would be nominated for vice president and then they would be president the second year, so they were feeling inexperienced. The fact that I had been there for a while meant that I provided some continuity and stability to that executive board meeting. People would ask me how it was done. Someone said I was a voice of sanity on that board. I don't know if I really was, but I grew tired of chairing the Investments Com-mittee and being on the board, and moved on to other non-SAWH activ-ities.

V. K.: You mentioned Ben Wall and some of the difficulties that you had with him. Some people say, "Oh, Ben Wall, really he was very reasonable; we just were asking the wrong kinds of questions." What was your rela-tionship to Ben and Neva Wall?

J. G.: Neva Wall was always friendly to everybody. I don't believe there was any question about that; she really doesn't care about these kinds of decisions, and she's a wonderful person. I think Ben is representative of a whole generation of the people who were running the SHA at that time. They're now seventy-five or older, most of them, and that generation of men in the SHA had been very active in the civil rights movement, were southern liberals to a large extent, and were gentlemen. There was a certain way of doing things and dealing with people that involved a gracefulness about that interaction. They would say, on the basis of merit, if we had done as well, we would have been selected too. They had already had two women presidents before any pressure was brought to bear upon them, they were rightly proud of the stands that they had taken with regard to race and thought that they had done what they ought to do with regard to women in the profession. Some of them had had women graduate students, and, in their eyes at least, supported them. I would say, and I think many of them would say, that for women to be acceptable they had to be the very, very best. The very, very best women were treated quite well—Ella Lonn, for instance, and Mary Elizabeth Massey. But I believe that generation also thought that most of the women who were in the profession weren't top-notch. In their judgment they thought they were using the same scale for men and women, but in my judgment, the men who were moderately important scholars would do quite well in the profession, might even become president of the association, but women who were moderately successful scholars were of no importance whatsoever. So that's how I categorize that generation. Of course, they felt that it was inappropriate for there to be a pressure group to pressure them to do more because they felt they had done quite well with regard to women.

It's interesting because the next generation of men on the council were men who are now probably around sixty-five or seventy, who then were in their late forties and fifties and early sixties. These men were of a different generation and were harsher and harder, much more hostile to women, and much more difficult to deal with as a group. That generation, that slightly younger generation, was more verbal in their hostility to women. I'm sorry I wasn't present on the council then. But the younger men were not an improvement over the older men. I don't know what's happening now in terms of generations, but I know that men can still become extremely defensive whenever something is suggested that maybe it's not going right. If the SAWH or the SHA Committee on the Status of Women suggests that things ought to be done a little differently in order to provide more equity in the association, there is anger and resentment, and there is defensiveness, which can get quite personal. The job of equity for women is not won, the job is not done.

If I had to make an extreme comparison, I would talk about paternalistic racism versus hostile nonpaternalistic racism, and I would say the same with regard to gender relations. That older generation was paternalistic in many ways, as all of us are to our students, right? There's that mentor thing. And then there was a generation which was not so paternalistic, which was more just batting heads against each other, and I think we're still at that place in terms of the SHA council. There have been men who were strong supporters of the SAWH. Gerhard Weinberg was one. I know that there were, and are, sympathetic men on the council, but they tend to be quiet when this sort of interaction starts on the council. The men who are speaking out, expressing resentment about the SAWH or the SHA Committee on the Status of Women, interact with the woman who is reporting on the activities of the SHA Committee on the Status of Women. This group usually doesn`t know her very well, and it's kind of an unpleasant interaction. The others are uncomfortably quiet; they don't usually come to anybody's rescue, although some do speak out in support.

I think that it's an awkward interaction that takes place between people in power and others who are pressing for change, and it takes a very gracious person to say, "Well, OK." That doesn't happen very often anywhere, and it doesn't really happen often in the SHA either. Although it does happen sometimes; let me point out that John Boles, managing editor of the *Journal of Southern History*, attends all the women's sessions and solicits papers to be sent in for possible articles in the journal. There are other men who take steps to try to accomplish things that would be beneficial, to provide equity for women in the association, and, of course, they work for their own female students as they work for their own male students. So a lot of that is good. But even some of these same men, in a different situation when somebody is suggesting they're maybe not doing it exactly right, get real defensive. I think that the SAWH needs to continue the pressure when we discover things that aren't going especially well. It would be nice if the people who are in power could bring themselves to respond graciously to that pressure. But I understand that; I've been there. Somebody criticizes me, I sometimes lash right back at them, so the job is not done. There is a role for SAWH, not only in promoting study of the history of women but also with regard to equity issues.

V. K.: You had mentioned when you were talking about the male leadership of SHA and their reaction to the women that they had been active in the civil rights movement. Was this reflected in the membership of the SHA?

J. G.: Many of the leaders of the SHA were, although I don't know about how active. Many of them were active in their local communities. The SHA itself had been concerned about civil rights for blacks. There were a few black members of the SHA, but the 1960s was a time in which you had a lot of black interest in doing things alone, in separate black groups. So there wasn't a whole lot of black membership in the SHA. That was also true of the SAWH.

V. K.: Was SAWH concerned about trying to include black women?

J. G.: I don't know in that first year, because I didn't become active until at least five or six or seven years later. There were a couple of things that SAWH did to try to get more black women involved, and one of those was to try to make contacts. There is a black women's historical organization, the Association of Black Women Historians, and efforts were made to approach through that structure—to bring to the attention of the black women that they were welcome to the SAWH. Some of the people who were officers in the SAWH, who had a great deal to say about who would become the next vice president, promoted choosing black women scholars to be vice president and then president of the SAWH.

V. K.: Darlene Clark Hine was the first in 1985; Elsa Barkley Brown served as president in 1993; Jacqueline Rouse served as president in 2001.

J. G.: That's right. So, I think that the SAWH was primarily interested in hearing women say what needed to be done and moving on that, in other words, solving our own problems. That was the focus; that was the way it was created, but not too soon after that, there was a reaching out to be inclusive, to involve black women in the SAWH, which has been to some small extent successful. But here again, black women probably find more comfort in a black women's organization than in an integrated organization. Many of the women who were in the SAWH had been active in the black civil rights movement in their hometowns and universities. Like those men I described who were white southern liberals, these were largely white southern women liberals. Once the organization got off the ground and got going, it was part of the agenda to involve black women in the process and to make certain that our equity efforts included black women. You don't have to try to get people to do the history of black women; that was already happening without a lot of pushing by anybody. It's an interesting subject.

V. K.: Were there any women in the SAWH who were mentors or were particularly influential in getting you involved in it?

J. G.: I don't see it that way. My understanding of how it worked when I first entered the SAWH is that Mollie Davis and Barbara Schnorrenberg were at the center holding the organization together. Barbara had a formal position as secretary-treasurer and *Newsletter* editor. Mollie was our eyes and ears. Mollie had social connections in the SHA, which enabled her to know what was going on. Mollie had a certain idea of the direction that we needed to go, especially in terms of equity for women in the southern historical profession, and always had her eye on that ball. She was always finding out for us what was happening before we had women on the council—what the problems were that you couldn't see unless you knew people. So Mollie was out there finding out information without even trying; it's just the way she is. She is a very social person, very aware, knew about the men, knew about the older women. Mollie provided continuity throughout the years from the very beginning, and Barbara Schnorrenberg did too soon after the very beginning.

When I came in, I continued to provide continuity, as did Barbara Schnorrenberg and Mollie, except that Mollie's role was constant but not official because she didn't have an official position and wasn't attending the SAWH Executive Committee meetings. That's my vision of how SAWH worked in the early years; most of the rest of the people kind of came and went until Carol Bleser. Carol became a very central, very important person. Carol was a publisher, and she laid her beginning publishing career on the line by affiliating with us. That's a risky kind of a thing to do, because the men looked down their nose at women who affiliated with the SAWH. Carol became a long-term important part of the process. A. Elizabeth Taylor was willing to help at any time. She was getting quite old, but she was willing to help at any time. Rosemary Carroll was kind of like Mollie in that she had an informal role and still does, for as long as I can remember, but had not continued in a formal position maintaining a membership on the Executive Committee. A lot of the younger people are not aware of their continuing informal roles.

Carol K. Bleser

Carol K. Bleser is currently the Kathryn and Calhoun Lemon Distinguished Professor of History Emeritus at Clemson University. She earned her Ph.D. in American History from Columbia University in 1966. She is the author of *The Promised Land: A History of the South Carolina Land Commission, 1869–1890* (1969) and the editor of *The Hammonds of Redcliffe* (1981) and *Secret and Sacred: The Diaries of James Henry Hammond* (1988) and both edited and contributed to *In Joy and in Sorrow: Women, Family and Marriage in the Victorian South, 1830–1900* (1991). More recently, she edited *Tokens of Affection: The Letters of a Planter's Daughter in the Old South* (1996) and coedited *Intimate Strategies of the Civil War: Military Commanders and Their Wives* (2001). Bleser has written numerous articles on southern women, the Civil War and Reconstruction, and family and social history. She also served as General Series Editor of Southern Voices from the Past: Women's Letters, Diaries, and Writings, for the University of Georgia Press. She presently serves as Series Editor for the University of South Carolina Press series Women's Diaries and Letters of the South. In 1982, the American Historical Association appointed Bleser a Commissioner to the National Historical Publications and Records Commission (NHPRC), where she served until 1990. In 1996, the National Archives gave her the Award for Distinguished Service in Documentary Preservation and Publication. She was the founding chair of the President's Commission on the Status of Women at Clemson University, 1993 to 1997. In 1998, she was the fifth woman to serve as President of the Southern Historical Association. She was President of the SAWH from 1979 to 1980.

Interviewer: Constance B. Schulz
Transcriber: Cheryl Morrison
The following interview took place October 16, 1996.

C. B.: I think my first interest in studying history was probably as a child checking out a book, Kenneth Roberts's *Northwest Passage*, with the help of my father from the adult library. That was followed up by wanting to read *Gone with the Wind*. I knew when I was about eleven years old that I wanted to be a historian. I thought the stories in history were better than anything I'd ever read in fiction. So, my mind was set as a very young child as to my career. I graduated from Converse College in Spartanburg, South Carolina, and there I had a woman professor who had the greatest impact on my career. Her name was Lillian Kibler, and she was from Newberry, South Carolina. She had been a high school history teacher and had gone back to graduate school during World War II, when Columbia University could not fill its ranks of graduate students with men since they were in the war. She had the opportunity to go to Columbia, and she studied with Allan Nevins. She then came back to South Carolina, and her entire remaining career was spent at Converse College teaching young women. Dr. Kibler wrote a brilliant biography of Benjamin F. Perry, a South Carolina Unionist before the Civil War. In her retirement years, she wrote the history of Converse College. She was always looking for students interested in history, and, of course, at the time I went to Converse there were many women who did not intend to go on to have careers, so she had an opportunity to influence my decisions and convince me that I should go on for a Ph.D. and that I should apply for a Woodrow Wilson Fellowship, which I did. I won one. Then I made the decision I wanted to live in New York because I wanted to have the opportunity to study at Columbia University but also to have the opportunity to be able to explore the city of New York. But, I must say that Dr. Kibler not only influenced my decision to go on for an M.A. and Ph.D., but she told me where I should live in New York, which was Johnson Hall, the women's graduate student dormitory. The thought always was that when I completed my degree, I would come back to Converse College and teach. Instead, I met my husband in graduate school; he was getting his Ph.D. in physics, and I stayed up North and I did not come back until many years later in 1985 when I came to Clemson University.

C. S.: It sounds to me as if a very important formative role for you, then, was the Converse College experience, of being a woman in an all-women's college.

C. B.: Absolutely! I think a coeducational institution is fine for men, but for women it is less so. It is important for young women to be able to try out their wings where they can play these leadership roles on campus. And I do see the difference. Here in Clemson there has never been a woman who's been president of the student body.

C. S.: Was that need for separate opportunities for leadership particularly important for a southern woman, do you think?

C. B.: I think it's important for all women. They did a study about Radcliffe women, and most of the women who went on and had successful careers attribute their achievements to the single-sex school. I can see some real advantages for women. I think you're right, the perception that southern women perhaps need a little more drawing out than northern women is true, but the studies indicate that women who went to Mount Holyoke, Smith, and Radcliffe attributed their success to attending a women's college.

C. S.: Let me ask, when you went to graduate school, whom did you choose to study with and what did you choose to study? I'm curious because you are known as a southern historian. When did that became your focus of study, and whom in New York did you find to work with?

C. B.: I wanted to study southern history, and I wanted to study at a leading northern institution. The only way to achieve both goals was to study Civil War and Reconstruction. So, when I went into Civil War and Reconstruction, there were extraordinarily few women in the field. There still are not very many, because many women don't want to teach the military aspects of the Civil War. When I went to Columbia University, Eric McKitrick became my mentor. In the early years, he was a major supporter of me, and, yet, he confided to me that when I came to Columbia, they really did not think "Miss Magnolia" was going to last very long, coming out of Converse College in Spartanburg, South Carolina. I went on to win many scholarships. If you chose Harvard or you chose Yale, they guaranteed when you came in with a Woodrow Wilson to carry you straight on through to the completion of doctoral coursework. It turned out at Columbia, that it was just the one year, then what were you supposed to do? Eric McKitrick supported my applications for university fellowships, which I did receive. And so, although I was one of the very few women in history at Columbia University at the time, I was getting these grants in the early sixties.

C. S.: So you went to Columbia as a graduate student in 1961?

C. B.: 1960. I got my M.A. in 1961. I finished my M.A. in eight months. That was due to the good training again of Lillian Kibler, who said, "Have your topic well in hand before you go."

C. S.: Did any of your work in those early years involve women? Did you see that, or was there anyone there who saw that as a field appropriate to study?

C. B.: No, no one. It was almost an all-male environment. Living in a women's graduate dorm was a real benefit, because in all of my classes I would frequently be the only woman. All my peers would meet over coffee, and they were extraordinarily hostile to women being in their environment. Then when I would win fellowships, they really were hostile. But encouragement from my professors was always there.

C. S.: Were there any women faculty at Columbia at that time?

C. B.: No. Not in history.

C. S.: None at all. So, if you'd not had Lillian Kibler at Converse and a whole host of others?

C. B.: Yes, that's right; there would have been no role model for me at all to see that a woman could be a historian.

C. S.: How did you move from there to a first job? Was Eric McKitrick instrumental in getting you a job? Did you have a particular place where you wanted to teach? What was the mechanism?

C. B.: I married in graduate school. My husband was a physicist who went to Brookhaven National Laboratory on Long Island. We were just newlyweds, and I was looking for a job on Long Island, and I made many applications. I do recall my first experience with rejection. The amazing thing is that I had not had any rejection all through school. I had been nurtured; I had been attended to, and to the end of my life, I will have to say that in my educational experiences I was nurtured. I applied for jobs and started getting rejections, and the rejections stated that there were no women in their institutions.

C. S.: As students or as faculty?

C. B.: As faculty. And their letters stated that there were male faculty who did not think they could work with a woman. Now, this was just before that became illegal.

C. S.: But they put it in writing?

C. B.: Put it in writing, and I could name some universities, but I will not put that on tape. Some of them are very well known schools. To show how much I just didn't believe that argument, I thought they were really saying that I didn't have the qualifications to be hired, and they were trying to let me down easy. My husband gave me a copy of Betty Friedan's *The Feminine Mystique*. That raised my consciousness to the fact, No, they mean this. This is the way the world really is. And so, it took until I wanted to go out to be employed that I really found the hostility toward me as a woman in academia.

C. S.: Well, it sounds like there had been some hostility among your fellow graduate students.

C. B.: Yes, you are right, but I attributed it more to the fact that I was one of the few women in school with them. I attributed it to the fact that they couldn't think that anybody coming out of South Carolina could compete. A lot of these people had gone to Harvard, had gone to Yale as undergraduates, and now wanted to live in New York City and couldn't understand how anyone from a "backwoods" school could succeed. That was part of the problem; it was very difficult to convince anyone at Columbia. And that showed the provinciality of Columbia, that anyone could walk and talk at the same time and come from South Carolina.

C. S.: How did you get the first job then if all of them were saying no? What happened?

C. B.: Well, there was a small school; it was part of Adelphi University; they had recently established a branch, Adelphi Suffolk College, and it was in Oakdale, Long Island. We moved to a little town called Sayville; my husband commuted to the Brookhaven National Laboratory, and I commuted only a few miles to the Oakdale campus. It was an experimental school. I still didn't have my degree; I was done with my coursework. I also must say that when I'd run out of university fellowship money, I won a Woodrow Wilson dissertation fellowship. I do remember that when I put in for the dissertation fellowship, and I mentioned that I was going to get married, they wanted to know why my husband couldn't support me. I wrote back and said, "Because he's just getting out of graduate school and would not be able to on $8,000 a year." They awarded it to me. You were really on the cusp there, people had always assumed that women did not go on for Ph.D.s, and, if they did, they certainly had a husband or a family to support them.

C. S.: Did you have both men and women students at Oakdale?

C. B.: Yes.

C. S.: Were there any other women faculty there?

C. B.: Yes, in fact, the person who hired me was a Dr. Ying-Wan Cheng. She had her Ph.D. from Radcliffe, and she had done her undergraduate work at Vassar and had an interesting personal history. She grew up in China. In fact, at the start of World War II, her father was on the World Court at The Hague, and so she was sent to the United States to be educated and never went back to China until very recent years. A lot of people wanted to teach at Oakdale because it was just about forty miles out of the city, so they got many very qualified people there.

C. S.: Were you a novelty among the students as a southerner?

C. B.: By that time I didn't project "southern"; one of the things I learned at Columbia was to play down my southernness. It was not an asset in academic circles in the North.

C. S.: What made you decide to leave Oakdale? Was it a better offer, or was there a sense that you wanted to work with a different kind of student?

C. B.: Well, these were all commuting students. But I won an NEH fellowship in 1967 to do my own independent research. So, I took the year off from 1967 to 1968.

C. S.: What were you working on that year that the fellowship was to support?

C. B.: I was trying to work on a collection of essays on Reconstruction and revise my doctoral dissertation for publication.

C. S.: Did you come back from that, then, to that campus?

C. B.: No, at that time—and this again was a joint decision—my husband had a wonderful opportunity to go to Fermi National Laboratory in Illinois. So, you can see in the very early years of my marriage, I'm following the pattern that most women follow—follow the husband's career. So we moved to Chicago. Now, there my mentor tried to help me get a job. He would call up a chairman and say, "She's really top-notch; you should be happy to have her, and after about thirty minutes, you'll forget she's a woman." And he thought that was the highest compliment that one could be paid.

C. S.: In academic circles, at least. Did you get a job in Chicago?

C. B.: Yes. I taught at Chicago State. After I'd accepted the job, there were the riots over the death of Martin Luther King. The campus was located on the south side of Chicago, and that college was a target. Those were very interesting years in which I was really teaching inner-city kids. So, no one was thinking about being female or male or anything like that, except that I felt *I* was more threatened because of my gender. I did have police officers who would follow me to school to make sure I got there all right, until we finally worked out a way that I hired a driver to take me to school and bring me back home. It was a campus under siege in the late 1960s. Therefore, I was determined that I wasn't going to stay very long. Things got really tough in 1969. I left in 1970, but very early in that year I was on my way to teach a big lecture class, and someone in the corridor pulled out a knife and said, "Your money or your life." I thought it was a joke and said, "I think you need to get a new line." I just didn't believe that this could be happening, and then I realized it was happening. I always knew to carry enough money with me, so the person then took my money and put the knife away and fled down the hall. And I went and taught my lecture class. I had telephone threats and all sorts of things like that, but, fortunately, I was in the process of getting out. My husband, by this time, was desperate for me to get a job where I would be safe and secure as well as employed and stimulated intellectually rather than stimulated by fear. We decided I would take the first good job that came along. I was offered three jobs in the Northeast in 1970. I went to Colgate University, which was going coeducational in 1970. I was the first woman hired into a tenure-stream job in the university; so it was one hundred ninety-nine males and one female as full-time faculty.

C. S.: Were there many women students?

C. B.: Not in the beginning. Now, it's almost half and half.

C. S.: Through all of this, your training had been in Civil War and Reconstruction. Were you self-consciously also doing southern history?

C. B.: Oh, always! We got off the track on that. My doctoral dissertation, which became a book, was the first volume in the Tricentennial Series with the University of South Carolina Press. I was studying black land ownership in the state of South Carolina during Reconstruction [*The Promised Land: the History of the South Carolina Land Commission, 1869–1890*]. I was just slightly ahead of the times as black history soon became a field that was truly developing. But, again, this was the study of an experiment in South Carolina, so I was doing southern history. That's what I did all the time I was at Columbia University. You just had to find ways to study and teach southern history within a broader context.

C. S.: But you continued to do that as you moved to Chicago and then back to upstate New York.

C. B.: That's right. When I went to Colgate, I taught the middle period of American history, but I devoted as much time to the South as to the North, which was considered an unusual approach at the time. Colgate is where I introduced my first course in southern history. I would have a hundred and twenty students subscribing for these courses, and I think that was partly because the South was viewed as a foreign culture in upstate New York.

C. S.: Did Colgate hire other women while you were there, and was there a sense of collegiality among the women faculty, or were you scattered across different departments without opportunities to interact?

C. B.: There were very few women in the early years of coeducation. For instance, in my discipline in the first six years there was no other woman hired. It took Colgate a long time to make a commitment to hire women, and eventually they required that all their hires had to be women unless you could demonstrate such and such. So, they made a real effort to get women. But most of the time I felt very isolated. So, I took many leaves. I would get fellowships, because I did feel it was a very lonely place. It was only in the late 1970s that they started to bring in women in any numbers.

C. S.: What was your first involvement in a historical professional association? Did that begin in graduate school, or did that come later when you were working?

C. B.: My first real involvement was in 1965 when I was a graduate student. I attended my first Southern Historical Association meeting. It was in Richmond, Virginia. Since then, I have been an active member, and I remember that meeting so very vividly.

C. S.: Were you giving a paper, or were you urged to go by Professor Mc-Kitrick?

C. B.: No, Professor McKitrick didn't attend most meetings, and he didn't encourage his students to do that either.

C. S.: So you did that on your own.

C. B.: Well, not exactly. I had come down to Columbia, South Carolina, in 1963 to do my doctoral research. Almost all my research records were at the state archives. It was Charles Lee [director of the South Carolina Department of Archives and History] who introduced me to my dissertation subject. They were in the new building then. What had happened was that as they moved into the new building they discovered these Reconstruction records on the land commission for African Americans becoming land owners. The day I arrived looking for a topic, I did not go to the search room but came into the building by another door and ended up in Charles Lee's office. He had these records and suggested them to me. He was very supportive of me. At that time there were less than twenty-five people working for the archives. That's when the archives used to be open just Monday to Friday, nine to five, and he would come in on Saturdays working on his own project, and he would telephone me and tell me he was going in so that I could go in and work too.

C. S.: Well, did he introduce you to the Southern Historical Association?

C. B.: No, it was actually Wylma Wates, the archives historian. She urged me to go to a Southern Historical Association meeting. So in 1965 I was in New York, but I did go. At that time, I hated to fly; I was terrified of flying. I'd taken the bus down and went to the meeting and met Wylma there. The big star of the meeting was Eugene Genovese. I went to the bus station to return home, and who else was at the bus terminal waiting to go back to New York but Gene Genovese. It turned out that he too did not like to fly. So the two of us rode back together from Richmond, which is quite a long distance on a bus. That was the beginning of a professional association with Gene, who promoted my work. Richmond in 1965 was my first introduction to the Southern.

C. S.: You've been a lifelong member of the Southern ever since.

C. B.: Yes. I think I have missed two or three meetings in thirty-one years.

C. S.: Was the Southern Historical Association particularly valuable to you because you were teaching and living in the North and trying to do southern history? Or are there other connections to it?

C. B.: It was an opportunity to network with many people who were doing the kind of work that I wanted to do, and, yet, in the North I did it in isolation, far from the sources and other southern historians.

C. S.: Were there many women scholars in the Southern at that time? Did you notice them, or do you remember noticing women as part of the work in the Southern?

C. B.: No, I don't. The Southern was a very male-dominated organization. I would go for the papers; I'd go for the friends I had made from other places. It was a place that was doing the kind of work I did. Now, the first organization I belonged to where I truly became involved in promoting women within the profession was through the Berkshire Conference meetings. So many of the ideas I had to promote women in the Southern came out of my experiences with the Berks.

C. S.: When did you start getting involved—beginning in 1970 when you went to Colgate or earlier?

C. B.: No, earlier. Dr. Cheng got me to go to a Berks meeting in 1968 just before I was moving to Chicago, and it was the spring meeting, a small meeting, now called the Little Berks, where thirty or thirty-five people gathered at some resort in New England and exchanged ideas, papers and concerns that women professionals have. I thought, I'm moving west, and I need to have an anchor in the East, and so I got very active in that group. Even when I was living in Chicago, I would come back for the Little Berks meetings. As a result, right after I went to Colgate, I was elected secretary-treasurer of the Berkshire conference. As secretary-treasurer, I was involved in the first effort to ensure that women got on the ballot of the AHA. That was when the AHA first introduced rules that you could get on the ballot by petition. The Berkshire conference ran the first petition with women's names on them.

C. S.: So, you saw from the beginning professional association membership as important.

C. B.: Absolutely.

C. S.: And were you also in the OAH in 1968?

C. B.: No, I was not a member then. I was in the AHA, the Southern, the Berkshire Conference, and the CCWHP/CGWH.
  The Organization of American Historians I got into about 1970, 1971. The big push with the Berkshire Conference to get women on the AHA ballot occurred in 1971. Unfortunately, the AHA was most upset, because they had their ballot already printed. They never thought anyone would take advantage of the petition process.

C. S.: And you used their rules.

C. B.: Yes, we used the rules, and we got on the ballot, and that meant they had to print another ballot. But what they clearly did, they never put one woman up against another woman; they always put a woman up against a very well known man. Not one woman won that first year, but some came close.

C. S.: But the Berks was really the formative organization in terms of getting involved in women's activism, at least for you.

C. B.: Yes. When I joined in 1968, they were very happy to see younger people coming in, because most members had been in this organization since the 1930s. They formed the Berks in the thirties because women were not invited to the smokers at the AHA. However, they kept losing members; and they weren't gaining any new blood, since the number of women in the field was declining. But then in the late 1960s women started reentering the profession and in the early seventies, when I was secretary-treasurer, we decided to hold our first full-size conference in women's history, which developed into what is now known as the Big Berks Conference with two thousand attendees. When you look at the number of women in the historical profession in the late 1960s, there were very few.

C. S.: Was this professional network, then, your connection to people like Willie Lee Rose and to people who had been senior women?

C. B.: Yes, and I had a special love of Willie Lee. She published, when I was in graduate school, *Rehearsal for Reconstruction*. Before it was published, I knew she was working in this area, and it was important to me since I was going to be working in South Carolina on Reconstruction. Eric McKitrick told me to call C. Vann Woodward at Yale, because C. Vann Woodward was her mentor, and he wanted me to explore with Woodward the feasibility of doing the topic. It must have been around late 1962. To me the thought of dialing up C. Vann Woodward and saying, "I'm this graduate student down at Columbia University, etc." But I did call him, and he detected that I was shy, and he said, "Oh! I'd love to meet you! I'd love to talk to you about this." And he said, "If you'll just let me know when you're coming up, we'll go have lunch and we'll talk; just give me a day's notice so that I can get a haircut." I thought that was wonderful; but I was terrified. I never took him up on this offer. But when I went to the first Southern, I met him there. We corresponded; I did correspond with him; I was comfortable writing to him. Later we became friends. He's the one who introduced me to Willie Lee at a Southern. I knew her work; she was very active, and she was one of the few women who would frequently be on panels. Her analysis was very powerful. Many men felt threatened appearing on a panel with her.

C. S.: Did you see her as a kind of a role model that you would like to follow?

C. B.: You know; I'm not sure. It's not so much that she was the role model, but watching a woman become totally accepted, it began to cross my mind that perhaps I could too.

C. S.: And to be free to be critical in the best sense.

C. B.: Yes, but she also had a wonderful sense of humor, an incredible sense of humor. In the best sense, and she was really sharp.

C. S.: You've told in another context the story of her being given special recognition at Colgate.

C. B.: Yes.

C. S.: Did you play a special role in that?

C. B.: Yes. That was after she had the stroke, which I think was 1978. We were at the Big Berks. It was one of their big meetings, and she was going to be giving a major speech, and we were going to have dinner together. Then someone came in and said, "Have you heard that Willie Lee had a stroke?" At that point, all I wanted to do was to go home. I mean I still get emotional because I think she got chewed up being the only woman at that level in the field. And being so prominent, she was asked to do so much, and she did so much. She carried the burden because there was no one else. And it's not our fault that there wasn't anybody else, but the system had only allowed for a few, and so, I do believe that her stroke was in part due to her life being too stressed out. In that sense, she represented to me what happened to women, to all of us as we took on all these burdens and tried to do everything right.

C. S.: And yet, you continued in all the organizations to try to create more roles for women.

C. B.: Yes, but I was hoping for more women in the field. You see, that's why I do these series on southern women's letters and diaries. In that way, I am frequently promoting women's careers. This will often be their first book publication, and I'm helping them get established and to make it easier for them than it was for Willie Lee and even for people like me who had to keep proving themselves again and again. I don't know whether the stroke of Willie Lee influenced my decision to become a series editor, but I thought it was important that Willie Lee got an honorary degree from Colgate.

Just at the time when her career was starting to be honored, she had a stroke. And, she hadn't gotten many honorary degrees, and I wanted to see that she got an honorary degree for her work and for her inspiration.

She was an inspiration. I tried to have her given an honorary degree at Colgate, but there were rules. You had to be present to receive it because they didn't want to be giving it to no-shows. I used to keep trying to make the case that this should be an exception because this was not someone who was just going to have more pressing business that day. She physically could not attend. Well, that wasn't accepted, but the president, George Langdon, said to me that if ever she got well enough, then they would give her the honorary degree. She came to a point in her rehabilitation where it appeared she could come, but by that time her husband was very ill. He could not attend; so her good friend and colleague at UVA, Bill Abbott, picked her up in Baltimore and brought her up on a plane. Friends joined them at Colgate, and the school did handle the event very stylishly. The president and the provost threw an elegant dinner for her afterwards. We invited many historians, and she was so pleased. At the ceremony, she could walk across the stage, and I was honored to do the introduction for the honorary degree. That was a special moment in my life.

C. S.: This seems off the subject, but it's a way of my leading back into the role that you took in the Southern Association for Women Historians. If I'm putting these things together correctly, you were going to Colgate the year that the Southern met in Kentucky and the women there formed the first Southern Association for Women Historians.

C. B.: Yes, and I was not a member of that, though I went to that meeting. By that time, I had mastered flying. I figured if I was going to have a commuting marriage, my husband staying in Chicago when I came back to upstate New York, I was going to be flying a lot, and I went to Kentucky to that meeting, and it was four planes I had to take. It was an all-day excursion to get to that meeting, but I did not know of the SAWH. I was at the meeting, because I was there for the SHA and my friends.

C. S.: How did you get involved in the Southern Association for Women Historians?

C. B.: More women were coming to the Southern; more women were being turned out as historians in general; so more southern historians were women. They were coming to these meetings, and you saw them at sessions. At some point I started to run into people who belonged to an organization, the SAWH, which they were trying to get more firmly established, and they were not being treated well by the establishment of the SHA. I knew Judy Gentry; I met Mollie Davis; I met Margaret Ripley Wolfe, and Barbara Schnorrenberg. They were all already heavily involved in the SAWH, so, in one sense, I came late to the table. Until then, I'd been active in the Berks, and by now, I was on the Committee on the Status of Women in the Historical Profession of the OAH. I was already thinking about women's status in the profession when I came into the SAWH, and it seemed to me to be very informal and not a very well structured organization.

C. S.: But, the connection in my mind was that you became instrumental in setting up the large fund-raising efforts to create the prizes.

C. B.: Yes, that's right.

C. S.: Now, that's much later, but the Willie Lee Rose Prize is really one of your legacies.

C. B.: Yes. All of this comes from the Berks. The Berks had prizes. I had been president of the SAWH in 1980. When I came to Clemson in 1985, the SAWH was really beginning to flourish. Theda Purdue, of Clemson, became president, and I said, "Well, you know, what you really need to do is have a regional meeting." Again, I'm thinking of the Berks, which had a regional meeting, the big meeting, which came into being while I was secretary-treasurer in 1972–1973. The first meeting of the Big Berks was in 1973. So, I suggested that the SAWH expand its horizons and gain greater visibility. With bigger meetings and greater visibility, we could institute prizes. The prize then becomes coveted, and the organization becomes something that is perfectly creditable and can advance the careers of women.

C. S.: Some of your background is with the Committee on the Status of Women in the OAH. Were there any particular issues that were raised in your mind by being active on that committee that you translated to the Southern?

C. B.: Yes. Mollie Davis was on the OAH Committee on the Status of Women with me, and so I established much closer ties to her there, and that was 1976 to 1978. Then in 1978, I chaired the OAH Committee on the Status of Women. What we were working on, and what we later tried to get the Southern to do, was to get more women on the program and to get more women on the Executive Council. Those were the issues of the OAH.

C. S.: Did you see the SAWH as being a mechanism to do that within the Southern?

C. B.: Yes, because one of the first things that we did when I was in the SAWH was to determine how many women were in the Southern. We did the same head counts as in the OAH. How many women are on the program? How many women are on council? When I was on the Executive Council of the Southern, which was 1981 to 1984, there were no other women, and the woman who had been on just before had been LaWanda Cox, who was also the lone woman. So there was very little representation of women. There I first saw how you bring this to the attention of the SHA. You just need to do a numbers count, and I certainly learned that at the OAH. Also, I served on Eugene Genovese's OAH Program Committee for the 1978 meeting.

C. S.: So that bus trip paid off!

C. B.: No. Program Committee work is just plain old hard work. Gene viewed me as someone who would attempt to get women on the program. That was my job, to get women on the program. I did a good job; there were more women on that program than had been on any program in years.

C. S.: You had a mandate.

C. B.: I had a mandate to do it from Gene.

C. S.: Your involvement with the SAWH comes when they're beginning to transform themselves.

C. B.: That's right.

C. S.: I see you as a key person in that process. You've already said that you brought to that some of the sense of the importance of hard information, counting the numbers. The importance of . . .

C. B.: Getting them focused.

C. S.: The importance of mentoring younger people.

C. B.: Gaining them acceptability.

C. S.: Can you talk some more about when you began to take a leadership role, what you did, or what you set in motion in the Southern Historical Association, and the SAWH as a tool for doing that?

C. B.: When I was elected to be president of the SAWH—I was president in 1980—it was their tenth anniversary. I was appalled at the conditions under which we had to meet each year. The Southern slighted us. I thought, we've got to get credibility with the SHA. We had to make the SHA realize that since they're always concerned about membership, there may be a lot of women who will not come to their meetings if they feel that this is an unfriendly environment. The SAWH could actually increase the membership of the SHA. It would be mutually advantageous to both.

I also proposed the idea of letting us give prizes to gain legitimacy. We needed to raise funds. I became active in raising money. Then we had the thought, How do you impress upon the Southern that they might not be doing a good job of including women? You see, in 1980 there was an incredible denial on the part of the Southern of the fact that they were not accepting women into the core of the organization. As I have said, I would sit there at the council table, the only woman, and try to say this is terrible the way it is. The year before I joined the SHA Executive Council, when I was president-elect of the SAWH, I asked to make a presentation before the council about the possibility of establishing a Committee on the Status of Women.

C. S.: So, you're really responsible for getting that now-permanent committee in the Southern.

C. B.: Yes, that's right.

C. S.: Was there opposition to that?

C. B.: Yes, of course.

C. S.: Was there support for it? I guess the other part of that is, it's there, there must have been support.

C. B.: Yes. Well, what happened, LaWanda Cox was still on the council in 1980. I had cleared this with her before I went to them. I didn't realize what I was walking into the day I went in to meet with the council about this. I said I was coming on the council next year, and look at who was going to be on council, just one woman. Who's at the table now? Just one woman. I don't want to name all those on council who opposed the idea, but certainly Ben Wall opposed it. As secretary-treasurer, he was a very powerful man in the organization, and he did his best to stop it. Ben could not believe that the organization he loved so much did not treat women fairly. He had always been a good friend of mine, but he had a blind spot. However, there were council members who were allies. The final decision at that meeting was to appoint a committee to decide whether there would be a Committee on the Status of Women. The next year, three of the four subcommittee members agreed to recommend forming a Committee on the Status of Women. The real opponent did not attend the meeting.

C. S.: You were president of SAWH, you were on the council, and now you have this committee in the Southern.

C. B.: Yes. And I will say, sitting on the council, in the beginning, the person who was really supportive was Sanford Higginbotham, editor of the *Journal of Southern History*. He was such a sweet man, and he was a close friend of Ben Wall. He would try to explain to me that Ben really did believe in women's rights. You know, Ben marched in all the civil rights movements. Ben moved forward on the cause of African Americans. He could never see himself labeled as not being supportive of women, and that I had to see it in that light, but at the same time Higg would constantly work to see that Ben did move forward on women's rights. And so, Higg was a great supporter, telling me to keep on. When I first went on the council, things would be said at the table in my presence about women and, in particular, about this new committee of the SHA, such that one would assume that I was not there.

C. S.: I don't know if you played a role in this. One of the things that made the Southern Association for Women Historians more visible in the Southern is the reception and the party that they throw. Do you remember when that began?

C. B.: I do not know when that began. I do know that in 1980, SAWH was ten years old, and I was president. I felt we should throw a party for our tenth anniversary and have a big reception, and we should make sure to send handwritten invitations. We invited every person on the program, which was still very male-dominated, all the Executive Council, all committee members, and every other prominent member. We didn't have much money at that time; I don't remember what our dues structure was. We just collected money, and I do remember Barbara Schnorrenberg coming over with the whole backseat of her car filled with food to have at the party, and then we went out to the liquor store and bought liquor. We had rented a suite for four of us. We had three rooms, and we had a huge fine spread of food, because we tried very hard. The interesting thing for us was to wonder would they come. And of course, they did. Even Ben Wall came with his wife, Neva. They were all there, and if there was a turning point, it occurred then, when everyone came.

C. S.: After ten years.

C. B.: After ten years. Oh yes, one other thing I took pride in was the program at that meeting. We did a program on the three women presidents of the SHA. We had an extraordinarily big turnout for that session. I always remember that. They had us in this, I swear, you did go through the boiler room to get to this room in the back, but it was jam-packed.

C. S.: We have mentioned that you worked to set up the prizes to reward scholarship and give legitimacy. How difficult was it for a new organization like the SAWH to raise the money to support the prizes? Did women have a disadvantage in achieving that goal?

C. B.: Maybe in a bigger organization it would have been harder, but you see the most magnificent thing about the Southern, everybody helps. I really love that organization. Here I have been sounding critical, but on the other hand, it has been my support system for my entire career. The only objection to the prizes, and it was a really harsh objection, was that I wanted the Willie Lee Rose Prize to be a prize given only to women. There, one saw a lot of hostility on the part of men within the SHA to limiting it.

C. S.: But it was the SAWH that was setting up the prize?

C. B.: Yes. But the SHA members were being asked to donate, and most of them were men. Some said that was illegal; others that Willie Lee would not have wanted it; that it depreciated the value of the prize if it was limited to only one gender, etc. There were some SAWH members, I think, who agreed with that. That was one place that I may have lost friends. I felt that since women would raise the money, would serve on the selection committee, and after doing all that work, if you are going for the best book in southern history, there will be so many more books written by men, in most years you will give the prize to a man. Thus, I was determined that it was to be a prize for women. I thought, look at the heavy burden of Willie Lee Rose's career. She had done so much for the profession, had done all that serving on committees, and look what it had done to her. It should absolutely go to a woman; I clung to that. Willie Lee thought so too, and many prominent southern historians, including C. Vann Woodward, agreed, and it got funded.

C. S.: This is sort of jumping ahead; we haven't gone back to talk about your establishing the Women's Committee or the women's studies program at Colgate. Is that when you really became interested in the history of women, as such?

C. B.: I was already working on a new book, *The Hammonds of Redcliffe*. I was very interested in the four generations of Hammond women. That led me into southern women's history. I thought, my goodness, they were really promoting women now at Colgate, and we didn't have any women's studies program or visibility. So, I convinced our new provost that we had to have a program; we couldn't find anyone to take the job, so I agreed to be acting director for one year. I thought I would have to do it for life because they weren't allocating the money to fund the job. I had friends in other departments who informed me that a chair had been created for someone in the economics department, and they weren't going to fill his job. So I asked, could not that money just be moved over to women's studies. And they said, "No, it's an economics slot." But I said that women's studies involves all of the fields. So, you have the money. It was a good sum of money to fund our program. The end result was that they created the directorship, and Ann J. Lane was the person who served as the first permanent director of women's studies.

C. S.: So you've played an important role in bringing women into lots of institutions.

C. B.: Yes. And then I left Colgate for an endowed professorship at Clemson, and so Ann Lane said, "Thanks a lot."

C. S.: Do you see that there is still a need for the SAWH? Does it have different goals from when you were playing those active roles? Where is it going?

C. B.: I worry about the SAWH. It handles its professional responsibilities with great ease. But it is becoming so structured and less personal. It's losing its ability to deal with the many individual cases of discrimination against women. I know, since I am the chair of the President's Commission on the Status of Women at Clemson University, that discrimination continues to exist. Our findings show that women faculty still feel beleaguered and need a support system. We're becoming perhaps a little smug in thinking that we don't need to do anything to assist women, that everything is now open to women, that there is no discrimination. That sort of thinking is a myth.

C. S.: Do you think that's an effect of the organization or of the younger generation of women?

C. B.: I think it may be both. Linda Kerber made that very clear when she gave an address at the OAH in which she said that most young women absolutely will not believe that revolutions can go backwards, that their gains today might not be there tomorrow, and that all they need to do to be successful in the profession is to emulate men. She said, "I believe they're in for a rude awakening."

C. S.: So you see yourself as a continuing revolutionary in this sense.

C. B.: Well, I don't know. I think of myself as a realist. I think attitudes have not yet changed enough. I just think that when we start to think globally, nationally, and internationally, that we are losing what's happening to our individual members. We used to gather in a room and select our officers. Now we've had to mail out ballots. I guess that's the price of success, but where is the place where we're supporting each other?

C. S.: And that has to be on an individual level.

C. B.: I think so.

Elizabeth Jacoway

Elizabeth Jacoway is an independent scholar who has taught at the University of Florida, the University of Arkansas at Little Rock, and Lyon College. She earned her Ph.D. from the University of North Carolina in 1974 and is the author of *Yankee Missionaries in the South: The Penn School Experiment* (1980). She is also the coeditor of *Southern Businessmen and Desegregation* (1982), *"Behold Our Works Were Good!": A Handbook of Arkansas Women's History* (1988), *The Adaptable South: Essays in Honor of George Brown Tindall* (1991), and *Understanding the Little Rock Crisis: An Exercise in Remembrance and Reconciliation* (1999). She has authored numerous articles and encyclopedia entries and has received several grants, fellowships, and awards. She has served on the board of editors for the *Journal of Southern History.* A founder and past President of the Arkansas Women's History Institute, she has also served on numerous organizational boards and review committees, including the National Endowment for the Humanities. She was President of SAWH from 1980 to 1981.

Interviewer: Constance B. Schulz
Transcriber: Staci Richie
The following interview took place on January 6, 2003.

E. J.: I am Elizabeth Jacoway in my fantasy life where I am a historian. In the real world I am Betsy Jacoway Watson, and I live in Newport, Arkansas. I'm the mother of two college boys, and the wife of a small-town lawyer. I got my Ph.D. at the University of North Carolina in 1974, I worked under George Tindall, and I never had any thought at all of becoming a professional historian. I pursued a degree in history because I was just fascinated by everything that I had studied there. I was actually reared to be a traditional southern lady, and the game plan was for me to marry some federal judge and have teas for the rest of my life.

C. S.: Teas, and entertain important people in the community.

E. J.: Yes, and I didn't really have much quarrel with that whole approach, except that I found it very constricting, but everyone else in my circle seemed to think it was fine, so I just thought there was something wrong with me. My father insisted that I go to graduate school, and I chose the University of North Carolina because I went to the wedding of a girl who had gotten her master's there. The boys in the wedding were so cute; I decided that's the school for me.

C. S.: Are you a native of Arkansas?

E. J.: I grew up in Little Rock, and I was in the eighth grade at the time of the Little Rock crisis.

C. S.: Did you go to Little Rock Central High School?

E. J.: The year of the Little Rock crisis, 1957, a new high school opened out in the west of Little Rock, Hall High School. It was designed for the city's elite to protect them from having to be a part of integration. That was really the Achilles heel of the whole program in Little Rock: because the elite, the businessmen and professional men's children, were not involved in integration. Those men were not involved, and therefore it became really as much of a class issue as it was a race issue in Little Rock.

C. S.: So you weren't at Central High School?

E. J.: I went to Hall High School.

C. S.: Later in your own career as a historian you wrote about African American education in Reconstruction. Were you aware of those issues in the eighth grade?

E. J.: No, I lived through the Little Rock crisis with my eyes closed. Even though my uncle, Virgil Blossom, was superintendent of schools, I was such a part of the patriarchy that I just assumed that the men who were in charge, the authority figures, knew how to take care of things, and everything would be all right, and that wasn't my business to think about it or reflect on it. That's really the way I was reared. I was not supposed to think. But then I went to Randolph Macon and had an absolutely wonderful experience there.

C. S.: Were you a history major?

E. J.: I went there two years and was thinking about majoring in history and wanted to stay there, but my father insisted that I come back to the University of Arkansas. He was afraid I was going to fall in love with somebody up there and move away. And his word was, I had learned how to live in the ivory tower, he wanted me to learn how to live in the supermarket. So I came back to Arkansas and majored in sorority life, and I never cracked a book. It was a lot of fun; I had a wonderful time! But, again my father, the controlling figure in my life, figured out when I was a senior that I was not an educated person, and he insisted that I go to graduate school, and he told me I was going to get a degree in history. So I went to Chapel Hill, and I chose American history because I only had to have one language. Actually I had gone over there to get a master's of art in teaching, which is what my father told me to do. I sat in there for a week, and I said, "I cannot do this." I just walked across the campus into Jim Godfrey's office, chairman of the history department, and said I would like to be a history graduate student. He said, "What are your scores on the GRE?" I told him, and they were good, and he said, "You're in." So I literally came in through the back door. All the classes had already been going on for a week, and it was *unheard* of that there would be an opening in George Tindall's seminar, and I got in. This was in 1966.

C. S.: In 1966 were there other women in the graduate program?

E. J.: Yes, there were. It was about 50 percent women. But I was in that seminar, and really, if George had looked like a radical, I would not have paid any attention to him. But he looked like all of my father's friends. He was, you know, sweet, and white-haired, wore a bow tie and a tweed jacket, and he didn't say anything that sounded radical. He is *far* to the left of my parents. But he hooked me before I had understood what had happened. And, I was there for three weeks, and I had a Damascus Road experience and realized that I was a racist, that I had lived through the Little Rock crisis, I had not thought about it. I knew that I had grown up surrounded by good people, and I knew that my father and his friends were the leaders of the community; *how* could this have happened? And how could I have been a part of it and not thought about it? And that was the genesis of my Ph.D., and my parents were not at all pleased.

C. S.: Did George Tindall have Penn School as one of the possible topics, or did you find it on your own?

E. J.: No. I found it on my own. I told Daddy I wanted to write about the Little Rock crisis for a master's thesis, and he said, "Oh, no, I'm still making a living here, we're not going to stir that pot." George Tindall got a Fulbright and went to Vienna. Joel Williamson took me over, and I went in to see Dr. Williamson. He thought I was just a cute little girl from Little Rock, and he put me to work on a project that no one ever heard of and that couldn't do anybody any harm. It turned out that the Penn School Papers had just been accessioned and had actually just been processed at Chapel Hill. They were an absolute goldmine. And I did my master's thesis out of that and got so bitten that I just had to know how that story turned out. So I really got a Ph.D. largely because I wanted to understand that story and be the one to tell it, and I *needed* to do it.

In the interim I had married Gus Burns, who was a graduate student there, went to Florida, where I taught in an integrated school the first year it was integrated. I taught all these precious black children, and I realized more and more: I have got to understand this. So my life ever since then has been a quest to understand southern race relations. I'm now back to square one, and I'm writing the book about the Little Rock crisis that my daddy wouldn't let me write. I've written five out of fifteen chapters.

C. S.: You were the first one who took the Penn School seriously and wrote about it. Did your dissertation immediately become a book?

E. J.: It's *Yankee Missionaries in the South: The Penn School Experiment*, and it was published in 1980 by Louisiana State University Press. Everybody was surprised: I mean that this cute little Chi Omega from Little Rock had published a book with LSU!

C. S.: Do you mean everybody in Little Rock or everybody at North Carolina?

E. J.: Well, I had kind of gotten people's attention at North Carolina, finally, and I think my professors were not so surprised, but I didn't take myself seriously as an academic. I felt like I was there through the back door, and all these other people were the serious scholars. I was just there because I was really interested and didn't ever intend to teach or even never thought I'd write.

C. S.: Did you, when you were in graduate school, come to the conclusion that you wanted to teach at the college level?

E. J.: No. I finally did teach, just out of poverty. I got a graduate assistantship the last year I was in Chapel Hill, and I just loved it. I found out that I was good at it. I got so much energy from it, from my students, at that point I realized I could; I could do this. So I did and taught at the University of Florida and then at the University of Arkansas at Little Rock, and then I remarried and moved up into rural Arkansas.

C. S.: Did you teach first graders or very young children?

E. J.: No, I taught seventh grade at a junior high school in Interlachen, Florida.

C. S.: Have you continued to teach in Arkansas?

E. J.: No, I have not. I taught for three years at the University of Arkansas at Little Rock when I first moved back here in 1975. After I got married in 1978, I finished up *Yankee Missionaries* and worked on a new book, *Southern Businessmen and Desegregation*. I had gotten a grant from NEH in 1976 to start the Little Rock book, and I started with the question that, of course, I would start with: Where were the businessmen? Where was my dad? Where were his friends? How did this happen? And that grew. The more I worked on it, the more I realized that a pattern was established in Little Rock that really was copied across the South, and so I started finding other people who were doing similar things, and I just got together with my friend Dave Colburn and said, "Let's do a book of articles." And so that was *Southern Businessmen and Desegregation* that LSU did in 1981. I was working on those two book projects, finishing them up, and then I got pregnant, and I had two babies in two years. Because Newport is a little tiny town in rural Arkansas, everything that I wanted for my children I had to create. So I started a Montessori school, and I started an Academic Booster Club when they got into public school, and my husband is a lawyer and president of the Rotary Club and president of the Chamber of Commerce and stuff like that, so I did the wifely things that I had been so well trained to do, and all that has pretty well kept me busy.

C. S.: Let me back up a little. When you finished your Ph.D. or finished the work in North Carolina and moved back to Florida, were you actively looking for a teaching position? What was your experience, going on the job market as a southern woman in the 1970s?

E. J.: That was about 1972. I had finished my coursework and my exams. But the problem for me was, I was atypical in every way, every category. I was married to a man in the history department at the University of Florida, so they didn't want to hire me in the history department. Florida at that point had an interesting program, University College, for undergraduates. All undergraduates went through two years of University College. So they found me a slot to teach there. I was not out on the job market on my own. I had a man running interference for me. I had the work towards the degree; I had the dissertation almost written; I was legitimate. They hired me to teach courses that were unattractive courses that they really needed someone to teach. I taught one called comprehensive logic, and it was just absolutely horrible!

C. S.: So you weren't necessarily teaching history courses.

E. J.: I was not teaching history courses. They had an undergraduate curriculum called American institutions that was sociology, religion, and history, and so I taught some of that.

C. S.: When you went to Arkansas and taught in Little Rock, how was that? Was there a job announcement, or was that again just something you lucked into?

E. J.: I had gotten a divorce and wanted to move home. They announced they had a slot in southern history, and I applied for it and got it. I taught there for three years. But again, I got outside the pattern because I taught there in the fall of 1975, and then my NEH grant year started in January of 1976, so I was gone for a year.

C. S.: So your professional ties really have been quite scattered: North Carolina, Florida, but since 1975 pretty strongly in Arkansas.

E. J.: Yes, and as a consequence, the SAWH has been a very important vehicle for me, and even more so the Southern Historical Association. Those two organizations have been the vehicle that I have used to stay visible, such as it is.

C. S.: Well let's go back. How did you first learn about the SHA, and how did you go from there to becoming involved in the SAWH?

E. J.: My first husband was a southern historian, and he was just always involved with the SHA. Having gone to Chapel Hill, I was very aware that the Southern Historical Association meeting was always something to go to and that the *Journal of Southern History* was something you always read. And so, I just started going to the SHA, and it was the most exhilarating thing I had ever done. Every paper was better than the last! I just loved everything about it. And it's so fascinating to me now; I look at the program and say, "Haven't I heard all these papers?" My first SHA was 1972 at Hollywood-by-the-Sea, Florida, and I've been to every one since then but two. That was just a wonderful experience. I loved getting to know so many people, and year after year realizing that you keep seeing the same people, you get to know new people, and it's small. I didn't realize until I gave a paper at the AHA in about 1980, that it's an entirely different animal, so alienating. The SHA has just become so dear to me. I came to realize a long time ago that everybody comes and gathers there, and then they all scatter and go back to their own world. They don't know, they don't stop and think that I don't go back to a job somewhere.

C. S.: You're part of a group that's been variously called independent scholars, or even "underemployed historians," a label that is one of my favorites. Did you have any sense in the Southern Historical Association that people knew and that you were set aside because of not being part of the academic club?

E. J.: No, I have never felt that. Of course, I'm a part of the Chapel Hill Mafia, so all those connections are just wonderful. Another part of it has been that I have stayed active, and I've published five books, so I have never had the feeling that I was by the wayside. But I have always had the feeling in SAWH, amazingly enough, that I was invisible. And it's very interesting to me, it has always been interesting to me, that an organization that says it is promoting women has been so unsupportive of a woman who doesn't follow the traditional male pattern. As an independent scholar I have made a choice that not a whole lot of people have made: to try to have it all, to have a career, and be the kind of mother I wanted to be to my children.

C. S.: How did you find SAWH?

E. J.: They found me. I can't really remember any earlier awareness of SAWH, but on my wedding day, in 1978, Martha Swain called me and said that Jacquelyn Hall was supposed to have given the talk to SAWH that fall in St. Louis. Something had come up, and she was not going to be able to do it, and would I be willing to talk about the Southern Oral History Program at Chapel Hill? Jacquelyn had given them my name because I had done some interviews for them.

C. S.: Was that the project that became *Like a Family: The Making of a Southern Cotton Mill World*?

E. J.: No. She was just doing a whole series of outstanding, or interesting, southern women. And I did a couple people for that—Daisy Bates and Vivion Brewer in Arkansas. So I gave that talk, and then Martha and I just got to be famous friends, just instantly. Martha was president that year, and the way the thing used to work was that the president chose who was going to give the paper, and the president chose the next year's president. The next year's president was Jody Carrigan, but Jody didn't really have anybody in mind, and Martha suggested me. I accepted it, and I was thrilled to have the opportunity to become involved, although I didn't have any understanding at that point, particularly, of what the association was trying to accomplish. In the early years I'm talking about, even by the time I was involved, it was just done out of somebody's hip pocket. It was very, very unstructured and small. And a small group of us were involved in trying to tighten it up. We used to meet in Mollie Davis's and Carol Bleser's suite. That was where the Executive Committee always met, and the year I was president, we actually got a room for the Executive Committee meetings. That was something that I thought was important.

C. S.: You were describing your early involvement and Martha Swain getting to know you and inviting you to give the talk and then inviting you to be active; you very quickly went into the leadership role.

E. J.: My sense of it was that Mollie and Carol were pretty much the old hands in the association when I came onboard. And Martha and Jody were kind of new at it, and Judy Gentry had been around for quite a while, being the treasurer and handling all the money, and Barbara Schnorrenberg had been around for quite a while editing the *Newsletter*.

C. S.: What were some of the things you wanted to do that you felt were necessary or useful, and how did they fit with your interest in and devotion to the Southern?

E. J.: I hesitate to say too categorically what I was thinking at that point. I had come to feminism very late, as you can imagine. I kind of came in through the back door. And when I was in Chapel Hill, I did not feel discriminated against as a woman; there were lots of women graduate students and there was lots of support for them. So I didn't feel that I had been mistreated, and I didn't feel mistreated in the profession, and it was interesting to me when I started working with Mollie and Carol that they felt so mistreated. They talked about it and raised my awareness of things that I had always taken for granted, that, sure, women are treated this way, but you just have to overcome it; you just have to work harder. I finally realized, you know what? I shouldn't have to work harder. I credit them with really raising my consciousness about what could be expected. But at that stage of the game, women's history was really on the threshold of becoming something important, but it had not done so yet. It was new, and it was marginal. I kept hearing from other women, especially from Mollie and Carol, that this was something that deserved equal treatment. So I remember in my year as SAWH president, I got us a room to have the Executive Committee meetings. Another thing that I did, just out of my gracious southern background, was to formalize this. We needed to make this a more elegant and important occasion than just a bunch of women sitting around trying to complain about things, and so I brought wine and cheese, and we kind of had a little party. Just a few years later Theda Purdue turned that into the SAWH reception.

C.S: What that sounds like to me then, is that you were being radicalized, and the epiphany, the "Road to Damascus" experience that you describe in terms of southern race, didn't immediately translate into any kind of radicalism on women's ideas.

E. J.: No, no, not at all.

C. S.: Although you yourself were doing research in women's history, first with the work on the Penn School.

E. J.: See, I didn't think of that as women's history. I thought of that as institutional history, the story of the school that just happened to be run by two women.

C. S.: But when you did the project for Jackie Hall on noted women in Arkansas, did that trigger anything in your mind?

E. J.: No, and I'll tell you why. I grew up in a family of really neat women. My grandmother was the daughter and the wife of a United States congressman. Her sister was married to William Pettus Hobby [Governor of Texas, 1917–1921], and my grandmother, Peggy Jacoway, just thought of herself as a public woman. In 1941 she wrote a book called *First Ladies of Arkansas,* and I grew up thinking that women wrote books. My mother was president of everything in Little Rock and was one of the founders of the Arkansas Art Center, and I grew up thinking that women could do anything. Although my father was very patriarchal in the sense that he wanted to have the last word, and really called the shots on things like where I was going to go to school, it was clearly understood in my family that my mother was the real power. I took all that in, believing it's OK for women to be intelligent, it's OK for women to write books, and if they marry the federal judge and have the teas they're also doing the things that shape the community. I didn't feel oppressed, and I wasn't oppressed, and so I didn't see a need to be radicalized. I didn't understand for a long time that that was atypical and that other women were not so blessed.

C. S.: Well, but then you say that dealing with Carol Bleser and with Mollie Davis, they raised your consciousness. Did you see yourself as becoming either a feminist or a radical feminist?

E. J.: I am not a radical feminist. But I see myself as a feminist in the sense that I feel women should be given equal opportunities and equal recognition. And I think that is what SAWH did, as much as anything. I think that is so wonderful, and I really credit Mollie and Carol with it, although there were a lot more women that I didn't know. I didn't know Arnita Jones, and I didn't know a lot of these early founders. I'm sure they were a part of this, but the early message that I got and that really contributed to my awakening was the sense that the Southern Historical Association had not been open to women. In the 1970s there were not women in leadership positions, there were not women on committees, and so that was my understanding of the early goal of SAWH. I'm sure it was broader than this, but my understanding was that we wanted to open up the SHA to women, and that we wanted to use SAWH as the tool to make that happen. One of our early strategies that worked so brilliantly was just a rule among the early women, that you always go to the business meetings at the SHA. And that came out of somebody's understanding that Ben Wall had complained at some point that the women didn't have positions because they really weren't interested in the association. Well, doggone it, we made it our business to get interested in the association, and by 1982 or so, our whole organization was at that business meeting. And it worked. I turned to Martha Swain this year [November 2002] at the business meeting, and she and I were the only old SAWH hands there, and I said, "Where are all the women?" She said, "We've won." And I think that's exactly what happened, when we started going to the business meeting, we started showing an interest in the SHA. We started promoting the SHA among women, and a part of the result was that women were rewarded. By making ourselves visible and by insisting, in a nice, southern ladylike way, with our male friends that we should be on the Executive Council, we should be on the *Journal of Southern History* board of editors. We should be on committees, and our men friends started appointing us.

C. S.: Did the women who did this then, in their turn, mentor younger women, do you remember? How important was the mentoring of younger women historians when you became president and were in the leadership of SAWH?

E. J.: It was very important. And one of the early things we did was to try to promote graduate students and get them involved in the organization and have graduate student sessions at the SAWH conferences, and have a stipend for them to come to the Southern Historical Association meeting.

C. S.: How important have the Julia Cherry Spruill and the Willie Lee Rose prizes been in terms of your understanding of the role of SAWH in doing some of the things that you're talking about?

E. J.: I think that they've been very important, which is why I wanted to make them large stipends. The year they were established, I was president of the Arkansas Women's History Institute, and I had established the Susie Pryor Prize in Arkansas that year with a $1,000 stipend. I pushed real hard for us to give a large stipend for the Rose and Spruill prizes. I thought that a little $250 prize is not really something that you're going to go after. But a $1,000 prize, that's going to make people sit up and say, "Hey, I'm going to go for that." I don't want to give too much credit to SAWH, because it also happened that women's history came of age at the same time, and there were lots and lots of people out there producing good work. But I think that our two prizes have done a wonderful amount of work in making women's history and women visible and in making us credible.

C. S.: How difficult was it to raise the funds to support the Rose and Spruill prizes?

E. J.: Well, we need to step back. We were talking about creating a prize, and of course the question came up immediately: Is it a prize for a book written by a woman, or is it a prize for a book in women's history? And who should we name this after? Very quickly the decision was made; maybe we need to have two prizes, and we fought over who to name it for, not fought, but talked long and hard. We all thought that it ought to be named for Julia Cherry Spruill, and then Carol also said, "Oh, but we've got to have a prize for Willie Lee Rose." And so we said, "Well, let's do both," and Carol said, "OK, I will raise the money for the Willie Lee Rose prize." I had been friends for some time with Anne Firor Scott, and I knew that she loved Julia Spruill, so I said I would ask her if she would raise that money, and she very graciously agreed to do that. So really those two women raised the money.

My sense was that Anne Scott had done more than anyone at that point to bring southern women into the profession and to make that a valid field of study. So, when I was president I invited her to give the talk at our program, and I encouraged her to take on the Julia Spruill fundraising effort. In those ways, she became active in the association, and I feel that that was a contribution that I made to bring in some disparate practitioners of women's history together in a manner that I feel good about. I think it was good for everybody.

C. S.: How important is it, do you think, that eligibility for a prize is still only available to women? How crucial is that?

E. J.: Well, that's another issue that I wanted to bring up, because some time after we created the prizes, Hugh Davis Graham wrote a letter in the OAH *Newsletter*, attacking us for having a prize that was only given to a woman. And I answered him in the *Newsletter* with the argument that it is valid to have an organization that recognizes work that's done by women. He was saying, "Are we going to have organizations that represent work only done by gays, and blacks, etc." [Graham, "Race, Ethnicity, and Scholarly Prizes," OAH *Newsletter* 15 (May 1987)]. And of course . . .

C. S.: Now we do!

E. J.: But, my answer was, "Yes, it's valid and it's legitimate; it's there to do. You can have any kind of organization you want if you'll raise the money and you're willing to do the work." [Jacoway, OAH *Newsletter* 15 (May 1987)]. I continue to feel that it is valid, and needed.

I want to mention another thing that has been important to SAWH. I worked really hard with Willard Gatewood to get SHA to come to Little Rock in 1996, and so I was very involved with the SAWH reception that year. One of the things that I did with First Vice President Elizabeth Turner was to initiate the books exhibit. When she was president, Liz appointed a book exhibit chairperson, so that has gone on to be a good idea, and I'm tickled that I was able to help with that.

C. S.: Good. I had forgotten that that's where that began, and it's been a huge fund-raising success. I think it has also had huge success in making the university presses more aware of SAWH as a separate organization. As you look at the SAWH and SHA today, and I know you're still active in both, how important is the continued existence and presence of an organization primarily about women or for women?

E. J.: I think that the fact that it is so wildly successful speaks to the need that a lot of women feel to have a place where they can go and feel some sense of triumph and feel that they are valued. At the same time I think it would be a grave mistake ever to let the SAWH take away from the role of or the work of the SHA. I think it's very important to keep that connection.

C. S.: Why do you think that?

E. J.: The work of the SHA is much broader and therefore much more important and more valuable, and I would hate to see us harm that in any way. But at the same time I think women have every reason in the world to know, and to believe, that if they don't stand up for themselves, no one else is going to. As long as we have found a way to bring some attention to ourselves and validate our own work, then I think that it's important that we continue to do that.

C. S.: Do you see a need for new directions or new goals? Do you think that the SAWH has been successful at what it's done and needs to change, or has it been successful in what it's done, and it needs to keep doing it?

E. J.: I think the latter. I think it's been wildly successful. Again, largely because women's history came of age just at the time the SAWH was there to encourage it along. I think it's always a good idea to have a committee carrying on a dialogue within an organization about what should we be doing, and where do we want to go from here. But I think, given my understanding of where we were—at least during my period of leadership in the organization—we've accomplished what we set out to do: to become visible, to be taken seriously, to be given opportunities for leadership within the larger organization, and to have women's history recognized and taken seriously.

Jo Ann (Jody) Carrigan

Jo Ann Carrigan is currently Professor Emerita at the University of Nebraska at Omaha, where she taught from 1970 until her retirement in 1996. She is still actively involved as Adjunct Professor in the Department of Preventive and Societal Medicine, University of Nebraska Medical Center, working with Ph.D. students in an interdisciplinary medical humanities program. She studied with John Duffy at Louisiana State University, where she earned her Ph.D. in American History in 1961. Since 1959 she has written over twenty articles on the subject of public health and medical history in the South. Her major work is entitled *The Saffron Scourge: Yellow Fever in Louisiana, 1796–1905* (1994). She has received numerous awards and fellowships, including the Andrew Mellon Postdoctoral Fellowship and the Newberry Fellowship in State and Local History. She has served as Managing Editor of *Louisiana History*, was a member of the Executive Council of the Southern Historical Association, and is a consultant and authority for various associations and agencies. She was President of the SAWH from 1981 to 1982.

Interviewer: Constance B. Schulz
Transcriber: Victoria Kalemaris
The following interview took place October 26, 1995.

J. C.: I grew up in southwest Arkansas in a little town called Washington in Hempstead County, not far from Hope. It had been the Confederate capital of Arkansas after Little Rock fell to the Union forces, and so I grew up in the midst of history, hearing about all the stories from my grandmother. I liked history from childhood, sort of lived in history growing up in the 1930s and 1940s. And then I went to undergraduate school at Henderson State Teachers' College in Arkadelphia, Arkansas, and I was a little uncertain what I was going to major in, toyed with a few other fields but wound up staying with history. I taught one year in a high school in Arkansas. Then I went to graduate school at Louisiana State University in Baton Rouge in 1954, and I took the master's there. Then I took off one year and went back to Henderson and taught, and then I finished the Ph.D. in 1961. From there I went to Pittsburgh on a postdoc Mellon Fellowship at the University of Pittsburgh, at the School of Public Health, where John Duffy had gone. John Duffy is really the one who got me into medical history when he was teaching at LSU.

I had been interested in southern history generally. I didn't even know such a thing existed as medical history but through some of his lectures. Of course, there was no such thing as a course in medical history at the time, but he gave lectures in colonial history and on his own work on epidemics in colonial America, which he had done on the Ph.D. level. That's when I got interested; I did papers, and he encouraged me to go on and do research in it. So that's how I got into medical history. Duffy had moved to Pittsburgh the year before I finished the Ph.D. So we had mentoring in absentia, by mail. Professor Edwin Davis, the department's specialist in Louisiana history, chaired my Ph.D. committee after Duffy left. Jobs were not easy to get in 1961 for a woman just finishing. I applied for several jobs as well as the postdoc. So I did the postdoctoral fellowship then, and a job opened up back at LSU to fill in for someone who was going on leave just for a year. That's how I went back to LSU in 1962 on the faculty.

C. S.: Was that a position where they were particularly interested in your medical history training? Or it was a general position?

J. C.: No, no. I think this was because they knew me, and they figured I could fill in; you know I was versatile. Actually what I was doing was filling in for someone in Louisiana state history, American history survey, and Western civilization survey. I was a workhorse. I had never had a course in state history, but, of course, I had done a dissertation on yellow fever in Louisiana so that made me not only a medical historian, but a state historian; you know how that works. I went for a one-year appointment and then I stayed. A job opened or materialized, and I wound up the next year editing the state history journal as well as teaching the undergraduate and graduate state history and I think Western civilization or maybe American survey. I stayed at LSU seven years, I believe, and taught at the University of Alabama one summer. Then in 1968 or so I came to the Missouri Valley History Conference in Omaha to read a paper; and then I think I came back in 1969 and either chaired or commented or wrote another paper and got acquainted with some of the people here. In 1969 I was interviewed for a job here while I was at the conference. They had an opening in urban history, and, again, having worked on New Orleans made me an urban historian. They were also interested in medical history because the chair of the department had connections with the medical school here, and they were interested in encouraging some sort of cooperative arrangement there. I decided in 1970 that I needed to move. I had been at LSU too long. And I think while it was not a bad position, going back where you were a graduate student can sometimes be a difficulty.

I got stuck in the niche of state history, and while it was interesting for a time, I never got to teach southern, and I never got to teach medical, and that's what I wanted to do. So I moved to Omaha in January 1970 to the University of Nebraska at Omaha. That was a bit of a culture shock too, driving up from Baton Rouge in January from about 65-degree weather to 30 below, and there had just been a snowstorm.

C. S.: Well, you've gotten yourself to Omaha and to the position that you still hold twenty-five years later, and your anniversary pretty much coincides with that of the SAWH.

J. C.: That's right. I came here as an associate professor, and then I was promoted to full professor in 1971. I was the first woman full professor in the Arts and Sciences College.

C. S.: In the entire college?

J. C.: Yes, they had I think one woman full professor in the Education College and one in the Business College, but I was the first in Arts and

Sciences. I've taught a little of everything here. It's kind of interesting. It is mainly a teaching institution. We have a master's program, but we're a service institution; there's expectations of research but limited resources.

C. S.: Have you chaired your department?

J. C.: No, I have had the opportunity to several times, but I have always declined. I don't think I really have that kind of administrative talent. What I have done is coordinate the Missouri Valley History Conference several times. The Missouri Valley History Conference really doesn't have an organization. It is a conference that is sponsored by my department at this university and has been for thirty—it's running on close to forty—years now. It started out as kind of a regional group that people drove to in one day, and now it really covers all fields, and we pull people in from all over the country. It's an ongoing thing and works mostly for people in the region, but we do pull people in the program from all over.

C. S.: What would some of your roles have been in the Southern Historical Association?

J. C.: Yes, let me get back to that. The reason I think maybe I wasn't there in 1970 is that when I moved up here, I didn't go to the Southern for several years. I went to the Northern Great Plains regional group, which meets usually in October. For several years I went with most of the people in the department to that, and I thought, well, I'm here and I'm going to be cut off from the Southern. I thought I might get more involved with local history research, but actually I continued to be more interested in the Southern. I went to the OAH meeting in Los Angeles in 1970, and that was the first semester I was here. And that's where I first began to encounter something about women's consciousness, because I was a latecomer to feminism. I went to some of those alternate history sessions at that meeting, and one of them was a women's caucus, and that was the first time there had been such a thing. It was very strange and interesting, and I thought these women were very radical, but it was the first thing that opened my mind to start thinking about some of these things. I mark that 1970 meeting as my first step toward having some sort of consciousness about women in the profession. It forced me to begin to think more about my own experiences—the problems that I had just ignored or denied and just didn't want to see.

C. S.: What did you feel at that point were some of those problems?

J. C.: Not having quite the same opportunities. I had a good record as a graduate student, and some of my mentors, I think, really tried that year I got my degree to get a good job for me. This is 1960, 1961. They would tell me that, "Well, they think you have a good record, but that department just doesn't want to hire a woman."

C. S.: So they told you that.

J. C.: Yes, and it was much more, in fact, I never got it in a letter, but I knew people, even some years later, who actually would get this written in a letter, "You have a very good record and so on but the department is not ready to hire a woman." That's kind of hard to take, but you can't dwell on those things, and so I would just put it aside. But things like that and the fact that I was qualified to teach areas like state history that I've never had a course in. Anytime I would agitate to teach southern or medical, well, the medical school is in New Orleans so we don't need medical history here, and there were always other people brought in to teach southern. It made me think about a lot of things that I hadn't really thought about in terms of very specific comments—how I should try to get a job in a good girl's school. Some professor had told me this at one point somewhere along the way, because as a woman I would never get a job at a university. Since then I've thought that wouldn't have been a bad move, but this was the attitude; this would have been in the mid-1950s when I was working along on the Ph.D.

C. S.: Was there any attempt to steer you either to or away from dissertation topics because of your gender?

J. C.: No, I can't say that. This was the irony of it, when you were a graduate student the feeling was that you could do anything. You were fine as a graduate student, it was just when you went to get a job, there was a problem. No, I never felt that at all. When I showed some interest in medical history, I was really encouraged to go on and do it. Of course in the late 1950s, early 1960s how many people in history departments were doing medical history? Not very many.

C. S.: That's right and some of that may be the personality of John Duffy.

J. C.: That's exactly right.

C. S.: Some of that is his own open-mindedness in many areas.

J. C.: Yes, I'm sure this is true. So anyway the 1970 meeting at the OAH when I went to the women's caucus and heard some of this, there were some young women graduate students, and they were telling their tales of woe. I knew what they were. It's just one of those things where you deny things that are too painful; that's really what it amounts to. And when I began to dredge things up after this meeting—just little comments about what a disadvantage it was to be a woman in the profession—this is when you begin to have trouble with job possibilities. There didn't seem to be any trouble being a student, but when you get into the job market then you run into trouble. I felt very fortunate there to come back to LSU when I hadn't been able to get a job, and I felt fortunate to get the Mellon Fellowship. Anyway, the 1970 meeting started me thinking about it, but I think my mental set was, I did it, I made it in spite of all the obstacles, what's everybody fussing about? It took me a while to really break through that. The next big move was getting to teach women's history here, and that was more or less by accident, and I wasn't too happy about it at first. There were three other women in this department when I came.

C. S.: That's remarkable!

J. C.: Yes, it was one of those cases where we had a chair who was interested in building the department, and at that particular time it was easier to get more highly qualified women because men had other opportunities. I was the fourth woman to be hired in a department of fourteen. The department doubled in size within a two-year period because Omaha University became part of the University of Nebraska system, so there was a doubling of size, and then we hit the peak and we've never moved since. In any case, there was a women in the department, Jacqueline St. John, who was a very strong feminist and had just organized the first NOW chapter in Nebraska the year I got here, and she had agitated and had really pressed to get a course in women's history in the early 1970s. She was persistent and eventually overcame the resistance in the department. It's a pretty freewheeling department, so she actually got a two-semester course approved by the department and all the way up through the college on the history of women in the United States.

C. S.: How early was this?

J. C.: 1972. The fall of 1973 was the first semester it was to be taught, and this woman colleague of mine got sick. Her father died, she went back to

Syracuse, and she developed pneumonia and was hospitalized, and so she had not returned at the start of the semester. They said, "Somebody's got to teach this; go in and do something." It was a one-night-a-week class. We do a lot of those here, a lot of part-time students here. We don't have dormitories, so it's definitely an urban campus, a lot of night classes. I had worked up a lecture for some other purpose on the suffrage movement, which is about all I knew about women's history, and I went in the first night, and I talked about the suffrage movement. Then Jackie didn't get back another week, and they said, "We've got forty students in here"; it had closed out as full—thirty-nine women and one man. This was a great class. I went back in, and I talked about women in medical history. By the third week it was clear that Jackie's health was such she was going to have to stay home that semester. So under quite a bit of pressure I taught it. I was the only woman American historian now available because the other two women in the department were in European history.

C. S.: And there wasn't much in the way of secondary sources out there to pull lectures out of.

J. C.: There was a lot more than I realized. Jackie likes to remind me that when she was putting together her book list, I said—and she will never let me forget this—"You mean there's more than two or three books available?" I had read *Century of Struggle,* the Eleanor Flexner book on suffrage, I think that was the only book I had read or even knew existed, but Jackie had a bibliography that would choke a horse. She had really found a lot of stuff and had a lot of required books on the list. The department relieved me of a section of American history survey. I was quite reluctant, but I could also see that we had to save this. By the second or third week I was intrigued too. I worked to keep ahead of the class and to prepare the lectures and do the readings. The course really transformed me. This was a great class of women. There were a number of traditional students in there, but there were also a lot of older women, very active. Some were already active in the local chapter of NOW. One of them went on later to run for the Senate and didn't make it, but it was a very, very active group, and they were a lot farther along than I was. I think maybe they taught me more than I taught them, but we had a great time.

When Jackie came back she said I had been transformed. I've since taught the course several times. That was in 1973. I became pretty active here in various women's causes. Being the only woman full professor for a while, I was very busy on committees. You know how that went, token woman on committees. I worked with a program for International

Women's Year and several things like that. So it was a busy several years there in the mid-seventies.

The first memory I have of getting back into the Southern was in New Orleans or Atlanta. I don't have any specific memory of going to that 1970 meeting. I think I had met Mollie Davis at the Washington meeting in 1969 or 1968. I think that's the first time I'd ever met Mollie. You know, I saw her at meetings, and I went to the Newberry Library to the summer workshop in quantitative history in 1977. Mollie was there, and Kitty Prelinger was there, and Joan Hoff Wilson was there, and D'Ann Campbell. This was the next step along the way. The next year after that, I think it was D'Ann that actually got me back into the Southern because I had just about quit going to the Southern and went more to the OAH or the Northern Great Plains regional group, mostly because of location and because we have very little travel money. D'Ann got me to go to the Southern; she was on the Program Committee the year that the Southern was to be in St. Louis—1978. She got me to chair a session.

So I went to St. Louis, and I think I've been to every Southern conference since then maybe with one or two exceptions since 1978. And in 1978 I probably went to whatever meeting the SAWH had, and I think that's probably when I really got into it but not very active. I still wasn't taking an active role in either the Southern or the SAWH until Mollie and Barbara Schnorrenberg—Betsy Jacoway might also have been involved—did a little arm-twisting in 1980 to get me to agree to be the next SAWH vice president. At that time they were doing a vice president a year ahead. Mollie and Barbara had started working on me at some point, that I should do this. I had always attended the meeting, but I hadn't really done anything, and I didn't really see myself in it, being out of the South. I was still interested in southern history, and whenever possible doing a little research in it. This was the stage at which the organization was really having trouble getting people to be officers. That's hard to believe now. It really amuses and delights me to see the degree of involvement now. You actually have people to vote on as opposed to those times when people had to arm-twist.

C. S.: So you trace your own activity in the Southern Association for Women Historians beginning about 1980.

J. C.: Yes, that's right.

C. S.: Is that really also your point of reinvolvement with the Southern, or had you really not been involved with the Southern either in the intervening years?

J. C.: Well, there were a few years there when I was not involved. I was on the Membership Committee as the Nebraska, Midwest, member in 1973 and 1975 even when I had not been going to meetings. The St. Louis meeting was in 1978; that's really when I started going again, and I chaired a session. I was involved again before I was involved in SAWH because Thomas B. Alexander, when he was president, appointed me to the Program Committee in 1980. Really it was 1978, 1979, 1980 that I got more involved in the Southern.

C. S.: Was there a sense then that the Southern was welcoming to women or perhaps more welcoming to women than it had been from your early years in it in the late 1960s?

J. C.: Yes, I think so. Tom Alexander did make a real effort to include women. There had just been so few of us in the earlier days. I had gone a time or two as a graduate student, and you could look around the room and maybe there were half a dozen. Most of the women there were the wives that happened to be there with their professor husbands. There was also a kind of funny standoffishness, too. The women professors or students really didn't find it easy to come together. And that's the reason that I thought the SAWH was such a good idea; it was a forum. There was a shyness or something; you just stuck by your mentor or whoever was there from your department, and it just wasn't that easy to make contact with the few women that were there. And it was more difficult if you're shy anyway, as I was. I felt that the Southern was opening up certainly by the early 1980s.

I know the SAWH had been going almost a decade really before I got into it, and I sensed from visiting with Mollie that it was to try to get more activity in the Southern, to encourage women to be a little bit more forthcoming and present papers on the program, to recommend women for committees, to come forward and be more active. I think it was certainly the forum for women to come together and plan sessions or to find out what research other people were doing, and to be a kind of pressure group, to make a southern women's presence felt. The Southern was more open, but that doesn't necessarily mean it was wide open. I think there were presidents that were beginning to appoint women to committees and so forth, and there were some women, or at least one woman, on the Executive Council usually, but I think there was clearly resistance to having a regular Women's Committee of the SHA. We had an ad hoc committee for several years in a row.

C. S.: In the Southern?

J. C.: In the Southern, there was some pressure by women to have that, and I know that there was pressure from the SAWH and the women Southern members.

C. S.: In some ways this is really very valuable because your memories of what SAWH was doing and what its goals were in the early 1980s give us some sense of continuity and shifting from its absolute foundings. You've described yourself as a feminist or had become more interested in the feminist movement. Do you see the SAWH as having been part of a strong feminist direction or being radical in the sense that's often described for some of the early feminist or women's history organizations?

J. C.: No, I didn't see it that way, and I think most of the people that were involved in it when I was were very professional in a sense and were simply trying to open up the avenues for participation in the Southern as an organization and on the program.

C. S.: And if that was radical that was the extent of your radicalism.

J. C.: That's right. I didn't see it. I know that some of the older male historians might have seen it as radical because it was radical to have a group of women that were agitating to do anything. I do remember that there was some sense of distress or concern about whether the members of the SAWH were really members of the Southern or not. I know that I never got this directly from Ben Wall, but I have seen some correspondence that indicated Ben was concerned that there were all these outsiders—really that were members of SAWH—that came to meetings but were not members of the Southern and were trying to tell the Southern what to do, tell the Southern it ought to have a committee, and it ought to be pushing for women to get jobs. And I do remember there was some suggestion that the Southern should be more active in urging history departments in the South to open more opportunities for women. Ben thought that some people that had helped organize the SAWH in the beginning were not really members of the Southern. To the best of my knowledge, everybody that I knew in SAWH was there because they were members of the Southern, and the whole purpose of the SAWH was to work with the Southern and through the Southern. We saw it as the spin-off in a way from the Southern and designed to cooperate with it and be a part of the Southern, but some of the men, I think, saw it as some kind of outside agitator or something. Ben was concerned in the early years because he had apparently asked somebody a time or two that was involved for a membership list and never got it. So he thought that there was some kind of secrecy about the membership list.

C. S.: One of the things we are interested in is the role that Ben Wall played or the relationship between the Southern and Ben Wall. His wife, Neva, also played a key role in the Southern. Is it appropriate for you to talk more about your relationship with Ben or with Neva during your period as president?

J. C.: When I was president, it seemed to me there was very little relationship. Ben never asked me for a membership list. I don't think I would have felt any reluctance in giving it to him or giving him all the information. At that time I was pushing people, anybody who was interested in SAWH, to also become a member of the Southern because that was the only way we were ever going to have any influence in the Southern. But as to my knowledge of Ben, I first became acquainted with Ben when I was in graduate school at LSU, and he came up one summer and taught summer school. When he was at Tulane, he came up to LSU sometimes and visited with the graduate students. That was years ago, and so I had known him way back and had been seeing him at conferences all the years. When I was president, I really didn't have any correspondence. He didn't ask me for any information; maybe the only information was that he wanted me to make sure that Neva had whatever we were going to do on the program in time to put into the *Program*.

C. S.: So there was some real cooperation at that point?

J. C.: Yes, by that time it was being published. What we were doing was being listed in the *Program*—the time of our business meeting, and in the concurrent sessions part of the program, it would have whatever we had planned for the program. By that time we were having a panel; or the year I was president we actually had the SHA Committee on the Status of Women talk to us. It was an ad hoc committee, but it was LaWanda Cox, A. Elizabeth Taylor, and Mollie Davis. We had the three of them as a panel in 1982, "Women's Issues: Report and Inquiry by the Committee on the Status of Women, Southern Historical Association," to talk about what the Women's Committee of the Southern was doing and how we might better cooperate and what the goals of our group should be. So we had an open discussion rather than a formal scholarly presentation.

It seemed my relationship with Neva was always very cordial and, of course, still is, but that goes way back. I know that some people in the group felt that Ben was kind of an obstacle to establishing a Women's Committee. I think he might have been one who wanted to keep it ad hoc, not to make it a permanent, standing committee because we didn't need it, you know, that kind of thing. But when he was president, he appointed me to chair the Membership Committee, and when he did become president, I think he appointed a lot of women. I think he really went out of his way to demonstrate his support for women, whatever had been the case earlier.

C. S.: When you were president, was there a visible group of minorities, either men or women at the Southern, and do you recall whether the SAWH at that point was aware of or had an interest in encouraging either the study of minority women's history or the recruiting of minority women into the profession and into the organization?

J. C.: Yes, there were, I think, fairly large numbers of both black men and women. That was really the only minority group that I was thinking about at the time or was aware of. And yes, I think we were—at least certainly by the time I was involved in the organization—very much interested in including and bringing in black women. Darlene Clark Hine became president, and I think did a lot to bring other black women into the organization.

C. S.: Is your memory of the years before then that the women in the profession were aware of and interested in reaching out to African Americans?

J. C.: I'm not sure that I can really answer that. We had a black studies department here at University of Nebraska at Omaha, and in the 1970s there was an African American woman chair of that department that I was close to, and she was working on her Ph.D. and I was working with her. She was in anthropology, but she had a lot of historical material, and so I was interested in reaching out. And we also had an office of minority affairs here, and the black woman who was running that office was in one of my seminars. So, I was aware of black women working in the field and some of the problems they were encountering, but as far as how it was in the Southern, all I can say is that by the time that I got into the position as vice president or president of the SAWH, we were talking about it. Before that I don't really remember having that much interaction at Southern meetings with black women historians, but I think there were definitely a few there.

It seemed to me that somewhere there along in the early 1980s, the institutionalization and the expansion of SAWH really sort of took off. I don't know what all the problems were in that first decade, but I suspect it was a matter of just hanging in there and trying to make a little space and at least get on the program and gradually pull people in. I know that in those early years when I went to meetings there wasn't a huge crowd there, and I did have to be persuaded myself to be an officer. I did it more out of a sense of duty than anything else because I saw people had put a decade into something, and it deserves to keep going; you can't just have the same people that do it all the time. This was before formal nominating committees or anything else; because this very small Executive Committee, which was vice president, president, and some past presidents, and Barbara Schnorrenberg, who was the secretary-treasurer for ages, did practically everything. It was like whoever was vice president did membership drives; and it was the responsibility of the president to put together the program and indeed to nominate the next, to locate someone as it were, to arm-twist if necessary, to get a vice president down the line.

And so we recruited Margaret Ripley Wolfe at East Tennessee State University. I happened to know her through the Missouri Valley History Conference. She had come here as a young Ph.D. and given her first paper, and I was aware of her career and had seen her at conferences over the years. She seemed like a really efficient go-getter type, and so I put her name forward as the vice president for the next year, and she, I think, had as much to do with really shaping up that group as anybody.

I think that she and Darlene Clark Hine really set it on an expansion path, a path of expansiveness simply because in the earlier period we had just been holding on. The main thing I was involved in was the publication prizes. But Margaret is an organizer and an administrator type, and she was the one that said, "We've got to have bylaws; we've got to have clear bylaws; we need a constitution; we need a base. Everybody is paying for this out of their own pockets, you know the postage and all. Barbara Schnorrenberg's minimum budget is from the little dues we collected; we ought to collect more dues. We ought to decide what our goals and objectives are." We needed to be more organized, and I think Margaret did that. This was in opposition to what I think was that kind of women's ideology thing, which I have gone along with at times but have never agreed with. That is, you just kind of muddle through and reach consensus, and you don't vote, and you don't have bylaws, and you just keep talking until everybody agrees with everybody. That's not very efficient, and I think maybe we did a certain amount of that. Margaret got some *Robert's Rules of Order* into it and also urged that we try to find a base, some school that would give us some support as far as the *Newsletter* and the secretary-treasurer and this kind of thing. And then Darlene furthered that with membership, a real effort at membership. I think Betty Brandon is the one who got Darlene involved in SAWH.

C. S.: So you see that as a turning point, 1983, 1984, and the leadership of Margaret Ripley Wolfe and Darlene Clark Hine.

J. C.: Yes, I really do; now that might be just my perspective on it, but things really took off after that, and then a lot of people made a real effort. You know, earlier we just did everything ourselves, and they made an effort to involve other people, to have committees, to get local arrangements committees, to have those receptions that really gave the organization high visibility, to involve lots of other people, to have a nominating committee, have more than one person running for an office, to think about getting a lot of members, get a big membership committee. I think this was a kind of institutionalizing shift that was really important.

C. S.: Can you talk a little bit about the prizes?

J. C.: Carol Bleser, Judy Gentry, and some of the others that were involved before I was first began to talk about having prizes. But by the time I was president, we were beginning to make the arrangements. I was on a committee, I believe, when I was vice president. The committee was to decide how we were going to do this. What kind of prize it would be and who it would be open to and what it was for and what it would be called. There were really two points of view that I think were general among the various members of the committee. One was that it should be for women, that the prize should be limited to women historians because, after all, this was a women's group and we were trying to encourage women historians. And the other was that it should be open to everybody. If we were going to have a prize, it should be open to men as well as women. Then there was some question about whether it should just be women's history or whether it should be southern history in general. We went back and forth on this. We seemed to be at loggerheads, and I remember in one of these meetings I made a suggestion that we should try to do both, that we have a prize for women only for the best book in southern history, and that we have a prize that was open to everybody, men and women, for a publication in southern women's history. I guess I was a consensus person in spite of myself. I was trying to cover all the bases, and I thought it's a bigger challenge to raise enough money for two prizes, but this at least would cover everybody, and who could complain about this? We would be supporting women in southern history, that is, a woman historian writing southern history, and also encouraging work for everybody, male and female, in southern women's history. And to show you how much things have changed since, at the time we decided to allow either a book or an article because we weren't sure there would be enough books on southern women's history published in a two-year period. We had our doubts there would be enough of a volume in a two-year period. I really see a change there. I don't know how much the Southern Association for Women Historians has to do with that, but certainly there has been a big change. Let me just throw this in; there was an objection. Hugh Davis Graham wrote a letter, published in the OAH *Newsletter*, objecting to a prize for women only, the first time the Rose Prize was announced. And then Betsy Jacoway, who was chair of the Rose and Spruill Publications Prize Committee, wrote a letter justifying what we had done and that it was a women's organization after all. If it was the Southern or the OAH that was limiting prizes to women then that's one thing, but we also had another prize that was open to everybody. I thought she wrote a wonderful justification of it.

Betty Brandon

Betty Brandon is currently Professor of History at the University of South Alabama. She earned her Ph.D. in American History from the University of North Carolina at Chapel Hill in 1969, where she studied under George Brown Tindall. She is the author of numerous articles and encyclopedia entries and coeditor of *Southern Women: Histories and Identities* (1992) and *Hidden Histories of Women in the New South* (1994). She is Senior Series Editor for the University of Missouri Press's Southern Women and has published over forty-eight book reviews. She was President of the Alabama Association of Historians from 1998 until 2000 and has served as representative to the National Coordinating Committee for the Promotion of History. She was President of the SAWH from 1982 to 1983.

Interviewer: Constance B. Schulz
Transcriber: Victoria Kalemaris
The following interview took place on October 11, 1995.

B. B.: I graduated from the University of South Carolina in 1962 and went to the University of North Carolina at Chapel Hill for my graduate studies, finishing the master's in 1964. After teaching two years at Elon College, I returned to Chapel Hill and completed the Ph.D. in 1969. I accepted an appointment at the University of South Alabama in September of 1969 and have been here throughout. This is my twenty-seventh year.

I was present at the meeting in Louisville in 1970. I like to say I was present at the creation, the founding meeting of SAWH. And by that time, I had become interested in women's history and within the next few years had developed a course, which I have taught periodically at the University of South Alabama. I wanted to be involved in the organization and to meet people, to have a closer network. I had been a member of the SHA since 1964, when I first went to Elon, and I had been attending the annual meetings of the SHA. My first one was while I was still in graduate school, the meeting in 1963 in Asheville. So it just was natural, I think, that I would get involved in SAWH. I knew some of the people who were instrumental in the founding. I always have regarded it as having a completely compatible and complementary relationship with SHA.

C. S.: Had you been active in SHA or just simply had attended the meetings?

B. B.: I don't think I had held a committee assignment or any active participation.

C. S.: Even the infamous Membership Committee?

B. B.: That was 1972, Connie, when I chaired that. It was 1972 that we had the meeting, and it was actually for George Tindall's presidential year, which was 1973. So that was my first membership assignment, and as Mary Elizabeth Massey always said, that was where she started, and so many people actually did begin with some affiliation with the Membership Committee. I think I had been attending the annual meetings, and it was a little later in the early 1970s that I became involved.

C. S.: As part of your coming to get involved with that first meeting in Louisville of the SAWH, was there any sense of dissatisfaction with the SHA?

B. B.: Not from my point of view, but I am not very perceptive about that kind of thing. Somebody just told me that so-and-so belongs to such-

and-such a faction in a certain discipline and somebody else is part of the antithetical faction. I had no idea; I just simply do not pick up on that. I thought that we were organizing to be closer, to bond with our particular interests, our gender. It never penetrated my thought that this was some sort of withdrawal or rebellion from the organization. In fact, I've always regarded the two organizations as completely compatible and coexisting.

C. S.: When that group first met, were there articulated goals for the SAWH at Louisville?

B. B.: My memory is that it was more social than professional, that people wanted an opportunity to talk with other women or people interested in women's history. I don't remember that the idea of professional interest emerged right away. I remember in 1972 at Hollywood-by-the-Sea, Florida, at the Diplomat Hotel that there was a social gathering that Mollie Davis and Connie Myers and William McKee Evans organized, and I don't believe that there was a formal paper session. I remember that as being an evening gathering and then again with more as I remember these early years of socializing, of conversation, of getting acquainted. It seems to me that the organization evolved. But networking, conversation, discussion—those are my initial memories.

C. S.: Had you attended the Berkshire Conference? Did you see that as a model at all?

B. B.: No. I was pretty regional in those years. I hardly ever went to the AHA because it was so big, and it seemed so difficult to get through. The first Berkshire I ever went to was in 1987 at Wellesley. So I didn't see this as particularly modeled on any other organization.

C. S.: And so you saw it as really to meet the needs of southern women.

B. B.: And interested people. Now Bill Evans was there very early, so I never had any sense of gender exclusivity.

C. S.: So even SAWH included men from the beginning.

B. B.: In my mind and, as I'll say a little bit later when I was president, that was one of our objectives to change the name to reflect that.

C. S.: OK. Do you recall at that early gathering whether the women who were there were primarily women beginning to do women's history, or was it from its beginning a much broader attraction to women in general whether they studied women's history or not?

B. B.: My memory is that it was the latter. It was more oriented toward women who taught in the South, women who had some interest in the SHA. The focus on women's history came later, because I think maybe even some of the early people were in European history.

C. S.: Had you had any training in women's history?

B. B.: I guess somebody mentioned Seneca Falls, and it was an identification on a test or something, but there was no content about women in any of the graduate or undergraduate courses.

C. S.: I remember. That was true for me too. Were there any women on the faculty here at University of South Carolina that served as role models for you?

B. B.: No, I don't think there were any women in the history department at that time. I don't remember having classes from any women at USC or at Chapel Hill; I never had a course from a woman. Isn't that shocking? Barbara Schnorrenberg did have an appointment at Chapel Hill, but she wasn't teaching graduate courses, and she was in British history. But there was nobody in any of the fields in which I was working.

C. S.: We had listed some people who were present or who others have mentioned as having taken a leading role. You've mentioned Connie Myers and Barbara Schnorrenberg and Mollie Davis. Are there some others, other than the ones that we had listed, that we ought to include or that you remember?

B. B.: I remember LaWanda Cox. Now this is somewhat later, I don't remember her in 1970 but in later years; certainly in the 1980s, she was profoundly supportive. And the year I chaired the SHA Program Committee, which was the Charleston program in 1983, LaWanda was just incredibly helpful and sensitive and understanding. And I remember talking with her. I think it was in Philadelphia, and we were having a little meeting, and she had a number of suggestions about overtures that we could make by that time, and I think one was extending a life membership to Neva Wall. My memory is that LaWanda was quite insightful and a real builder of bridges and someone who wanted to promote extended involvement and participation by people. I have just an incredibly high regard for her.

C. S.: You mentioned Neva Wall. What kind of a role or position did both Ben and Neva Wall play in the very early years? Were they supportive, and what particularly was the role of Neva?

B. B.: The year that I was president, Neva was the person who did all of the administrative work, and I remember that she secured the biggest room in the hotel for our 4:30 meeting. That was 1983, and I was so pleased by that. I remember that very vividly. I think that there has been a certain amount of ambivalence on some people's part that maybe there was some sort of division, that if there were too many subgroups, it might be divisive; it might be contrary to the unity within the large organization. But I think on the whole there has been support. I've heard Barbara Schnorrenberg say this, that the meeting in Louisville was just way out on the fringes somewhere, and I remember Helena Lewis looking for chairs and saying, "I'm going to go liberate some chairs." We didn't have a real room as I recall. So it seems to me that there is a very dramatic contrast. And Neva did all the assigning of rooms and the designation about the sessions, and I think that always the copy has gone into the *Program* as it's been submitted by SAWH.

C. S.: Do you recall either an interest and a concern about women of color or African American women? Were there any present in that first decade who were involved with SAWH? Was there a concern among the women that there should be?

B. B.: I do not remember anyone, but this was certainly a concern and it was a chief concern of mine, and this is something that I really take great pride in. I was president when the nomination of Darlene Clark Hine to be vice president and then president took place. She was the first black president of SAWH, and this has been something that I really take great interest in because I think that the more unity, the more support we can have, the stronger we'll all be. And I remember when this year's Nominating Committee was working, one of the members of the committee talked with me, and I was trying to suggest some people, and that was a point that I made then that I would really like to see us reach out to try to find more minority members. I think the presence of the Association of Black Women Historians maybe has been a little bit of a complication in terms of an affiliation there, perhaps does not lend itself to participation with SAWH. I think that's something I'd like to see us work more on.

C. S.: Do you recall seeing black women at the Southern or available to be recruited into SAWH?

B. B.: A very few. There was Sara Dunlap Jackson, an archivist with the National Historical Publications and Records Commission (NHPRC), and Sylvia M. Jacobs, a professor in the Department of History at North Carolina Central University. But there were very few as I remember it in those days, the early 1970s.

C. S.: As a woman historian with networks within the region in SHA and SAWH, has that enabled you to do more, to be more effective in some of this outreach to noncollegiate and more local communities and to bring women's history into their consciousness?

B. B.: Oh, I think so because the more you know about who's doing what research, who's publishing what, the more you are able to make suggestions when you have public programming. I know, for instance, that the Alabama Women's History Network sponsors drew on people from Texas, Mississippi, and Georgia, and I think it was through SAWH and SHA that those contacts originated. I just think the more people you know, the more opportunities you have to take advantage of somebody's knowledge and experience. To me that is still one of the major benefits of SAWH, that you simply know more names, more types of research.

C. S.: One of the comparisons has been with the Berks, which is perceived as being radical. Do you think the SAWH ever saw itself as being part of the feminist movement and in any way a radical break-off from SHA. Was there a sense of feminism in particular? Was that seen as being radical in the early years?

B. B.: Again, I think that attitudes and approaches have something of a regional quality to them. I really think it's possible within SHA and SAWH to accomplish a great deal with subtle ways of doing it. I think if you look at the number of women who have held positions on the SHA Executive Council, have chaired the committees of SHA since 1970, I think that some of that has to be attributed to SAWH in terms of getting people visible and making them active. And I think we've had remarkable success in terms of the percentages of women on the council.

But it seems to me that it's by being visible, by being available. I don't think SAWH has ever taken the lead in any sort of boycott or policy or ideological statement. I think we've just slowly and over time grown and evolved and become a presence. I mean this is a very high percentage.

Every time when you look at the membership of the SHA Council, it's pretty striking to me the number of women who are involved and continue. New women take their places every year or every three years.

I wanted to say that I thought Barbara Schnorrenberg was the hub of the SAWH, and for many years she worked in her home without a regular affiliation, teaching part-time. More than any one other person, Barbara was responsible for producing the *Newsletter*, keeping the organization going. Her commitment has been quite remarkable, but she just did that in her home—very hard work on her part. Rosemary Carroll at Coe College has been a stalwart. And over and over A. Elizabeth Taylor was such a tremendous source of support. I remember again, one of the first committees I ever chaired, she made a point of speaking to me, and I thought that was so special that she would remember what I had done and similar to what LaWanda Cox has done all through the years. I think the two of them have been major sources of strength and encouragement.

C. S.: So that when they talk about mothers and grandmothers, LaWanda and Elizabeth Taylor are grandmothers.

B. B.: I would think so. Then in the second stage, it would be Barbara Schnorrenberg, Mollie Davis, Connie Myers, and Martha Swain. Then two people who were very close to me in terms of helping me become acquainted with the administrative work were Betsy Jacoway and Jody Carrigan. I think they were the two presidents immediately preceding me. Betsy continued to serve SAWH without regular appointments at that time; she has been extraordinarily active and has stayed so involved. Jody is an example of a historian who has been able to give us a lot of breadth from Nebraska.

C. S.: Yes, Nebraska's not quite the South, but she's remained interested.

B. B.: Exactly, and she's there all the time, and that was just a wonderful year. I have been very pleased by the work that they've done.

C. S.: Tell me some more about Connie Myers because she seems to claim now that she really didn't play much of a role.

B. B.: I don't quite understand because in my mind she was right there with Mollie and Barbara, and I certainly vividly remember that 1972 party in Hollywood-by-the-Sea, Florida, and the invitations came from Bill Evans, Mollie Davis, and Connie Myers. I don't know exactly who initiated it. She was certainly present then and very much involved. And I looked to her, I think she was one of the people who gave me encouragement at a very early year. I remember one time I was on a program at the meeting in Omaha, and she was there. I think that was 1971, and we talked there, and I felt a real sense of sisterhood and affiliation. I remember her very, very positively as someone who was there, a driving force, making things happen.

C. S.: A name that's been frequently mentioned is Willie Lee Rose.

B. B.: Yes, again I think she was a model. I don't remember her being actively involved. But I think she was a model along with Anne Scott. These were the women historians on a high plane in the South. My impression is that we looked to Anne Scott and we looked to Willie Lee Rose as the accomplished professional women historians.

C. S.: Did you have a sense that they were welcome in and part of the leadership of the SHA?

B. B.: Not exactly. I don't think that they were unwelcome, but I think that there were tendencies to look to certain places for the presidents, and I think here's where SAWH deserves a lot of credit; we have opened up other careers. I don't think the list of potential nominees is ever going to be quite as limited as it was before the 1970s. I would say that if Willie Lee's health had not deteriorated, I think that she could have been president of SHA. I think it took some publicity, some education, and I think SAWH should be credited with some of that.

C. S.: When you were president, what were the major concerns you faced? Do you see the SAWH as having had a change of goals since your earliest affiliation with it?

B. B.: A widening I would say, much more depth and reaching out, much more ambitious goals. I know not too many years ago, Jody and I were somewhere and she said, "Do you remember the time that we met in my hotel room and we had $2.50 in the treasury?" And now look at these prize funds, and the conferences, and the *Newsletter*, and the publications. So I am just elated at the scope of the activities. I think that in the beginning those were perhaps dreams that someone might have imagined, but the fulfillment of them is just remarkable—the positive steps that have been taken. I think that's it, that originally it was small steps that said, "Let's get to know people; let's see who's available; let's have a social network." And then, Wow, it took off. I think the fund-raising for the prizes did a lot of that because more people heard about the organization when they were requested to make contributions. That was a very wide net, as I remember it, for the prizes, then the first conference, getting the Ford Foundation grant for the first SAWH conference in 1988, and then getting the contract with University of Missouri Press—all of that.

C. S.: Do you think that has been the result of a growing interest in the history of women in the South, or did the SAWH play a role in increasing the interest in the history of women? In other words, has it had a scholarly as well as a networking and social goal component?

B. B.: To me it works both ways—that there is some interest and the activities encourage and promote that interest, and then when the activities are available, particularly the conference, that just gives opportunities all over the place. Look at all these graduate students who now can go to conferences and read papers and have a chance of getting an article published by a real university press in a real anthology. That's an opportunity that's bound to have ripple effects. And beyond that, I believe that the interest in women's history is bound to grow.

C. S.: When you were finishing up your graduate work and getting ready to go out and become a teacher, did you feel that your gender played a role in the way you were received by the committees interviewing you? How did you feel about being a woman on the job market in the early 1970s?

B. B.: In graduate school, I had always been completely protected, and I mean in the neutral sense. I didn't ever think anything was gender-based. I competed for scholarships; I competed for grades. I was taken seriously.

C. S.: And this was in Chapel Hill.

B. B.: Yes.

C. S.: Who was your advisor there?

B. B.: I started with Fletcher Green for my master's, and I was one of his last master's and then George Tindall for the Ph.D. Tindall was a student of Green. There was such courtesy and support, and I still have tremendous loyalty and feelings totally devoted to the Tindalls. Blossom Tindall has always been a tremendous presence, doing everything that she could. And every time I see her we have such warm memories of the days in Chapel Hill. Then I went for an interview in the fall of 1968 at a school that I really wanted; I really wanted that position. And I was working hard and going through all of the stages and interviewing with all the administrators in the department, and it came to, I think, a dean. We had a little conversation. One of his questions was, "Do you expect to be married?" That was really kind of troubling to me because I knew he would not have asked a male that question. I really felt that gender was an issue in that interview. But when I came to South Alabama, I felt that again, if anything, it was an advantage. They wanted a woman; they were delighted to have a woman in the department. More doors, I think, have always been opened for me, so I don't feel that I have ever been discriminated against other than that one little moment, that one question that I thought was gender-biased. On the whole, throughout everything I've ever done, people have been completely supportive, have given me every opportunity, so I have not experienced any kind of gender discrimination.

C. S.: Do you think that the SAWH, by calling attention to women in the profession, has helped to deal with some of these issues?

B. B.: I think so, and that was what I was saying earlier. I thought that the subtle way of having women out and visible who are efficient and productive and can deliver, doesn't that neutralize some of the bias? It seems to me that's a way that you can make gains and that more women can follow these earlier models. Maybe it alleviates some of the anxieties about radical feminism or whatever the doctrinal inclinations might be.

C. S.: Recently, the SHA has dropped its charge to the Committee on Women to count how many book reviews, how many reviews of books by women, how many articles, how many members of each committee are women. Is that an issue? Do you think that the days of counting are over?

B. B.: Well, that might be a little premature from my point of view, but I think that we can monitor that. People can be cognizant of that, and if it begins to look as if some of the old patterns are recurring that we should be aware and prepared to respond to it. Was there any explanation for why this happened, or was it just thought that it was unnecessary or misleading?

C. S.: There was a sense that the results were misleading.

B. B.: Oh, I think probably in the *Journal* that could very well be the case because so much of that is beyond anybody's control in terms of who submits what and what books are being reviewed within a given year of publication. I can understand that completely. It might be possible though still to have a kind of informal survey of panel participants.

C. S.: And should SAWH continue to have that as part of its role and part of its goal now that there is a Committee on Women in the Southern Historical Association?

B. B.: Again, I don't see any conflict between the two, and it seems to me that if there's duplication, that's all to the good. The more mindful people are of what can be done, the larger the numbers grow, the more women should be pleased. So I would say that's still an appropriate work for SAWH.

C. S.: What would you say are the goals of SAWH now, and what should they be for the future?

B. B.: I think my highest interest is in minority involvement, more black women officers, more of the dialogue, some of which came out of the First Southern Conference on Women's History in 1988 at Converse College in South Carolina. I'd like to see us be more inclusive and be able to make room for women and men who support the work of southern women's history and women historians in the South. Above all else, I'd say let's find more black women members, more minority members and have preparation for officeholding, and then I think just build on the conferences, build on the publications, build on the prizes. We have the Taylor prize now, so that's three major endowments.

C. S.: When you talked about your term, you said you wanted to have men involved, and you've mentioned Bill Evans. Can you suggest other men besides Bill Evans who were involved in the early years, and can you elaborate on that a little more?

B. B.: Bill is the first man that I remember from the very earliest years, and then Vincent DeSantis from Notre Dame. I don't know exactly how involved he was, but he was certainly visible at meetings over a long period of time. And then later, Wayne Flynt and Paul Gaston have been dues-paying members at some point. Those are some of the first names and first people that I remember. What we did in 1983 was to change the name in what some people thought was an inconsequential way, but it was meaningful to me. Rather than referring to the Southern Association *of* Women Historians, the name was changed to the Southern Association *for* Women Historians, and I introduced that in order to be more inclusive and to parallel what is now the idea: that it's not restricted to women, but it's for women and for anyone who supports women's work in this regard. That was actually changed at the meeting in 1983.

C. S.: Had you played a role in other committees? One of the things that is not really clear is whether there were committees or much of a structure before 1983. Had you had a leadership role in other ways before you were chosen?

B. B.: No, I think it was so informal in those early days. There were no program committees. Barbara Schnorrenberg was the treasurer; she had all the financial responsibilities as well as secretary, so there was no financial committee as I recall. Really the endowments, I think, modified so much of that and transformed that into much more of a structured situation. I don't remember that there were committees, I went and then I was asked to be vice president.

C. S.: And then you moved up.

B. B.: Right, and that was the way it worked. The idea of this ballot and three people for each position—we didn't have that many in the early meetings to have had that kind of competition. But I just don't believe that there were committees until the endowments. And then the Converse conference just took off, and there had to be so many more committees after that. But the 1984 meeting was our first really swell party, as I recall, and I was so proud of how attractive that was. Then in the next year, in Houston in 1985, we had a conventionwide breakfast for everybody. Darlene Clark Hine was president that year, and Ginger Bernhard did the fund-raising and put all that together. That was delightful, and the whole convention was invited to breakfast. My impression was that the SAWH was more a mechanism for information, for support, for conversation. Then, over time, that has been transformed but not obliterated. It seems to me that the networking part of it is still very crucial, and that people want to have the chance to talk with other people and to know who's researching in what areas. They're just much more professional and much larger in scope.

C. S.: Is there still a need for a separate women's professional organization? We talked about what the goals should be; is it still necessary?

B. B.: I think so because women need support, and it doesn't destroy the possibility for cooperation. It merely enhances; it's a way of helping to prepare women. I think if you serve in a capacity in SAWH, you're more experienced, if you're then offered an opportunity to be involved in SHA. So I see no conflict, I see only gains. It seems to me that it is a way of giving support, giving experience, giving encouragement—all of which are very crucial.

C. S.: Have you been yourself active in other national historical organizations—OAH, AHA?

B. B.: Yes, and right now I am representing SHA on the NCC, the National Coordinating Committee, so that gives me a level of activity that's larger than what I've done before. That's primarily what I'm doing right now, going to the meetings of the OAH and the AHA in that somewhat official capacity. That's very informative, I've learned a lot about what's going on.

C. S.: Has the SAWH been actively linked in your experience as president in 1983 or even before that with other regional women's organizations or with a national organization such as the Coordinating Committee on Women in the Historical Profession?

B. B.: We were one of the affiliates, and all the member organizations supported a reception at the AHA. SAWH has always been involved in that, and I remember years and years ago that Barbara's name would be on the inside cover of that *Newsletter* as the contact for the affiliate. I do think that it's been a remarkable growth when you consider the amount of time to have the recurring conferences, to have the book publication contract with the press, to have the prizes to offer. I just think that if we're able to increase our membership with particular emphasis upon minority scholars and interested people that that will give us the strength through numbers that should enable us to go on for many years.

C. S.: Perhaps to reach out to new, younger members.

B. B.: Yes, indeed. That's why I think that the opportunities for the graduate students are great because that didn't exist a generation ago. Now they have many more chances to be on programs, to meet people at an early point in their careers. I still think that if you can be an example to somebody else; that's just about the most rewarding contribution you can make. If graduate students can know that there are these more experienced professionals, and most of them women in the field, then if they have something they need to talk about, if they need some sort of assistance that we can give, we're here. That's what I cherish most of all, so, more numbers, more strength. Quite a story I think for twenty-five years.

Transformers

As more women entered the historical profession, and as the field of women's history emerged at the cutting edge of late-twentieth-century scholarship, the role of specialized organizations like the SAWH inevitably changed. Partly as a result of SAWH lobbying, the SHA itself had changed, creating a Committee on the Status of Women in the SHA in 1982, chaired first by A. Elizabeth Tayor. Mollie Davis and LaWanda Cox also served on that first committee. From the twenty-five or thirty women who met in 1970, SAWH membership had grown to four hundred members by 1990. In this new environment, the activities of the SAWH and other women's scholarly organizations also changed. The women who transformed the SAWH during these years no longer had to fight for women simply to have places at the table, to have their voices heard. Now they wanted to assure a balance, an equity, of women's contributions in the profession as a whole. They undertook new initiatives to achieve these goals: awarding prizes for scholarship in the field of women's history; recognizing outstanding scholarship by women historians of the South; monitoring women's participation in the activities of the SHA as presenters, as members of committees and boards, and as authors and reviewers in the *Journal of Southern History*. The creation of a standing committee for the encouragement of graduate students recognized the increasing percentage of women in history graduate programs. The leadership also recognized the need to diversify by reaching out to African American women.

In the face of changes for women within the profession as a whole, some began to raise the question of whether a separate organization specifically for women was necessary. At least one male scholar openly challenged the equity of a prize for which one's sex was a key qualification. Leaders of the SAWH insisted that as the push for inclusion in the mainstream organizations achieved success, the need for an organization like theirs became more important, not less. They reaffirmed their loyalty to the Southern Historical Association, with which they shared an annual meeting and members. But they continued to build and strengthen a separate organization that welcomed men as well as women but served as a focus for scholarly and professional issues affecting southern women historians and the study of southern women's history.

The women whose interviews make up this section had the administrative experience and the vision to move the organization into a more structured form, reforming its finances, creating endowments, and recruiting history departments to serve as the administrative home of the organization. Margaret Ripley Wolfe in 1983–1984 instituted important financial reforms; Darlene Clark Hine, the first African American president of the SAWH, drew on her administrative experience at Michigan State to initiate constitutional changes to strengthen its structure; Joanne (Jan) Hawks, president 1986–1987, helped to ensure the survival of the history of the organization by negotiating the deposit of its papers with the Southern Historical Collection at the University of North Carolina at Chapel Hill.

Margaret Ripley Wolfe was the first of those who took on these responsibilities. Jody Carrigan recalls that it was she who began the process of transforming an informal organization into a more structured professional body: discussions of the need for a permanent home began under her watch, as did the appointment of a committee to study and revise the bylaws. Wolfe was by then an established scholar in the field of southern women's history. Her education and long career in Tennessee and Kentucky gave her experiences, first as a graduate student and then as a teaching professional, a slightly different geographic perspective on the changing attitudes toward women as historians.

Darlene Clark Hine was nominated for the presidency of the SAWH by Betty Brandon, and her term from November 1984 until November 1985 marked an important turning point for an organization that grew up during the civil rights struggles of the 1970s but had not been particularly successful in reaching out to African American women. Although she recalls that some men discouraged her study of the history of African American women as "unimportant," Hine has emerged as one of the leading historians of African American women's experiences, and as one of the most visible and influential African American women historians. By 1984 she had completed graduate work in Ohio, had taught at the historically black South Carolina State University, where her husband is still on the faculty, and had been hired to teach African American history at Purdue University, where she eventually rose to become provost. Her administrative experience and her long experience with the SHA were important factors in shaping the new directions of the SAWH.

A native of Georgia, Joanne (Jan) Hawks returned to graduate school after marriage, motherhood, and high school teaching to earn a Ph.D. at the University of Mississippi. Shortly thereafter, her appointment as dean of women began her life-time professional career at Ole Miss. She taught women's history courses there beginning in the 1970s and founded its Center for Women's History. She argues with a certain wry detachment that it was her very familiarity there that made it possible for her to accomplish what she did: when the laws made it clear that women had to be included in the curriculum and on the staff, she was a known quantity rather than an outsider and trusted not to be too radical in a community where the very notion that women should be the focus was anathema to many male historians. Her association with the Southern Historical Association, and thus with the SAWH, did not begin until the late 1970s. Like Wolfe and Hine, she brought important administrative experience to the organization. Where earlier leaders had emphasized the "political" role of SAWH, insisting that women should be visibly present in the SHA as presenters, members of committees, and in leadership positions, she felt that it was important to refocus on how the organization could support scholarship about and by southern women.

$\mathscr{M}\!\mathit{argaret}\ \mathscr{R}\!\mathit{ipley}\ \mathscr{W}\!\mathit{olfe}$

Margaret Ripley Wolfe is Senior Research Professor of History at East Tennessee University, where she has taught since 1969. She earned her Ph.D. in American History from the University of Kentucky in 1974. She is the author of three books: *Lucius Polk Brown and Progressive Food and Drug Control: Tennessee and New York City, 1908– 1920* (1978); *Kingsport, Tennessee: A Planned American City* (1987); and *Daughters of Canaan: A Saga of Southern Women* (1995). She has contributed to fifteen other books and has published more than forty articles in a variety of professional outlets. She serves as General Editor of the Women in Southern Culture series for the University Press of Kentucky. A member of the editorial boards of the *Journal of East Tennessee History* and the *Tennessee Historical Quarterly,* she also serves on the State Review Board of the Tennessee Historical Commission. She served on the Executive Council of the Southern Historical Association from 1998 to 2000. She was President of the SAWH from 1983 to 1984.

Interviewer: Constance B. Schulz
Transcriber: Victoria Kalemaris
The following interview took place January 22, 1996.

M. W.: I grew up in a household where there was a considerable amount of interest in history, particularly on my father's part. He had been a World War II veteran and was interested in military history and also current events. So a discussion of politics and international matters as well as local history and southern history was a routine thing in the household. As far as my own education, I have a bachelor of science degree and a master of arts from East Tennessee State University and a Ph.D. from the University of Kentucky. I was hired immediately out of the master's program at East Tennessee State University. That was not a common occurrence at all, particularly in the history department, but an opening occurred just about the time I was finishing my degree. I had been a good solid student. Without sounding egotistical or enormously pompous, I had been one of their outstanding students, so when the opportunity came up, I certainly accepted the offer. At that time, I had not firmly made up my mind whether I wanted to pursue a Ph.D. in history or whether I wanted to go for a law degree. I had taught one year in public schools in Hawkins County, Tennessee, while I was completing my thesis, and had a job in the county if I wanted to continue. I was certified in English and history, but ironically, I'd ended up as an elementary school teacher because I was a young female, and the local school board member had some concern about whether a twenty-one-year-old would be able to deal with high school students. I guess that was sort of an antiquated viewpoint I had to contend with. As it turned out it was, I think, a very positive experience for me. I'm not sure about the students. I taught fifth grade. In any event, the next year I had a teaching assignment in a high school, but before the year actually started, I was offered a position at the university and took it. I taught there for two full years. Then the summer of 1971 I went up to the University of Kentucky to see if I liked the institution, if I liked the program. I came back and taught another full year; then took a leave of absence; and during the academic year 1972 to 1973, I was in residence at the University of Kentucky. I came back, taught in the summer, full load, worked the next year, wrote my dissertation, and finished in the summer of 1974. There were no women's history courses at either institution while I was enrolled in the master's program or the undergraduate program at East Tennessee State or the graduate program at University of Kentucky. Shortly thereafter the University of Kentucky hired a woman to deal with women's history, Nancy Schrom Dye, who later became president of Oberlin College. She came just about the time I was into my dissertation-writing year, and I didn't have any dealings with her. I met her, and that was the extent of it, but George C. Herring, who was on my committee and who is a well-known expert in diplomatic history and wrote on the Vietnam War, encouraged me to pay attention to women's history because it was emerging. And really what I know about women's history has come from the attendance at professional meetings, women's caucuses, women's conferences, and my own initiative. It was not out of a formal training program at the Ph.D. or master's level.

C. S.: When you were at Kentucky as a graduate student or even when you were beginning teaching at East Tennessee State, were you encouraged to attend professional meetings generally but also particularly the Southern Historical Association?

M. W.: No, I wasn't. It would never have occurred to any of the men I dealt with at either place to encourage me to attend a professional meeting.

C. S.: Did you do it on your own? When did you begin attending?

M. W.: I began attending the Southern in the fall of 1973 and have attended almost every year, not quite every year, but almost every year since. I also began attending the Organization of American Historians convention in the spring of 1974, and I had belonged to these organizations a little bit earlier, but my attendance at these meetings really dates from about 1973.

C. S.: I'm curious because you mention professional associations as being instrumental in your own scholarship in the history of women. Were you particularly aware in those early meetings of either sessions on the history of women or were you encouraged by meeting other women historians to become interested in it?

M. W.: The first woman who actually encouraged me to attend a woman's caucus was Nancy Weiss. She was at Princeton then. I attended a session that she chaired at the OAH. It had to do with Progressivism, as I recall, which was an area I was working in, and she told me about the women's caucus for the OAH. I attended; it was probably one of the best things I ever did in my whole career, and I met some people there, like D'Ann Campbell who was a graduate student at the time but taking a very active interest in professional matters, especially pertaining to women. And I met Jody Carrigan at that time; Jody has really been a mentor for me all these years and a good friend.

C. S.: When you were at the early Southern meetings, beginning in 1973, were you aware of the group of women who had begun the Southern Association for Women Historians? Did they seek out and encourage young scholars like yourself to be part of their network? How did you get to know about the SAWH?

M. W.: I sort of backed into that because I know I was not aware of it when I attended the first meeting of the Southern—the first one I attended in 1973. I was not aware of the SAWH. I think it was about 1974 or 1975 that I joined, so I was in fairly early, but I certainly wasn't among the founding mothers. It's possible that one of the women mentioned it. I don't particularly remember, but I think it was probably a listing in the *Program* that drew my attention.

C. S.: To what point in your own career would you date your strong interest in and more involved participation with the Southern Association for Women Historians?

M. W.: I routinely attended all the annual meetings that were concurrent with the SHA. Then, beginning in 1983, I became very, very active in leadership positions for a period of about two or three years. In the old days, the way the bylaws were set up, at that time, a person attended the SAWH Executive Committee meeting one day; the next day you were president, which was a little bit disconcerting. I remember it was quite a startling experience to show up at a pretty freewheeling meeting of the upper echelon of the organization one day and the next day, lo and behold, you're president. Also at that time in the organization's history, the nomination of the vice president, who would then become president, was pretty much in the hands of the president of the organization. And in my case, Jody Carrigan was president; she wrote to me and asked me if I'd be willing to be considered for the vice presidential position, and I responded, "Yes, indeed I would." However it turned out was fine because I expected I would be a member of the SAWH for a long time.

C. S.: What is your impression of the atmosphere or the receptiveness of women in the Southern at that point?

M. W.: I have changed, and the Southern has changed, so I don't know if my reactions to the Southern stem more from my being a novice to the profession or from the fact I was a woman or a combination thereof. I suspect a combination thereof. As a newcomer, I don't know that anything was being done to make me or the females feel really terrible about being there. I remember feeling a little uncertain and unsure just by virtue of being this new scholar who wanted to try to establish myself professionally. Over the years, the Southern has really become a home for me, and I feel like I'm going to a family reunion every year; but then I have gone all these years and gotten to know people and have developed professionally so I can't say that my insecurities stemmed from the fact that anyone was trying to do something to make me feel that way. Generally speaking, I've been extended a great many courtesies by male historians within the Southern.

C. S.: I'm asking that series of questions because your involvement comes a decade later than the founding generation, and I'm curious about what your perceptions were at the time that you became active. How strong was the need for an organization like the SAWH?

M. W.: I think it was just as important in the 1980s as it was in 1970, and I think it's just as important today. I think young female historians need a place they can call home. I think women need that kind of collegiality. I don't think we can ever take our gains for granted.

C. S.: What did you see in 1983 as the goals of SAWH? Were you aware in 1983 what the goals of the founders had been?

M. W.: I thought that the organization was operating according to the goals it had established as I understood them, which was to provide a home for women in conjunction with the SHA but a separate organization meeting concurrently to promote the professional interests of women within the SHA. I think the organization had been moving toward achievement of those goals. The thing is, the organization had grown; it had reached a time when some things needed to be done to formalize it a little more as a professional organization. That growth had certainly happened by the time that I became president. And we did some things that I think strengthened the organization.

C. S.: You began having a leadership role in 1983. What do you see as the important accomplishments that you wanted to make while in that leadership role, and how did you pursue them?

M. W.: In 1983, I began to become familiar with the workings of the organization a bit more, and I worked particularly as vice president with membership. At that time, we didn't have a great big committee, and I basically wrote to people and encouraged people to join. I think there was a concern on the part of founding mothers and everyone else that we expand the membership and that we be inclusive, that we get that message out; and I think that spirit has continued. It was one that all of us at the time were conscious of.

C. S.: Was there a sense by then that the SAWH had a responsibility not only to provide a home for women historians in the South but also to promote the study of women's history in the South, and did you take a role in that?

M. W.: There may have been a very loose consensus about that, but I was not involved in shaping that first conference. Also those initial endowment accounts to offer prizes had been set up prior to my presidency, though certainly I worked to try and expand those, and I contributed personally to them. But those were already in operation; so in terms of the time I was president and vice president and then chair of the committee to revise the bylaws, I could just list what I think were the accomplishments of those years.

C. S.: That would be great.

M. W.: First of all, we were to the point where we really needed an institutional home for the organization. Barbara Schnorrenberg had rendered invaluable service in keeping the organization going as secretary-treasurer, but we had really grown beyond that; we needed a more formal kind of situation. During the year I was president, Barbara herself reached the conclusion that she just could not do everything that needed to be done at that point and decided that she would serve one more year. We needed to find an institutional home. As it turned out, my nominee—and as I told you, at that time, presidents basically decided who the nominee would be, not for the immediate presidency but for the year thereafter—was Theda Perdue of Clemson University. Theda was able to negotiate a deal to base the SAWH at Clemson, and she and I discussed the institutional home matter when I was considering nominating her. We also discussed such things as sending out routine dues notices. The organization had not been doing that. Some people in the organization at that time thought it would offend members if they received dues notices. Of course, most of us need all the reminding we can get. But we went through those kinds of discussions back in those days. Another thing that occurred was that I launched the "Letter from the President" column in the *Newsletter*. That started during my administration in 1984. Also I did something I don't think any other president had done up to that point, at least I am not aware if it had been done. I gave a report at what amounted to the SAWH Executive Committee meeting the day before our business meeting and told them of some of the needs of the organization as I saw it. The person who was going to be incoming president should have a chance to be schooled in all of this and have some time to be prepared before just showing up for the Executive Committee meeting one day and being president the next. So the consequence of making that recommendation was that Darlene Clark Hine, who succeeded me as president in 1985, appointed me to chair the Bylaws Committee.

C. S.: So that really is the first set of bylaws.

M. W.: They had a set, but they weren't as elaborate. The ones my committee and I drafted were much more elaborate and set the scheme for the way things are now. Those were approved at the 1985 meeting. Then another thing we did in 1984, when I was president, was that we hosted a big reception at the Performing Arts Center in Louisville, and the person who was responsible for fund-raising and taking care of those details was Judi Jennings, who subsequently became a president of the organization. She was able to raise funds mostly in Kentucky. Now this was not the first reception the SAWH had ever had; they had one on the occasion of the tenth anniversary. This launched the idea that we would have a big social event every year because we found it was a gesture of goodwill within the SHA, and we thought it worked to our advantage. Of course, all throughout these years, there was great interest in expanding the membership and making the organization more inclusive.

C. S.: You yourself had been a public school teacher.

M. W.: One year.

C. S.: Did you make any effort, or was it of interest at that point, as it is today in the historical organizations, to do outreach to public school teachers?

M. W.: I saw no effort on the part of the professional historical organizations in those days to reach out to public school systems. In my case, it was not necessarily a lack of interest; it was just a question of where you would put your first priorities if you had a limited amount of time to do something.

C. S.: What about outreach to minorities?

M. W.: There was an interest in that, and I think all the members, or at least all the leadership people in the SAWH, were very conscious of that. I remember writing several letters to African American female historians while I was working on membership when I was vice president. Of course, Betty Brandon nominated—it was during her presidency—Darlene Clark Hine to be a president down the road, and that turned out to be a very positive development.

C. S.: Was there a visible presence—as you remember the early years of the Southern between 1973 and 1983—of African American either male or female historians?

M. W.: You would see a few African Americans but very, very few. Not a significant presence.

C. S.: Has the SAWH played a role, do you think, in increasing that presence in the last decade and in providing opportunities for leadership roles?

M. W.: Certainly in terms of nominating and electing someone like Darlene Clark Hine as president—that was a very positive statement, and, of course, she is a fine scholar, and I think presents a wonderful role model. So while I have no concrete evidence that the SAWH accomplished all of these things you mentioned, I would assume that, at least indirectly, the SAWH had a very positive impact.

C. S.: When you had an officer's role in the SAWH, what was the relationship at that point with the Southern? Did you have contact with Ben or Neva Wall in terms of getting SAWH on the program, and what was the response?

M. W.: I had contact with Ben in terms of arranging to have our program listed or our meeting listed. I had some dealings with SHA in terms of arranging rooms and tables and that sort of thing for meetings. I remember handling some of that for the Louisville meeting in 1984 during my presidency.

C. S.: And he was generally supportive, is that your memory?

M. W.: I don't know if *supportive* is the word I would use. He was a professional, and he did it, and he responded to the request. He didn't call me to see what I was going to do, but he certainly responded in terms of taking care of business.

C. S.: So there was a cordial relationship, and the Southern recognized and supported the legitimacy of SAWH?

M. W.: I would not say *cordial;* I would say *professional.*

C. S.: One of the concerns has been raised whether separate women's organizations serve to ghettoize women within the profession. Have you reflected on that at all?

M. W.: I personally see no evidence that it becomes a ghetto. There are all sorts of specialized groups operating within frameworks of major organizations or at least meeting concurrently, and these are just groups with mutual interests of some sort. So I see no problem whatsoever with women's groups meeting within that context and that framework.

C. S.: Do you have some particular memories of your own of people who were essential to the growth and development of SAWH beyond Jody and Darlene and Betty Brandon, who you've mentioned? And do you have in addition to memories of people, memories of particular events that you participated in that you've not already had a chance to talk about?

M. W.: Someone who certainly needs to be mentioned is Carol Bleser, who I remember making such a good impression as a professional, as a woman, always extraordinarily helpful to other female historians as well as male historians. She went to considerable effort, I know, to help any number of women get on the program, for example, of the Organization of American Historians when she was on that Program Committee in the late 1970s and just someone who has always been very positive and very helpful.

C. S.: So for you in many ways, the connections are equally the Southern and the OAH.

M. W.: I knew many of the same women within the context of both organizations, and when I first started attending professional meetings, I really thought that the Organization of American Historians had the best program. I enjoyed going to the OAH more. That is no longer the case. For me now, I think the Southern has far and away the best programs, and I much prefer to go to the Southern. I still go to the OAH, not every year but most every year, and I routinely go to the Southern. I also belong to the American Historical Association and several other professional organizations.

C. S.: Who were some of the men who were involved in the years in which you served as president in the SAWH?

M. W.: The person I remember who was around the longest is Vincent DeSantis, who was a longtime member. He probably was the one and only male member for a long time. And about the time of my presidency, Thomas H. Appleton, Jr., who was with the Kentucky Historical Society, became a member.

C. S.: And has remained so.

M. W.: And has remained so and has been a loyal supporter of women and the organization. Those are the two names in particular that I remember, but Vincent DeSantis had just been around forever and has been a member for a long time. I remember that some of the women used to say he was a spy, but I never thought that Vincent was a spy. He had always been most cordial, and I always thought very positive; but I remember that label being used. I thought it was funny then, and I still think it's funny. I think at the time I became active in leadership positions in the organization, he was our only male member.

C. S.: Since then of course there has been an expansion of that.

M. W.: I think one reason is that we women do not feel quite as threatened; and secondly, we give good parties. And also I really do think that socializing has done a lot of good for women. I hate to relegate women to tea parties and social events, but I think that sort of thing, no matter who is hosting it at professional meetings, has as much of an impact as sessions do. So much professional business is conducted in book exhibits and in social settings, and the socializing the SAWH has fostered has worked to our advantage as women and as an organization.

C. S.: And you see that as beginning with your presidency in terms of being quite self-conscious about hosting large gatherings?

M. W.: I was very conscious of it, and Judi Jennings did a spectacular job raising money and taking care of the details. I worked with her on it, but she was the principal person who was really taking care of details.

C. S.: In some ways, you could even argue that much of why we've had a separate conference is to provide more sustained opportunities for social as well as scholarly interaction.

M. W.: I think the principal motivation to begin with was professional, was scholarly. Of course, there is always the opportunity to socialize, too. But I wouldn't say they were equal. I think the people who really got the conference idea moving were very much interested in seeing this as an opportunity for scholarship. Theda Perdue was a prime mover.

C. S.: Can you think of anything else that you would like to contribute in terms of making sure we have the record straight on SAWH and its early years and your role in that?

M. W.: I know some of us worked very hard at that time, and we operated on a shoestring. Except for maybe a little postage, I had no institutional support when I was president. In fact, I made the personal contribution from East Tennessee State University; the university got the credit for it, but I made the personal donation for our contribution to that reception in Louisville, and I think it was something like $250. Judi had raised a lot of money from different institutions and groups in Kentucky. By the same token, my husband's company matched my contribution dollar for dollar, or it may have been two-to-one at that point, but anyway the institution here made money on it; but at that point, it would never have occurred to my male colleagues that my presidency of this organization was significant enough for them to assign some money to it. And also I remember that particular year at my institution that I had difficulty getting money from the department, from the institution, to go to the convention. I was chairing a session at the SHA, and I was president of the SAWH. I was able to piece money together from different sources, and my expenses were covered; but when I think back on those years, they were bittersweet years; they were tough years. I don't believe for a minute that I was alone; I think plenty of other women, who thought it was important to keep this organization going, made similar kinds of contributions in time and money.

C. S.: You're the first one who has really articulated that, so I think that's an important insight that we have talked about in terms of Barbara

Schnorrenberg keeping the treasury and all. But I think she and others like you put their own money into making the organization succeed.

M. W.: Right, and I don't imagine for a moment nor do I want to convey any impression that I was the only one who did this. But there were many women in those days, and I guess still today, who really put in a lot of personal time and then their own personal financing because they weren't getting institutional support. And we were, most of us, not being all that well paid in those days. But comparatively speaking, it was a pretty, pretty sparse time.

C. S.: You've made clear that you see a continued need for a home for women in the South, like the SAWH.

M. W.: Not just the South, all over.

C. S.: Do you see a change as the organization becomes larger and more formal in its organization? There have been new bylaws to implement some different methods. Do you see those changing the nature of the organization in a way that will be counterproductive to what it has provided to women in the past?

M. W.: No, I don't think that change is counterproductive at all. I think any organization is going to evolve. Certainly the SAWH had evolved from its starting point to a different kind of organization by the time I was president. We needed some structure to deal with that; that's the reason for the bylaw change. Any organization is only as good as the people in it, but sometimes the structure can be arranged to make it a little easier to do things. And certainly since the mid-eighties, when I was actively involved, the organization has continued to change and grow. I think change is a very positive thing.

C. S.: You worked with setting up an institutional home for SAWH at Clemson; did you work closely with Rameth Owens, and what was her role as you recall it? [Owens became secretary-treasurer after Barbara Schnorrenberg when Clemson became the SAWH institutional home.]

M. W.: The only influence that I had there was having the good sense to find Theda and to nominate her for vice president, and then she subsequently became president. That was a good selection. She's energetic; she can get things done. She enlisted Rameth Owens, who I think did really an extraordinary job getting those records in order.

C. S.: Right and for six years was really the mainstay of the organization.

M. W.: I can't take any credit for that other than just having the good sense to nominate Theda. She did that.

Darlene Clark Hine

Darlene Clark Hine is John A. Hannah Distinguished Professor of History at Michigan State University. She earned her Ph.D. in American History from Kent State University in 1975, where she studied with August Meier. She has authored four books: *Black Victory: The Rise and Fall of the White Primary in Texas* (1979), *Hine Sight: Black Women and the Re-Construction of America History* (1994), *Black Women in White: Racial Conflict and Cooperation in the Nursing Profession, 1890–1950* (1989), and *Speak Truth to Power: Black Professional Class in United States History* (1996). She has coauthored and edited seven books, anthologies, and encyclopedias, including *Black Women in America: An Historical Encyclopedia* (1993). She has also appeared in, and served as a consultant for, a number of PBS documentaries, including *Shattering the Silences: Minority Professors Break into the Ivory Tower* (1997) and *Eyes on the Prize* (1986). She was President of the Organization of American Historians for the year 2001–2002 and President of the Southern Historical Association for the year 2002–2003. She was President of the SAWH from 1984 to 1985.

Interviewer: Constance B. Schulz
Transcriber: Victoria Kalemaris
The following interview took place December 15, 1995.

D. H.: I was an undergraduate during the 1960s at Roosevelt University in Chicago. I received my bachelor's degree in 1968. It was during the time at Roosevelt that I changed my major from microbiology to history. And I did that as I became more interested in what was happening around me and especially in the civil rights movement. I became interested in the black studies movement and also the black power phenomenon. I simply could not understand why whites and blacks did not get along. I could not understand the meaning of racism or the manifestations of racism, and so I decided that I would study, and the logical place to begin was in the past. So I switched my major to African American history and upon graduation attended Kent State University. After I left Roosevelt University in 1968, I went to Kent State University to study with August Meier, who at that time was the leading scholar in African American history. I've always been interested in biography, so I initially wanted to do a biography of T. Thomas Fortune, but August Meier informed me that Emma Lou Thornbrough was doing that work, and so I chose another topic. He was working on a history of the NAACP, so we decided together that I would do a history of the NAACP and the Texas white primary cases, and that's what I did for my dissertation. I took it beyond just the constitutional and organizational history and spent a lot of time in Texas, where I interviewed the black individuals who had been involved in fighting against the white primary on the local level, orchestrated fund-raising activities, become plaintiffs, and who had organized and defended the cases in the lower courts. So the study actually was expanded into something beyond the initial conceptualization.

By this time, I had moved to Orangeburg, South Carolina, where I was working at South Carolina State College and teaching a number of courses, five courses per semester to be exact. I had done all but write the dissertation at that point. I went to South Carolina State College because my husband, William Hine, who is still there, had a job there, and they were very delighted to offer me employment as well. I had full-time faculty status at that time. I was also the coordinator of black studies. After two years, I applied for a position at Purdue University and got the job. I found out about the job because there was such a thing as a women's directory or coordinating committee back then. I remember that I had apparently filled out some kind of form so that whenever jobs were available, the CCWHP would send these forms to the various places.

So the people at Purdue contacted me and asked me if I wanted to apply for the job that they had in African American history. I went to South Carolina in 1972, so this would have been in 1974. I remember the first contact was held at the Southern Historical Association meeting in 1973 in Atlanta. I met with Harold Woodman. All of this is so circular. We met in the book exhibit, and we had our first conversation about the position. He was chairing the search committee, and I sent in my material, went up for an interview, and received the job. So I joined Purdue in September of 1974. I finished my dissertation because I only taught two courses, which meant that I had a great deal of time coming from a fifteen-hour semester. I defended it in the spring of 1975 and received the degree. I revised the dissertation. Harold Woodman knew Harold Hyman, who teaches at Rice University, and Harold Hyman was just starting a series with Kraus-Thomson Organization Publishers out of New York and was looking for monographs. So Harold Woodman put me in touch with Harold Hyman, who read the manuscript and decided that he liked it, and we revised it according to some of his specifications. Because of his constitutional history background and interest in constitutional law, I was able to strengthen those dimensions of the study. The first book was published in 1979 in time for me to receive tenure and promotion at Purdue. During this period, I continued to attend and to participate in the Southern Historical Association meetings.

C. S.: Had you shifted your own interests toward research into the history of women, or was there an interest on those campuses in courses or on history of women or integration of stories of women into the African American or the standard U.S. history courses?

D. H.: I did not become involved or interested in black women's history until about 1980. It was after the publication of my first book, and it was really by happenstance because it wasn't something that I had studied in graduate school or taught. The first real course that I offered was actually a reading course with two students. The two students were Kate Wittenstein and Thavolia Glymph. Kate and Thavolia wanted a reading seminar in black women's history, and I said, "Well, what kinds of books are we going to read?" So Kate and Thavolia said, "We'll develop a reading list, and we'll read what's in the library, whatever we can find." It was informal; we met in the school cafeteria for an hour or so each week and talked about whatever it was that we had read. One of the first books that we read, and Kate Wittenstein actually found this book and reported on it, was Anna Julia Cooper's *A Voice from the South by a Woman of the South*, which was published in 1892 and is considered the first black feminist text ever published almost a century later. After that I became more alert to black women's history, but still it was something that was not an integral part of my work. I had done it in response to these students. Then Shirley Herd called me in 1980, a call that launched the Black Women in the Middle West Project and all that followed. I remember being very, very arrogant and dismissive in telling her that there was no black women's history, and I had never studied black women's history and didn't know anything about it. There were no primary sources, documents. Why was she bothering me with this request to write a history of black women in Indiana for the National Council of Negro Women, the Indianapolis section? She was very persistent and eventually asked me the question that so stumped me that it transformed my life. She said, "You are a black woman, aren't you?" And I said, "Yes." And she said, "You are a historian aren't you?" And I said, "Yes." She said, "You mean to tell me that you can't put those two things together and write a history of black women in Indiana?" While I'm pondering this question, I'm also thinking, of course, historians can write histories of anything and anyone, but we have to first decide that those individuals or groups are worthy of study. And apparently historians had not considered black women of sufficient merit or interest to study them. At that juncture I said, "Yes, I think I can handle that."

C. S.: Were you aware of the activities of a group within the Southern Historical Association that was particularly interested in women as early as 1973 when you met there with Harold Woodman and others?

D. H.: No, I didn't have a clue. I did not know about the Southern Association for Women Historians. I did not have contact with any women within the profession during the seventies.

C. S.: Any women at all in the Southern? Even in the Southern itself, let alone the SAWH?

D. H.: Right; now I knew black women historians who were members of the Association for the Study of Afro-American Life and History because, after all, Mary Frances Berry and Nell Painter were very prominent black women historians. I knew them, but I didn't know any white women historians. I knew *of* Anne Firor Scott, and I knew of Gerda Lerner, but that is as far as it went.

C. S.: When did you become aware of women historians within the South who were active in the Southern—and by extension—of the existence of a women's group within it, which was the Southern Association for Women Historians?

D. H.: I became aware of the group in 1983 when Aubrey C. [Chris] Land was president of the Southern, and he had selected Betty Brandon to chair the Program Committee. I had lectured at the University of Georgia at one point in the early eighties, and I think Chris suggested to Betty that I be included on the Program Committee. So it was through that route that I became aware of the work of women, white women in the Southern Historical Association. By serving on that committee with Betty I became aware of the Southern Association for Women Historians. She was, I believe, president-elect. She became president, and then she nominated me to be president-elect. It was also during that period when Betty was the president of SAWH, she had asked me to recommend someone to give the annual lecture or presentation. We were meeting in Charleston, South Carolina. I had recommended Thavolia Glymph to give the address—partly because Thavolia is also from South Carolina. We were meeting there, and she is one of the brightest people I know. Indeed, I often tell people that she has the most awesome intelligence that I have encountered. As it turned out, Thavolia wasn't able to do it because of a death in her family. It was the day of the meeting that we discovered she wasn't going to be there. So Betty Brandon, understandably concerned, came to me and asked, what should we do? It just so happened that I had a paper with me. I must have been on the lecture circuit. Anyway, I had this paper with me, and I said that I would read it. So she said fine.

Now the talk that I gave eventually became the essay that's published in the book I edited, *The State of Afro-American History: Past, Present and Future,* that Louisiana State University Press published in 1986. In 1983, I had organized a conference on the state of Afro-American life and history that was sponsored by the American Historical Association and financed by the Lily Endowment. It was held at Purdue University. The plan was always to publish the proceedings of the conference. After the proceedings were put together, it was discovered that there was no discussion of black women in this or at the conference. Black women had been referred to, but there was no sustained discussion of black women. We had talked about slavery, urbanization, civil rights, emancipation, teaching, everything, but we had not talked about black women's history. The committee was comprised of Harold Woodman, Armstead Robinson, Rosalyn Terborg-Penn, Robert L. Harris, and Alton Hornsby. They said, "Well, Darlene, you have to write a state-of-the-art essay on black women's history so that this volume will at least reflect that." And so that's why I had been researching and putting together an essay and had one with me; I had been working on this state-of-black-women's-history essay to include in this volume. The essay was published as part of the volume, and it's entitled "Lifting the Veil, Shattering the Silence: Black Women's History in Slavery and in Freedom," in *The State of Afro-American History*.

My first published essay was one on female slave resistance, the economics of sex. That was published in the *Western Journal of Black Studies*. I had given that essay at a conference at the Association for the Study of Afro-American Life and History in about 1979. The reason I had given that essay was because Kate Wittenstein and Thavolia were supposed to give talks, but Thavolia couldn't make it. So Kate wanted to go on very badly, and she had a paper on the plantation mistress, and she wanted me to do something on black women slaves, which was what Thavolia was going to do. And so I said, "OK, I'll just put something together so that you'll have a chance to participate in this conference." And so that's what I did. That was really the first essay that I published, and Kate Wittenstein and I coauthored the essay because remember she and Thavolia had first proposed that reading seminar that we had had. And so that paper grew out of that.

C. S.: Given the amount of your scholarship and your commitment in a number of scholarly fields and encouragement of younger black women scholars, I'm curious why you chose to take on the commitment of leadership in both the Southern Historical Association and the Southern Association for Women Historians? What did you see that you wanted to offer or that those organizations needed to do that you could help them do that was important enough to take time from the scholarly work you were doing?

D. H.: I don't compartmentalize the professional dimensions of my work. Writing, teaching, and serving in these organizations are all part of the same continuum, and I knew that if African American scholars—and especially African American women historians—were to enjoy good and productive careers that they had to be part of the structure of professional organizations. This is the way professions work, and when I became involved in the Southern from 1974 on, I realized how important it was to meet and to interact with people in the field. African American historians, especially ones at southern schools, were always in attendance at the Southern Historical Association. I spent a lot of time during those early years with Jimmie L. Franklin and Arvarh Strickland. Of course, John

Hope Franklin was always there, and then the people who I was inter-
acting with in the Association for the Study of Afro-American Life and
History, people like Alton Hornsby and E. C. Foster, a number of African
American men were engaged. John Blassingame and James D. Anderson,
for example, were also involved. So when I found out about the Southern
Association for Women Historians through Betty Brandon because of our
friendship, I became determined that I would open up the organization
for black women as well. I was sure that black women did not know
about this organization. Now what you have to remember is that in 1980,
there were a number of us who got together and organized the Association of Black Women Historians. I had been involved in that organization,
so I decided that the role I could play to best serve both organizations
would be to open them up to dialogue and communication with each
other. And I could do that most effectively as an officer in the Southern
Association for Women Historians because then I could bring black
women into that organization and, by extension, also involve them in the
larger Southern Historical Association. You must remember that was
during the time that Gerda Lerner was also president of the Organization
of American Historians. She and I were engaged in a project on black
women historians. She had gotten some money from FIPSE, Fund for the
Improvement of Post-Secondary Education, to do a survey of black
women in the historical profession and also to involve black women in
the affairs of the Organization of American Historians. I was project codi-
rector with her on that effort. During the first five years of the 1980s, I
was involved with the OAH and with the Southern, and the objective
was the same—to involve black women scholars, to bring them to the attention of the powers that be, to make sure that they had space on program committees and in the conventions as presenters. So that was sort
of a time in my career that I simply devoted to organizational matters. I
think that the results of the efforts have been very positive. During the
latter part of the eighties, more black women joined the Southern Association for Women Historians, and certainly at the first conference that
was held at Converse College in 1988. And if you'll look back at the *Program*, there were a number of black women scholars there. I presented
one of the major addresses, and so did Elsa Barkley Brown. Stephanie
Shaw was there. So what happened, I would say that the awareness of
the organization grew among black women historians, grew tremendously because of the role that I played. You'll also remember that one of
the first black women historians to give a talk at the annual meeting,
other than as an officer, occurred during my presidency, and that was
Barbara J. Fields. We were in Houston, Texas. Then finally Elsa Barkley

Brown did become president of the Southern Association for Women Historians. So I think that the results have been quite encouraging.

C. S.: The story you're telling is really a very positive one of black women being actively sought out and encouraged. Did you ever have a sense either in your activities within the Southern or in the OAH that you needed to be a stronger feminist because of the special needs of women, or did you, in contrast, find encouragement of women and of scholarship on women from the powers that be?

D. H.: I've never encountered any major obstacles in the sense of people saying, well, you cannot participate. Privately, many of my white male colleagues advised me to stop doing black women's history. In the early 1980s, one professor told me that he thought that my work on the white primary and constitutional and political history was much more important and that no one was really interested in this history of black women that I was doing and that it was not going to get me promoted to full professor and it was not going to be taken very seriously. Others were a bit more patronizing in the sense that they said, "Well, you know Darlene, you're a fine historian and if you want to do these things to help the women for a while, then go ahead and do it, but remember that your true career interests will be in the more traditional areas of black history or American history, namely politics and constitutional history." Early when they said that, I recognized that, first, they were being friendly, and they thought that they were speaking to my best interests, and second, I also thought that I was putting my work on black professionals and politics on hold for a while, but it didn't matter; I would come back to it. I needed to do this work for all these younger people that I intended to train, because if there was no acceptance of their work, then I was training them for failure. So that's why I kept doing it because I wanted to make space for the younger generation coming up under me or behind me or after me. I wasn't really into being a feminist or on a feminist crusade, this was purely the way I envisioned the process, the professionalization process.

I came to Michigan State as John Hannah Professor of History in 1987. I would say that had I not done all of this work on women, and had I not been also involved in administration at Purdue University from 1980 through 1986, it may not have happened. I was vice provost at Purdue University, and part of the reason why some of the women in the Southern Historical Association—people like Jody Carrigan, Betty Brandon, Theda Perdue, and a number of others—were interested in having me involved as an officer in the organization was because I had this administrative experience. So when I became involved in the organization, I launched a lot of projects to strengthen the organizational infrastructure and to make it a much more viable structure.

C. S.: So you see your emphasis as that of organizational and administrative as much as bringing in black women.

D. H.: Right. I think they're both related, but I think the major contribution that I made in terms of the organization itself was along administrative lines. We found a permanent home; we got Rameth Owens to be the editor of the *Newsletter.* We organized the constitution. We launched that, and we began to have these very structured meetings and presentations. I also was very much interested in putting the organization on sound financial footing. So we began soliciting memberships, and the treasurer at the time got us a CD, our first CD. Judy Gentry did a report, a first report of the financial standings of the organization. So we worked very closely, and we developed life membership categories, and we took out life memberships and encouraged everybody else to do that. And for the annual meeting at which Barbara Fields spoke, we went to presses and asked for contributions to support the reception so that again it became a much more elaborate affair instead of just in somebody's room with a bottle of wine smuggled in. Well, that's what we had then. The idea was to make the organization much more visible because it drew nonmembers to the receptions. My being president of the organization at that particular juncture made it much more visible because a number of the good old boys at the Southern Association talked to me about the organization and were impressed that this was a serious effort. And maybe it was because I did have that administrative title at Purdue, and I was using these administrative experiences and talents to help this organization. After that, people wanted me to become more involved in the mainstream Southern Historical Association organization.

C. S.: So your involvement in the Southern really followed after your administrative and leadership role in SAWH.

D. H.: Precisely.

C. S.: Do you see that as a role that the SAWH can continue to play, to bring women into the Southern Historical Association, sort of the parent body? Or do you see other goals that the SAWH really should have?

D. H.: Well, absolutely, I think that one of the major goals—and I'm talking strictly in a professional sense of the Southern Association for Women Historians—is to provide skill training. I'm talking about leadership skills, exposure to ease the path into the larger organizational structure. Also, being an organized body, we are able to identify those women with talents and suggest them to nominating committees and other positions: those nonelected positions like membership on all kinds of book prize committees so that they can become more integrally involved in the Southern, the parent organization, although I don't see it as a parent per se, but it is the major organization.

C. S.: You're in the North. and your research in the Black Women in the Middle West Project has been focused in the North. What do you see in terms of the value of your continued involvement in organizations where the regional focus is in the South? You've remained interested in and very active in both the SHA and the SAWH. Are there particular reasons for that that the association needs to be aware of and interested in?

D. H.: First of all, I consider myself an African American historian, and I consider myself a southern historian because my first book was on Texas, and I'm fascinated by the South, and all of my roots are in the South, even though I am very urban and very northern. I would hope that there would be more cross-fertilization between the scholarship on women in various regions. I focused my scholarship in the location where I reside physically, but I think that intellectually I learned a lot from reading and talking to southern women who do southern women's history. Because of my involvement in the Southern Historical Association, I was able to come to appreciate regionalism as an analytical concept. I took that analytical concept of regionalism and applied it to my work in the Midwest. Indeed it helped to shape and define my work on black women in the Middle West. I will always remain connected with the Southern Historical Association because at certain intellectual levels and analytical and interpretive levels there are no—there should be no—barriers between the South and the North, the Midwest and the South.

There is much more work to be done. There is absolutely much more work to be done. The Southern Association has yet to create a committee on minority historians, although we held a preliminary meeting at this conference in New Orleans in 1995, one of many meetings. [Editors' note: The SHA created a committee in 2001.] We've had two black male presidents, John Hope Franklin and Jimmie Franklin. We have yet to have a black woman president of the Southern; we have yet to have a black woman president of the American Historical Association, although Mary Frances Berry was president of the OAH. [Editors' note: Darlene Clark Hine became president of the SHA in 2002.] In over a hundred years of historical organizational work, I can count on one hand the five black people who have been privileged to assume the pinnacle positions. Now as far as what's being done to encourage and promote the careers of junior-level graduate students and assistant professors, there's much more work that needs to be done. I don't see the Southern as having particularly reached out to black graduate students. Associate professors and people my age are coming and participating in large numbers. The Southern Association for Women Historians is reaching out regularly to women graduate students, but I don't see them making a special effort to get the black women graduate students. And I think that requires work.

Joanne V. (Jan) Hawks

The late Joanne V. Hawks was Director of the Sarah Isom Center for Women's Studies at the University of Mississippi beginning in 1981. She earned her Ph.D. in American History from the University of Mississippi and served as Dean of Women and as a member of the history faculty beginning in 1972. She is the author or coauthor of numerous articles. Her work concerned southern women, especially women legislators—black and white—in southern states. She is the author of *Mississippi's Historical Heritage: A Guide to Women's Sources in Mississippi Repositories* (1993), co-editor of *Sex, Race, and the Role of Women in the South* (1983), and a contributor to *Women in the South, Southern Women,* and *Stepping out of the Shadows: Alabama Women, 1819–1990* (1995). She served on various councils and agencies for the advancement of women in higher education. She was President of the SAWH from 1986 to 1987.

Interviewer: Victoria Kalemaris
Transcriber: Victoria Kalemaris
The following interview took place November 10, 1995.

J. H.: I'm a native Georgian. I grew up in a family with just daughters, and we were always pretty much told we could do anything. We also were raised very traditionally because I went to high school in the forties and college in the fifties. It was a very traditional time as far as our expectations, but still we were not made to feel like there were really any great limits on us. You think back on those things and wonder how much that affected you. Then going to a women's college, there we were challenged to do the best that we could. I look back on all those things now, which really I'm sure I didn't even think about in that way at that time, and realize that they probably shaped me, particularly in the area of being interested in women's issues.

I went to Agnes Scott College and graduated there with a major in history. After the year that I graduated there, I went to the Presbyterian School of Christian Education in Richmond, Virginia. At that time, I intended to get a master's in English Bible and thought I would be doing some church-related work. That didn't come about, and later, after I married and we were teaching school in Mississippi, we decided that we wanted to go back and get graduate work in our fields. Of course mine was history, and I was fortunate enough to get a National Defense Education Act Fellowship at Ole Miss. I was fortunate because the person who was one of the faculty members there had been my major professor at Agnes Scott, and I'm sure she helped me to get that. I went there in 1960 and finished the master's and the languages for the reading exams but really did not intend at that time to go on and get a Ph.D. We were intending to teach at the high school level. I taught in high school a couple of years. I had two children at that time. The second year that I taught in high school, I became pregnant with my third child and so dropped out of teaching for a year or two. When I went back to teaching, I went to Blue Mountain College near Memphis to teach at the college level, and when I did that, I decided that if I was going to teach at the college level, I'd like to finish my Ph.D. So I went back and took my comps and then did my dissertation. I was fortunate at the dissertation level in being able to get a fellowship from American Association of University Women to write the dissertation. Since I was married and had young children and we didn't have substantial income, those fellowships were very important in making it possible for me to get my education.

After I finished my doctorate, I went back to Blue Mountain College for a year. I had lived in Oxford, Mississippi, all that time. Someone in my church, who was the dean of students at that time, knew that the dean of women had married late in life and was leaving. He asked me if I would consider doing that. Of course, I had never considered this in my wildest imagination, but it was a chance to go back to the town that I lived in. He also said, "If you do this, I'd like to try to get you an appointment in the history department." I said, "Oh, that wouldn't be necessary," but I think he knew me a lot better than I knew myself, and I was fortunate that I did get a toe in the door of the history department, which, of course, I wouldn't have gotten as a graduate from that institution. I began teaching the second year that I was there.

Because I was dean of women, my colleagues and I would go each year to the National Association of Deans of Women. And at that time—it was 1972 when I started—they were beginning to talk a lot about women's issues and women's concerns. When we would go to national meetings, I would spend a good bit of time going to sessions on women's programming. That was really one of the things that I wanted to do with the dean of women's office at Ole Miss. It is a very heavily Greek-oriented school, with traditional-age women students, and I wanted to try to come up with some programming that might appeal to those that didn't fall into that category. I would go to meetings about programming, about the establishment of centers, and on women's studies programs. Early on I became interested in moving into that area, and one of the first courses that I taught was a history of women. I was allowed to propose and teach that course in the history department. The first time I taught it, I called it "History of the Women's Movement in the United States" because I wanted to attract students that weren't totally turned off by the women's movement and we could get some of those ideas in. I now teach it just as "Women in United States History" and teach some of the same things but with a little bit different orientation. That is what I started out with.

As opportunities came, I just tried to develop more in that academic area. I participated in two workshops at the University of Alabama. One was a FIPSE [Fund for the Improvement of Post-Secondary Education] workshop, and the second one was too. But the first one was on teaching women's literature from a regional perspective. We all developed courses in our discipline, so I developed my course on women in southern history out of that, and then later went back and did one that was on the history and culture of southern black women and developed a course on black women's history. I've only taught that once because in the Afro-American studies program—as I think is true in a lot of places—there is a certain amount of resistance to white professors teaching black courses. But they don't teach it. So I've still tried through the years to work out some way in which I could team-teach it with somebody, but that has not worked out, primarily because my main position now is administrative. I don't teach but one course or two courses a semester.

In 1978, I had a student come up to me in class, this was when I was still teaching the one on the women's movement, and she said, "Mississippi State has a Commission on the Status of Women. Should we have one?" I'm never very quick at thinking, but somehow that time, I said, "Well, why don't you ask the chancellor that?" She went to the chancellor's office; she was a journalism student and wrote for the paper, so they were careful in the way they dealt with her. She said, "Should we have a Commission on the Status of Women?" The chancellor then called me and said, "Should we have a Commission on the Status of Women?" because I was dean of women. I said, "Well, why don't we have a study committee and look at what we should do?" and so we did. We had a year-long study, and we wrote to find out what other institutions were doing; we did some surveys on faculty, staff, and students on our campus and got some ideas. Out of that, one of the things that we did was to develop the center for women's studies [the Sarah Isom Center for Women]. In order to come up with the money for it, they asked if I'd be willing to move me and my budget over into what is an academic support unit. We came up with the idea of a Center for Women's Studies rather than a women studies program because it's a very conservative institution, and we felt like we could be multipurpose if we were a Center for Women's Studies. It's not a women's center in the sense of what some women's centers are, but we do programming and try to build a resource collection, and I try to do research and we do teaching. We felt we would appeal to several different constituencies and be more likely to survive, and we have survived for fourteen years, so I think it probably was the way we should have gone. But we still haven't developed nearly as much in the women studies course area as we should have. We do not have a minor or even a concentration; we just have courses that are taught in several different departments, and we put out a flier every semester and show what's being taught on women that semester for people who are interested.

The other thing that we ran into was that about the time we were proposing this, the university was going through a kind of attrition of faculty, cutting back on things, budget-tightening. We probably have more professors who are interested in teaching courses than actually teach them because they're pushed into what they have to teach. They don't always have the luxury of developing a new course. That is an area that we need to work in, to try and develop more.

The other thing that we had when we first established the center was that we did a consultancy grant through the National Endowment for the Humanities and brought a woman down. They assigned us a woman who was at Indiana University as the director of their women's studies program at that time. She came and said, "If you're not going to have a minor or a major, get your courses to count for something." And so our introduction to women's studies course, which we call "Women in Society," counts as part of the lower-division requirements in liberal arts. That was a real smart piece of advice she gave us because a lot of students take it just because it looks like it might be something different, and we get a chance to present our ideas. It is listed as a women's studies course; of course, that turns some people off and keeps some men from taking it that might. But we do get a lot of students in there who we would not get and have a chance to at least present them with the ideas. Then in the history courses, because most of them are at the three-hundred level, they count as part of a major, or they count as upper-division electives toward a degree.

V. K.: So they are based within the department with just an emphasis on women then?

J. H.: Right. We don't try to accumulate any credit. The Center for the Study of Southern Culture had been established just a couple of years before we established this one, and we used their structure as a model. Theirs is a much more ambitious program than ours, but we decided there was no reason that we needed to try to accumulate credit hours, and so the students go to the department or whoever teaches that course. And that is at least some incentive for that department to let somebody schedule that course because the credit hours still count for them.

V. K.: We've talked to people a lot about their experiences in graduate school and their experiences in finding a job. You come at it from a slightly different perspective because you took a little time off before you went back to get your Ph.D. And you also had a family. It's come up that people faced the question of why do women need to get a Ph.D. in history? And when people were actually applying for jobs, as they were finishing their Ph.D. programs, the response sometimes was, "Do you intend to have a family?" "You're really qualified, but we're sorry, our department doesn't hire women."

J. H.: Well, I never really directly applied for a job. My career did develop differently. When I went back to Ole Miss, I went back into an administrative position and just had the good fortune to also get the history appointment as well. I really have never applied for anything. And I've told people before, I'm sure that what happened was the dean of students asked the history department if they would consider giving me a joint appointment. What the chair of the department said at that time was, "Now don't come to the first meeting, and after that we want you to feel free to participate in everything," which I have through the years. I've really tried to be a participating member of the history department. I know what he said to the people at that time was, "We've got to hire a woman and we at least know this one."

V. K.: You were the first woman in the history department then, at Ole Miss?

J. H.: Not the first woman but the only woman at the time that I went in. The woman who had been my professor at Agnes Scott, and my mentor in a lot of ways, was there when I was a graduate student. Her husband was in the department, so the two of them—they were both southern historians—had both been appointed in that department. But there was nobody there when I was there, and, of course, that was moving on toward Title IX days when they were looking at places that didn't have women. So, I'm just convinced that he said to them, "She's probably the lesser of the evils." Anyway, it did give me a foot in the door. But I have not had that experience really of having to go out and compete for a job.

V. K.: Did you feel that you faced any discrimination as a woman, either at Ole Miss or when you were at Blue Mountain, within the department?

J. H.: This same man who was department chair at Ole Miss at the time that I was appointed there, was at Ole Miss when I was a graduate student. This couple—the woman that I've been talking about that had gotten me into Ole Miss and then who had been my major professor—left and went to another institution. He had taken over my dissertation, he said to me one time, "I don't know why you women would even think of wanting to be in this field. The time is going to come when you're going to have to strap on a Colt revolver." It was something like that. But that sort of thing was the main thing we got. I'm sure that there were ways I was discriminated against both in being part-time and in being a woman. There was never anything very overt about it at all. I was allowed from the very beginning to begin developing and having them schedule these women's courses, so you know I felt very fortunate in that. Now I'm teaching all women's courses. Of course, I taught American history survey and some other things for a while when I first started teaching, but they finally came around to seeing that I probably was more valuable to them teaching just in the women's history area. I teach the two women's history courses, one each semester every year. I also teach the women's studies course in addition to that. I'm sure there's some of both sides of that, but I have felt like I've had a good bit of opportunity. I think probably at an institution like Ole Miss, it was at least in part that I was a known quantity and a lot of those things were probably in my favor to begin with.

I chaired this study committee that proposed the establishment of the center. A lot of what we asked for was approved and eventually carried out by the institution. We all were people who were very known quantities at the institution, had worked hard for it, and so I felt like we were able to accomplish some things that people coming in from the outside at that particular time probably could not have done. I would hear at these national deans' meetings every year about all these young women who came in and tried to establish women's studies courses, and, of course, they were very political. They didn't last any time; they didn't get tenure. I think I had some advantages in being able to get some things done that under other circumstances, I might not have been able to.

V. K.: What had your dissertation work been on?

J. H.: I was always interested in southern history, and my dissertation topic was to look at social reform movements in the South before the Civil War. What I was going against was the interpretation that was pretty widespread at that time that because of their fear of antislavery and abolitionist reform efforts in the South, they hadn't done anything much. Of course they had done a good bit more in areas like prison reform and education than what the generalization would seem to indicate. I took five states and looked at what kinds of reform efforts had gone on in those states—the temperance movement, prison reform, and all of those things. I wasn't even as interested in women at that time as I later became; and, you know, hindsight is always so much better. I'd love to have known how I would have approached that and what other kinds of things I would have noticed if I had been more attuned to looking for women.

V. K.: You said it was in the late seventies when you got back into the SHA.

J. H.: It really was not until I was at Ole Miss that I was able to do that.

V. K.: Do you remember how you found out about the SAWH?

J. H.: I'm sure just through the Southern; I just can't pinpoint what year I started going to that. I know it was in the seventies, but I had my last child in 1976, and it probably was after that. I just learned about SAWH through going to SHA.

V. K.: How did you get involved in the SAWH?

J. H.: I was not present at the founding, even though I think a lot of people think I was. I did not join the Southern Historical Association until after I went back to Ole Miss in 1972. So I have a feeling it was probably 1977, 1978 when I really started going to the Southern. Naturally, as soon as I found out about the Southern Association for Women Historians, since I was interested in women's issues and women's courses, I was attracted to that and have participated in it from whenever that was.

V. K.: I think by that time, they probably had their session listed in the *Program*. I know in the beginning they didn't, but it was around that time.

J. H.: I remember Anne Scott, and I think this must have been around 1980, when they began talking about establishing the book prizes. I remember she really made a pitch for the book prizes. She started talking about Julia Cherry Spruill and how hard she had had to work to do her book because she had no research assistants, no academic appointment. She started crying over it, and I thought, this is a good group of women; they care enough about other women that they're willing to let down their guard. That's one of the early meetings that I really remember. It was fairly well organized when I was first associated with it. I've attended the Southern Historical just about every year after I once started going and always went to the Southern Association for Women Historians session.

V. K.: For you, when you first joined the SAWH, was it the scholarship as much as the opportunity to be with other women that attracted you?

J. H.: Right, women that were interested in similar sorts of academic pursuits. I've always, I guess, been basically a historian regardless of what else I've done, and so I enjoyed being with other women historians.

V. K.: Because it seems that for some people, it was very much the socialization and the networking and the ability to be with other women; whereas for others it was the focus on women, this was a validation of women's scholarship.

J. H.: From what I've heard them talk about, I know that one of the reasons for the establishment of it was to try to have some impact on the Southern Historical. They were looking at the fact that there weren't many sessions that dealt with women's history, and there weren't many women in the leadership or on the program. So there was a political part of it that had happened by the time I got into it. At the time that I got into it, they were trying to increase their impact and their visibility, but those early efforts had already taken place.

V. K.: And you were president in 1987. Could you talk about the organization in the late eighties?

J. H.: I followed Theda Perdue as president and was succeeded by Judi Jennings. They had established the prizes by that time. The year that I was president was the first year the book prizes were given. They also had begun talking about having the Southern Conference on Women's History, and that planning had begun during Theda's presidency. That was one of the things that we were very involved with the year that I was president, and then it occurred the following summer. The organization was developing in those two directions at that time. Also at that time, they were beginning to try to reach out to graduate students to broaden the network beyond women professors and to include graduate students. Connie Schulz was very involved in trying to come up with money to enable graduate students to be able to come, to give a scholarship, a travel scholarship each year, to try to help them also network, and to become part of the network with the women professionals.

There was something else that they were doing that I think was very important at that time besides graduate students. That was to try to become more institutionalized—to get from a more informal structure and grouping to something that would be a little more formal. That's one of the things that's been very interesting about the Southern Association for Women Historians. I think it's had some real canny women in it who have helped it develop in some important directions so that it does serve a lot of different needs. One of the things they were trying to do was to keep people more aware of things. The *Newsletter* served to let people know where openings might be but also who might be doing research on a particular subject. If I had a paper on one thing, we might be able to develop a session. It was used as a means of contact to help women in a lot of different ways. And then they were working also the year I was president on the Committee on the Status of Women. Theda primarily was responsible for this because she was one of those who had some strong contacts within the hierarchy of the SHA through having been at the University of Georgia. She was trying to get the Committee on the Status of Women to begin with, to get that from that stage to a permanent committee of the SHA. They were both trying to use the SAWH as a means of serving a lot of the needs of women, but then they were also trying to get a better entree into the SHA. And it's been amazing to see how that has developed. I'm sure women still aren't where they should be in the SHA, but at every hour on the program, there are sessions on women, sometimes more than one. Not only are they there, but also they're scheduled in the ballrooms because they're expecting people to come to them. That's a big change from the past. In fact, I'm sure there are probably some men who are saying, "Do they not have anything but women's history on the program?" I'm sure part of that is just the times and the fact that everything is moving in that direction, but I have to feel like SAWH has been part of the pressure group or wedge that has helped that to come about.

We began putting together a list of all of the presidents from the past. The connection had been made to deposit the SAWH papers at the University of North Carolina, but not many people had been doing it. So I sent out a request to all of the former presidents that we could get in touch with to ask them to please contribute their records there so that we could have an institutional record of what the organization had done. Those were two of the things that we tried to do that year in addition to the others that we've mentioned.

V. K.: Were there any men in the SHA who you felt were particularly helpful for your cause or particularly a blockage?

J. H.: Of course by the time I was president, I don't remember our hitting any stumbling blocks. Maybe if we'd asked for a whole lot more, we might have. I'm sure there is a group of people, both men and women within the SHA, that wonder what in the world this is about. I mentioned my mentor and good friend, who the year that I took over as president of the SAWH wrote this nice little note, "Congratulations to you on doing this. Of course I don't approve of this sort of thing, but if that's what you want to do." It just flew all over me. I thought why write at all? I'm sure she represented a group of both men and some of the very traditional women within the organization who thought this was a bunch of wild-eyed women. I guess it's good that she wrote it to me to be aware of that whole constituency. When I got the note, I threw it across the room. I thought this is all I need in the way of affirmation. But anyway, I know those people were there. You know how southern men deal with southern women. It's not always a very abrasive sort of thing, so what I'm saying is, I think there probably were a lot of those who either were opposed or who had greater reservations who just weren't saying anything anymore.

V. K.: Obviously the dean of women organizations and the women's studies organizations wouldn't have offered much of a resistance, but did you find any sort of resistance or difficulty for women in the Mississippi Historical Society?

J. H.: Of course; it had the same kind of hidebound leadership that the SHA did, but gradually we began to get in there too in doing some sessions. I've done several sessions, and Marjorie Spruill Wheeler and others have too as time has gone on. We've gradually made our place there as we did in the SHA. That organization has always had some female leadership. They've had women as presidents; in that organization usually the president is a designated person, particular types of women have tended to be the presidents of that. It has opened up a lot more as time has gone on, and I don't think any of us really feel pushed to the side or discriminated against in it now. I've had three terms on the board. Other women have had that experience too, so I think it's probably in a lot of ways very similar to the SHA in what its original leadership was and the way it has gradually opened up.

V. K.: Did the women there form any sort of committee, or is it not really big enough?

J. H.: There aren't really enough of us, and that probably wasn't the way to work in that organization. You always have to decide. One of my research areas has been on women in southern legislatures, and, of course, we've always dealt with that question of did you form a women's caucus, and is it wise to form a women's caucus? Do you stir up more trouble for yourself? In something like the Mississippi Historical Society, I'm sure that would have done more harm than good. In the SHA, I think the reason SAWH was able to do it as successfully as it did was because I think those early women knew what they were doing, and most of them had connections. Of course Theda came along later, but she helped to do some things like get an ad hoc SHA Committee on Women the year that I became president. Because of her work, it became a permanent committee of the SHA, but they were women who had worked in it. She had been a graduate student under some of the people who were in the permanent leadership of SHA, and they had been able to gradually bring that about. Again, I think a lot of it was like some of what I said I was able to do as dean of women in getting some things changed at Ole Miss. They'd been around a while; they had been participating in the SHA. They were listened to more than probably some other people would have been.

V. K.: In your eyes, being a known quantity is something that really makes a difference.

J. H.: I think in a lot of southern situations, it is. I'm sure it's an advantage and a disadvantage. I'm sure that sometimes you don't push as hard or dare as much because you already know too much about what you probably can accomplish. But in my own situation, when I was trying to do the things I was trying to do at Ole Miss, I felt like if you keep moving steadily forward, you're a lot better off than if you move forward and get pushed back. Part of that feeling was coming from listening to the horror tales all of these other women who were telling about what had happened to them when they tried to make changes in their institutions. I have probably been too cautious, but at least we have kept moving in a positive direction. It has its advantages and disadvantages.

V. K.: Have you been involved at all as the dean of women with the graduate history programs at Ole Miss, and are there a fair number of women graduate students there?

J. H.: At Ole Miss, I think right now we have more men than women graduate students, but there has been more balance. And I have taught some graduate work. I'm not teaching any graduate work right now, but we have some people who are very interested in trying to groom and develop graduate students. One of those is Dr. Sheila Skemp. She has done a lot to try to nurture the women graduate students along with the men. We haven't had a whole lot of women graduate students who were interested in women's topics. That has developed very slowly. I can remember some years ago—and it's probably been ten or fifteen years ago now—a very good woman graduate student that we had. One of the other professors that she was going to work under for her master's said she wanted to do something on the woman suffrage movement in Mississippi. He was asking me about it because he was asking about a collection that was in the library special collections. But he said, "I don't want her to do that; she's too good a student to do that." So that attitude was around for a while. I said at the time, I should have kicked him, and if I had been a little more secure then, I probably would have at least verbally kicked him. I didn't say anything then about it except just kind of smiled. But that attitude's not around now. But many of the women students still feel like maybe that's too narrow a field or it'll narrow their opportunities. Unfortunately several of our women graduate students have not finished; usually it's because of family situations; they have the responsibility of children and all. So I don't know what would have happened to them if they had finished.

V. K.: At Ole Miss, and in the SHA and SAWH, can you speak to the presence of minorities, primarily African Americans?

J. H.: I think there's always been an awareness on the part of some of the people to make it much more open; we needed to encourage minority participation.

V. K.: Your presidency was after Darlene Clark Hine's, right?

J. H.: Yes. I think that that developed fairly slowly. I remember one thing that happened at that First Southern Conference on Women's History in 1988. Evidently, there were some sessions in which there was a good bit of conflict between some of the black presenters and some of the white presenters. I read something that somebody wrote recently, saying that they felt that sort of thing was good, to air things. I'm sure there has always been a certain amount of resentment that its origins were primarily a white southern women's organization. But I think there has been a real conscious effort to open it up, and I believe that we're improving on that as years go by. Certainly there has been a lot of effort even in the SHA to schedule programs that deal with minority research. I think there has been a steady improvement, what would appear to me to be a pretty steady improvement, I think. The numbers still are not what they should be.

V. K.: Have you in your role either as dean of women or now with the Center for Women's Studies been involved in any sort of outreach, Mississippi History Day, or even in your position in the Mississippi Historical Society in bringing women's history out into the state and the community?

J. H.: We have tried to, but the high schools are really not very receptive to it. And you're always treading that fine line, trying to keep from coming across as a radical. Really they get very scared by even the mildest sort of ideas now because of the birth control issue or the right-to-life issue. We have tried to say, we'll be glad to give programs, and we had at one time a curriculum workshop that we encouraged some of them to come to, but not too many of them participated in that. It's been a slow go. It really has. Just to give you an indication of where our high school has been since I have become the director of the Center for Women's Studies, we had a principal there (this probably has been ten or so years ago now), and a girl, whose father happened to be on the law faculty at Ole Miss, was running for student body president. There was a guy running against her. She said something to the principal about, "Surely, you're going to support me aren't you?" He said, "I really don't approve of women in leadership roles." I think they've moved beyond that. But this was the kind of thing we dealt with, and this was in a university town.

V. K.: With attitudes like that in high school, I can see why these women don't choose to do women's issues as graduate students.

J. H.: Exactly. Among our undergraduates at Ole Miss, there is such a strong sorority orientation, and part of that, of course, is that you don't want to do anything that seems the least bit daring to your sisters. So it's very hard even to get them to take courses; they're certainly not going to consider themselves feminists. Although they get very interested in the ideas that we talk about in the "Women in Society" course, and they sympathize with a lot of it, and they buy into a lot of it, but they're not going to call themselves feminists. That's the kind of environment we're working in.

V. K.: You feel that the SAWH has helped women in terms of the SHA and in the history profession?

J. H.: I feel like it has. We get that in talking about our Center for Women's Studies. Are you isolating yourself off and not trying to measure up? I was reading back over the letter that's in one of the newsletters in 1987. Hugh Davis Graham wrote and complained about the prizes, and Elizabeth Jacoway wrote back to try to explain. You always run into that. Are you doing special things for women, or do you not think you can compete with the men, and so you've got to have your little separate women's program. I don't ever finally know the answer to that. But I do think that there's a great importance of women working with other women. I'm sure there are some people who think having this organization sitting in the lap of the SHA probably is a laughable sort of thing. Who's to say how much SAWH has changed things in SHA and how much other factors have, but you can certainly look at it and see the change. The change may not be as great as it should be, but there has been significant change. Something has brought that about, and I just feel like SAWH has to be a part of it. It is an amazing story to listen to those early people talk about what they did. I found this out when I was first in the National Association of Deans of Women, and it's certainly true of this one too. Women like this are just such solid, good, down-to-earth people. They're wonderful people to be associated with, and I always keep wondering why anybody would want to be associated with women in the tea club or social club of that sort where it was a good bit more superficial. I have thoroughly enjoyed the association of women who enjoy having a good laugh about things but who also have some very serious dimensions to them, and I think that's one of the characteristics of SAWH.

Conclusion

For an organization, as for a marriage, the celebration of twenty-five years marks not an end, but the renewal of the promises and hopes that marked its birth, and the beginning of a new chapter or phase in its life. So, too, it has been for the Southern Association for Women Historians. The stories of the women who began and sustained it, who brought not only the organization but the field of southern women's history that it has nurtured to maturity, have filled this book. If theirs has been a sisterhood, their places are now being taken by their intellectual daughters and even a few granddaughters. Perhaps Anne Scott expressed it best: "I really think that if St. Peter asked me to justify myself that students are the justification, not the scholarship. It was helpful, but it won't be here forever. But students will have students will have students forever."

In reality, of course, the students do have help. The publication of these interviews will become, we hope, part of that help. Historians are among the first to point out that "history" does not "teach" lessons but that all of us learn from understanding the past. Just as mothers and grandmothers in a family tell stories of their experiences to their daughters and sons as a part of passing on family identity, women historians also need to pass on to the next generation a sense of their profession's past and to enable them to shape its future. At the beginning of the twenty-first century, these interviews give a powerful sense for women historians in and of the South of their origins in a not-so-long-ago time: when female mentors in graduate schools were few; when choosing to get married or to raise a family made it difficult to continue one's life as a scholar; when well-meaning and supportive male dissertation directors apologized to potential employers for a candidate's sex. The attitudes these women encountered when completing their graduate work in the 1950s, 1960s, and 1970s were not peculiar to the South, of course, but pervaded higher education. Nepotism rules against both members of a young academic couple being employed by the same university, insistence that male students could not be expected to learn history from female instructors, assumptions that women could and should accept lower salaries because their earnings were only supplemental to those of their husbands—such barriers were common, and the women who relate their stories in these interviews experienced similar incidents in many places.

Despite the difficulties they encountered, the women in these interviews endured in their determination to become historians and to share in the work of their chosen profession as equals. Their achievements came in many different forms. A few went on to help define the field of women's history, their names readily recognized by countless undergraduates and graduate students who read their texts. Others received the recognition of the profession through election to leadership roles in its associations, regionally and nationally. Yet others spent their professional lives within their own colleges and universities, relatively unsung by the profession as a whole, directing women's studies programs, mentoring young women in their departments, sharing their love of history with teachers in surrounding communities. A few made lives for themselves as historians outside academic walls, as independent scholars and public historians.

What also comes across is a sense of the support these women received from individuals throughout the South. In interview after interview, women describe helpful mentors (usually male) who believed in the scholarly potential of the young women whose work they directed. Universities gave the women opportunities to teach, and students responded to their enthusiasm. Curiosity about women's past lives was encouraged, and a new field for enriching scholarship about the past developed. Friendships emerged and were reinforced by contacts at professional association meetings. The Southern Historical Association played an important role for almost all of those interviewed. Many described attendance at its annual meeting as almost a given.

From all of these experiences in their own formative years, the women who created and sustained the SAWH brought to it a commitment to the advancement of the historical profession. They expressed that commitment by serving on committees or as leaders, by promoting the scholarship of others through generous gifts to endowment funds, and by encouraging younger or newer scholars through personal interaction at the SAWH triennial conferences.

The new generation of scholars to whom they passed the torch has already made great strides in advancing the importance of the study of women's history in and of the South. Merely looking at the list of women who have served as presidents of SAWH since 1985, or who have given scholarly addresses at those annual November meetings (see appendices), is to come face to face with the richness of scholarship on southern women's history during the past decade. This volume and all the books in the Southern Women series reinforce awareness of the importance of those contributions. Clio's southern sisters are doing well.

Questions and topics to consider for
your SAWH Oral History Interview

1. Your background history—education, professional career, etc. Anything in your childhood or undergraduate experience that may have led to an interest in history, women's history, or women's issues. Where were you in your professional life in 1970 (the year of the SAWH founding).

2. The frustrations, both for you personally and for women in the field as a whole, with established historical organizations that led to the creation of the SAWH.

3. Your recollections (if any) of the founding of the SAWH.

4. What do you remember as the early goals of the SAWH? Was the SAWH concerned with increasing the role of women historians who also belong to ethnic or racial minorities? Did the SAWH see itself as a part of the increasing radicalization of the feminist movement at the time? Did you see the SAWH this way?

The topics and questions were prepared in 1993.

5. Was there any opposition from established historical associations (to this new organization)?

6. Who were other leaders in the organization, and what were their roles? The following (names) have been suggested by others: Connie Myers, Barbara Schnorrenberg, Mollie Davis, A. Elizabeth Taylor, Rosemary Carroll, Arnita Jones, Betty Brandon, Charlotte Davis, Martha Swain, to name a few. Do you agree? Disagree? Comments?

7. Who from the SHA and other organizations helped the SAWH but was not a member in the early years? What role(s) did Ben and Neva Wall play? What role(s) did Dorothy Ross and the AHA committee on women play? What role did Mary Elizabeth Massey, who was president of the SHA after the creation of SAWH, play? These are some of the names that have come up in previous interviews. Comments? Additions?

8. What did you hope to see/get from the SAWH? What did you do to further these goals? If you were an officer, what were the major concerns that you faced and dealt with during your term?

9. Has the SAWH fulfilled its goals of 1970? Do you think the goals have changed since 1970? Have you seen an increased concern with the history of women in the South? Have you seen significant changes in the treatment of women and recognition of women's history at your university and in your state? Have you seen or been involved in outreach to high school history programs? History Day? What effect, if any, did your involvement in SAWH have on your activities on these issues?

10. Has the SAWH helped or hindered women in the field? Has it served to "ghettoize" them, or has it helped them to become a more active part of southern historians?

These questions are merely a guideline and are intended as a start to get you thinking about SAWH and your involvement in it. They are based on questions and issues raised in previous interviews. We will not necessarily cover all of the topics or cover them in this order. If there are any other issues you wish to raise, please feel free to do so in your interview. We look forward to our interview session. Please contact us if you have any questions or concerns. Thank you.

Appendix B

Southern Association for Women Historians

List of Chairs or Presidents, 1970-2004

1970–1972	Charlotte M. Davis	Cochair
	Mollie C. Davis	Cochair
1973–1974	Constance Ashton Myers	
1975	Arnita Jones	
1976	Rosemary Carroll	
1977	Helena Lewis	
1978	Martha Swain	
1979	Judith Gentry	
1980	Carol Bleser	
1981	Elizabeth Jacoway	
1982	Jo Ann Carrigan	
1983	Betty Brandon	
1984	Margaret Ripley Wolfe	
1985	Darlene Clark Hine	
1986	Theda Perdue	
1987	Joanne V. Hawks	
1988	Judith Jennings	
1989	Virginia Bernhard	

1990	Julia Blackwelder
1991	Marlene Rikard
1992	Constance B. Schulz
1993	Elsa Barkley Brown
1994	Janet Coryell
1995	Kathleen Berkeley
1996	Marjorie Spruill Wheeler
1997	Elizabeth Hayes Turner
1998	Catherine Clinton
1999	Drew Faust
2000	Any Thompson McCandless
2001	Jacqueline A. Rouse
2002	Sandra Gioia Treadway
2003	Jane Turner Censer
2004	Stephanie Cole

Appendix C

SAWH Annual Meeting Addresses

YEAR	SPEAKER/TOPIC	CITY
1979	A. Elizabeth Taylor	Atlanta
1980	Papers on the 3 women presidents of SHA (given by LaWanda Cox, Blanche Clark, Frederick Heath)	Atlanta
1981	Anne Firor Scott	Louisville
1982	Report on Status of Women in the Profession (given by A. Elizabeth Taylor, LaWanda Cox, Mollie Davis) The January 1983 SAWH *Newsletter* reports that Anne Firor Scott also spoke about the life and work of Julia Cherry Spruill, and Carol Bleser spoke on the life and work of Willie Lee Rose.	Memphis
1983	Scheduled: Thavolia Glymph "Black Women Historians: Race, Class, and Academia"	Charleston

	(unable to attend) Address given by Darlene Clark Hine "Lifting the Veil, Shattering the Silence: Black Women's History in Slavery and Freedom"	
1984	Tom Appleton, Nancy Baird "Vignettes of Kentucky Women"	Louisville
1985	Barbara Fields "Ideology and the Writing of Southern History"	Houston
1986	Mary Frederickson "Sassing Fate: Women Workers in the Twentieth-Century South"	Charlotte
1987	Joan Cashin "Women's Work and Culture in the Old Southwest"	New Orleans
1988	Suzanne Lebsock "White Supremacy and Woman Suffrage: A Virginia Case Study"	Norfolk
1989	Barbara Welter "The True Woman: Post-Feminist or Retro-Feminist?"	Lexington
1990	Catherine Clinton "Sex and the Sectional Conflict"	New Orleans
1991	Virginia van der Veer Hamilton "Clio's Daughters: Whence and Whither?"	Ft. Worth
1992	Theda Perdue "Pochahontas Meets Columbus in the American South"	Atlanta
1993	Thavolia Glymph "Civil War Memoirs and the Reinvention of Black Women's History"	Orlando
1994	Jean B. Lee "Experiencing the American Revolution"	Louisville
1995	Anne Firor Scott "Unfinished Business . . ."	New Orleans
1996	Glenda Elizabeth Gilmore " 'But She Can't Find Her (V.O.) Key': Writing Gender and Race into Southern Political History"	Little Rock

1997	Darlene Clark Hine "A Stronger Soul within a Finer Frame: Writing a Literary History of Black Women"	Atlanta
1998	Jacquelyn Dowd Hall "Writing a Way Home: History, Memory, and the Refashioning of Southern Identity"	Birmingham
1999	Stephanie McCurry " 'The Brothers' War'?: Free Women, Slaves, and Popular Politics in the Civil War South"	Fort Worth
2000	Nancy A. Hewitt "Seneca Falls, Suffrage, and the South: Remapping the Landscape of Women's Rights in America, 1848–1965"	Louisville
2001	Rosalyn Terborg-Penn "The ABWH, Black Women's History, and Black Women Historians"	New Orleans
2002	Jane Dailey "Sex, Segregation, and the Sacred from *Brown* to Selma"	Baltimore
2003	Marjorie Spruill "Countdown to Houston: The 1977 International Women's Year Conferences and the Polarization of American Women"	Houston

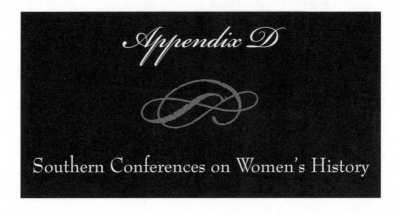

Appendix D

Southern Conferences on Women's History

First Southern Conference on Women's History—Converse College, Spartanburg, South Carolina, June 10–11, 1988

Steering Committee: Judith Jennings, chair

Kathleen C. Berkeley, Virginia Bernhard, Betty Brandon, Joanne V. Hawks, Darlene Clark Hine, Rameth Owens, Theda Perdue, Barbara B. Schnorrenberg, Constance B. Schulz, and Margaret Ripley Wolfe

Program Committee: Kathleen C. Berkeley, Barbara B. Schnorrenberg, and Constance B. Schulz, cochairs

Sara Alpern, Jo Ann Argersinger, Barbara Bellows, Elsa Barkley Brown, June Burton, Nupur Chaudhuri, Dorothy DeMoss, Elizabeth Fox-Genovese, Jean Friedman, Joseph Hawes, Martha Swain

Local Arrangements Committee: (no chair listed)

Julia Kirk Blackwelder, Virginia Daley, Joe P. Dunn, Bonnie Ledbetter, Brooks Simpson

Second Southern Conference on Women's History—University of North Carolina, Chapel Hill, North Carolina, June 7–8, 1991

Steering Committee: Janet L. Coryell, chair

Virginia Bernhard, Julia K. Blackwelder, Marlene K. Rikard, Rameth Owens, Constance B. Schulz, Sally McMillen, Christiana Greene, Lynn Willoughby, Sandra Treadway, Elsa Barkley Brown, Marjorie Spruill Wheeler
Program Committee: Sally McMillen, chair
Wanda Hendricks, Anna Clark, Mary Frederickson, Elizabeth Hayes Turner
Local Arrangements Committee: Christina Greene

Third Southern Conference on Women's History—Rice University, Houston, Texas, June 2–5, 1994
Steering Committee: Elizabeth Hayes Turner, chair
John B. Boles, Joan Cashin, Michele Gillespie, Nancy Hewitt, Cathy S. Monholland, Tiffany Patterson, Anastatia Sims, Marjorie Spruill Wheeler
Program Committee: Joan Cashin, chair
Cynthia Fleming, John Inscoe, Cynthia Kierner, Jane Landers, Stephanie Shaw, Martha Swain
Local Arrangements Committee: John B. Boles, chair
Virginia Bernhard, Lynda Crist, Jane Dailey, Merline Pitre, Linda Reed, Angela Zophy

Fourth Southern Conference on Women's History—College of Charleston, Charleston, South Carolina, June 12–14, 1997
Steering Committee: Amy Thompson McCandless, chair
Katherine Haldane, Laura Edwards, Constance Schulz, Victoria Bynum, Jane Turner Censer
Program Committee: Jane Turner Censer, chair
Glenda Gilmore, Judith McArthur, Thavolia Glymph, Jacqueline Rouse, Anastatia Sims, Sheila Skemp, Marcia Synnott, Jeannie M. Whayne, Betty Wood, Elizabeth Varon
Local Arrangements Committee: Katherine Haldane, chair
Amy Bushnell, Marvin Delaney, Rita Livingston, Randy J. Sparks, Katherine Fleming

Fifth Southern Conference on Women's History—University of Richmond, Richmond, Virginia, June 15–17, 2000
Steering Committee: Sandra Gioia Treadway, chair
Frances S. Pollard, Cynthia A. Kierner, Valinda W. Littlefield, Martha J. King
Program Committee: Cynthia A. Kierner, chair
Thomas E. Buckley, S.J., Lynda Crist, Elna Green, Wanda A. Hendricks,

Jessica Kross, Deborah M. O'Neal, Phyllis L. Smith, Sarah Wilkerson-Freeman

Local Arrangements Committee: Frances S. Pollard, chair

Cynthia MacLeod, Jeanne Christie, John L. Gordon, Jr., Robert C. Kenzer

Sixth Southern Conference on Women's History—University of Georgia, Athens, Georgia, June 5–7, 2003

Steering Committee: Mary Ella Engel, chair

Kathleen Clark, Laura Edwards

Program Committee: Laura F. Edwards, chair

Laurie Green, Laura Moore, Bryant Simon, Lu Ann Jones, Stephanie Camp, Victoria Bynum

Local Arrangements Committee: Kathleen Clark, chair

Diane Batts Morrow, Claudio Saunt, John Inscoe, Bryant Simon, Laura Mason, and Mary Ella Engel

Biographical Index

The purpose of this index of names is to help identify persons named in the interviews who may be unfamiliar to readers. Most of the names are of historians, and to help readers understand their significance and the connections to those whom we interviewed, we have provided a brief body of biographical and bibliographical information. A number of those listed below published more books than we have included here; we have tried in making a representative sample of titles to choose the most significant works or those that clearly identify them with their field. We have tried also to select the institution with which an individual was most closely connected. In a very few cases we were unable to find any information on persons named in the interviews. The name(s) in brackets following each entry refer to the interview(s) in which that person is mentioned.

CBS and EHT

Abbot, William Wright (1922–), Ph.D. Duke University, 1953. Professor, University of Virginia; Editor Emeritus, The Papers of George Washington;

author, *The Royal Governors of Georgia, 1754–1775* (1959); *The Colonial Origins of the United States, 1607–1763* (1975). [Carol Bleser]

Alexander, Thomas B. (1918–), Ph.D. Vanderbilt University, 1947. Frederick A. Middlebush Professor of History, University of Missouri–Columbia; author, *Political Reconstruction in Tennessee* (1950); *Thomas A. R. Nelson of East Tennessee* (1956); *Sectional Stress and Party Strength: A Study of Roll-call Voting Patterns in the United States House of Representatives, 1836–1860* (1967); *The Anatomy of the Confederate Congress: A Study of the Influences of Member Characteristics on Legislative Voting Behavior, 1861–1865* (1972). SHA president, 1980. [Carol Bleser, Jo Ann Carrigan]

Alpern, Sara (1942–), Ph.D. University of Maryland, 1978. Professor, Texas A & M University; author, *Freda Kirchwey: A Woman of the Nation* (1987); coeditor, *The Challenge of Feminist Biography: Writing the Lives of Modern American Women* (1992). [Anne Scott]

Anderson, James D. (1944–), Ph.D. University of Illinois, 1973. Professor, University of Illinois at Urbana-Champaign; author, *The Education of Blacks in the South, 1860–1935* (1988). [Darlene Clark Hine]

Antler, Joyce (1942–), Ph.D. State University of New York at Stony Brook, 1977. Samuel Lane Professor of American Jewish History and Culture, Brandeis University; author, *Lucy Sprague Mitchell: The Making of a Modern Woman* (1987); *The Educated Woman and Professionalization: The Struggle for a New Feminine Identity, 1890–1920* (1987); coeditor, *Challenge of Feminist Biography: Writing the Lives of Modern American Women* (1992); *The Journey Home: Jewish Women and the American Century* (1997). [Anne Scott]

Appleton, Thomas H., Jr. (1950–), Ph.D. University of Kentucky, 1981. Professor, Eastern Kentucky University; coeditor, *A Mythic Land Apart: Reassessing Southerners and Their History* (1977); coeditor, *Negotiating Boundaries of Southern Womanhood: Dealing with the Powers That Be* (2000). [Margaret Ripley Wolfe]

Bates, Daisy (1914–1999), Honorary Doctor of Laws, University of Arkansas at Fayetteville, 1984. Civil rights activist; interim editor for her husband, L. C. Bates, of the leading African American newspaper in Little Rock, the *Arkansas State Press;* author, *The Long Shadow of Little Rock* (1962); president, Arkansas State Conference of NAACP branches, advisor to "Little Rock Nine" who integrated Central High School. [Elizabeth Jacoway]

Begemann, Rosemary E., Ph.D. Emory University, 1973. Professor Emerita, Georgia College and State University. [Rosemary Carroll]

Berkeley, Kathleen C. (1953–), Ph.D. UCLA, 1980. Professor, University of North Carolina–Wilmington; author, *"Like a Plague of Locusts": From an Antebellum Town to a New South City, Memphis, Tennessee, 1850–1880* (1991); *The Women's Liberation Movement in America* (1999). [Judith Gentry, Anne Scott]

Bernhard, Virginia P. (1937–), Ph.D. Rice University, 1971. Professor, University of St. Thomas (Houston); author, *Ima Hogg: The Governor's Daughter* (1984); *A Durable Fire* (1990); *Slaves and Slaveholders in Bermuda, 1616–1782* (1999). SAWH president, 1989. [Betty Brandon]

Berry, Mary Frances (1938–), Ph.D. University of Michigan, 1966; J.D. University of Michigan Law School. Geraldine R. Segal Professor of American Social Thought, University of Pennsylvania; Assistant Secretary of Education, Department of Health, Education, and Welfare, 1976–1980; appointed chairperson, U.S. Commission on Civil Rights, 1993; author of six books on African American education and civil rights. OAH president, 1990. [Mollie Davis, Darlene Clark Hine]

Blassingame, John W. (1940–2000), Ph.D. Yale University, 1971. Professor, Yale University; author, *The Slave Community: Plantation Life in the Antebellum South* (1972); *Black New Orleans, 1860–1880* (1973); Editor, The Frederick Douglass Papers (1979–1999). [Darlene Clark Hine]

Boatwright, Eleanor Miot (1895–1955), M.A. Duke University, 1939. Teacher, Tubman Girls High School (Augusta, Georgia); author, "The Political and Civil Status of Women in Georgia, 1783–1860," *Georgia Historical Quarterly* (1941). [Anne Scott]

Boles, John B. (1943–), Ph.D. University of Virginia, 1969. William Pettus Hobby Professor of History, Rice University; managing editor, *Journal of Southern History*; author, *The Great Revival, 1787–1805: The Origins of the Southern Evangelical Mind* (1972); *Black Southerners, 1619–1869* (1983); *The South through Time: A History of an American Region* (1995). [Judith Gentry]

Brewer, Vivion (1900–1991), B.A. Smith College, 1921; J.D. University of Arkansas Law School, 1928. Opposed closing of Little Rock schools by Gov. Orval Faubus; organizer of Women's Emergency Committee to Open

Our Schools in Little Rock; author, "The Embattled Ladies of Little Rock" (1998). [Elizabeth Jacoway]

Brown, Elsa Barkley, Ph.D. Kent State University, 1994. Professor, University of Maryland; coeditor, *Black Women in America: An Historical Encyclopedia* (1993); *Major Problems in African-American History: Documents and Essays* (2000); author, "Negotiating and Transforming the Public Sphere: African-American Political Life in the Transition from Slavery to Freedom," *Public Culture* 7 (Fall 1994); SAWH president, 1993. [Judith Gentry, Darlene Clark Hine, Anne Scott]

Burns, Augustus (Gus) (1939–1999), Ph.D. University of North Carolina at Chapel Hill, 1969. Professor, University of Florida; coauthor, *Frank Porter Graham and the 1950 Senate Race in North Carolina* (1990). [Elizabeth Jacoway]

Burton, June K., Ph.D. University of Georgia, 1972. Professor Emeritus, University of Akron; author, *Napoleon and Clio: Historical Writing, Teaching, and Thinking during the First Empire* (1979); editor, *Essays in European History: Selected from the Annual Meetings of the Southern Historical Association, 1986–1987* (1989). [Judith Gentry]

Campbell, D'Ann (1949–), Ph.D. University of North Carolina at Chapel Hill, 1979. Consultant, Mary Baker Eddy Library, Boston; author, *Women at War with America: Private Lives in a Patriotic Era* (1984). [Jo Ann Carrigan, Rosemary Carroll, Margaret Ripley Wolfe]

Carroll, Berenice (1932–), Ph.D. Brown University, 1960. Professor Emerita, University of Illinois at Urbana-Champaign; author, *Design for Total War: Arms and Economics in the Third Reich* (1968); editor, *Liberating Women's History: Theoretical and Critical Essays* (1976). [Mollie Davis]

Chafe, William H. (1942–), Ph.D. Columbia University, 1971. Alice Mary Baldwin Distinguished Professor of History, Duke; author, *American Woman: Her Changing Social, Economic, and Political Roles, 1920–1970* (1972); *Women and Equality: Changing Patterns in American Culture* (1977); *Civilities and Civil Rights: Greensboro, North Carolina, and the Black Struggle for Freedom* (1980); *Paradox of Change: American Women in the Twentieth Century* (1991); *Never Stop Running: Allard Lowenstein and the Struggle to Save American Liberalism* (1993). OAH president, 1998–1999. [Rosemary Carroll]

Chaffin, Nora C. (1900–1981), Ph.D. Duke University, 1943. Author, *Trinity College, 1839–1892: The Beginnings of Duke University* (1950). [Martha Swain]

Chambers, Clarke A. (1921–), Ph.D. University of California, Berkeley, 1950. Professor, University of Minnesota, Twin Cities; author, *California Farm Organizations: A Historical Study of the Grange, the Farm Bureau, and the Associated Farmers, 1929–1941* (1952); *Seedtime of Reform: American Social Service and Social Action, 1918–1933* (1963). [Mollie Davis]

Cheng, Ying-Wan, Ph.D. Radcliffe College, 1960. Professor, Dowling College, Oakdale, New York; author, *Postal Communication in China and Its Modernization, 1860–1896* (1970); contributor to British Broadcasting Corporation Chinese program, 1950–1953. [Carol Bleser]

Clark, Adéle Goodman (1882–1983). Director, League of Women Voters; president, Virginia League of Women Voters, 1920. [Anne Scott]

Colburn, David R., Ph.D. University of North Carolina at Chapel Hill, 1971. Professor and vice provost, University of Florida; executive director, Reubin O'D.Askew Institute on Politics and Society; coauthor, *Florida's Gubernatorial Politics in the Twentieth Century* (1980); coeditor, *Southern Businessmen and Desegregation* (1982); author, *Racial Change and Community Crisis: St. Augustine, Florida, 1877–1980* (1985); coeditor, *The African American Heritage of Florida* (1995). [Elizabeth Jacoway]

Cook, Blanche Wiesen (1941–), Ph.D. Johns Hopkins University, 1970. Distinguished Professor of History and Women's Studies, John Jay College of Criminal Justice and the Graduate Center of CUNY; author, *The Declassified Eisenhower: A Divided Legacy* (1981); *Eleanor Roosevelt*, 2 vols. (1992–1993). [Carol Bleser, Mollie Davis]

Cox, LaWanda (1909–), Ph.D. University of California, Berkeley, 1942. Professor, Hunter College; coauthor, *Politics, Principle, and Prejudice, 1865–1866: Dilemma of Reconstruction America* (1963); *Lincoln and Black Freedom: A Study in Presidential Leadership* (1981). [Betty Brandon, Jo Ann Carrigan, A. Elizabeth Taylor]

Cunningham, Minnie Fisher (1882–1964), Graduate in Pharmacy, University of Texas Medical Branch, 1901. President, Texas Equal Suffrage Association, 1915–1919; executive secretary, National League of Women

Voters, 1921–1923; U.S. Senate candidate from Texas in 1928; gubernatorial candidate, Texas, 1944. [A. Elizabeth Taylor]

Davis, Charlotte (Kinch). With Mollie Davis first copresident of SAWH. [Rosemary Carroll, Mollie Davis, Barbara Schnorrenberg]

Davis, Edwin A. (1904–1994), Ph.D. Louisiana State University, 1936. Professor, Louisiana State University; author, *Plantation life in the Florida Parishes of Louisiana, 1836–1846 as Reflected in the Diary of Bennet H. Barrow* (1943); *The Barber of Natchez* (1954); *Louisiana, the Pelican State* (1959). [Jo Ann Carrigan]

Degler, Carl (1921–), Ph.D. Columbia University, 1952. Professor Emeritus, Stanford University; author, *The Other South: Southern Dissenters in the Nineteenth Century* (1974); *At Odds: Women and the Family in America from the Revolution to the Present* (1980); *In Search of Human Nature: The Decline and Revival of Darwinism in American Social Thought* (1991). OAH president, 1979–1980; SHA president, 1985; AHA president, 1986. [Mollie Davis]

DeMoss, Dorothy, Ph.D. Texas Christian University, 1981. Professor, Texas Woman's University; author, *The History of Apparel Manufacturing in Texas, 1897–1981* (1989). [Martha Swain]

De Santis, Vincent P. (1916–), Ph.D. Johns Hopkins University, 1952. Professor, University of Notre Dame; author, *Republicans Face the Southern Question: The New Departure Years, 1877–1897* (1959); *The Shaping of Modern America, 1877–1916* (1973). [Betty Brandon, Margaret Ripley Wolfe]

Donald, David Herbert (1920–), Ph.D. University of Illinois, 1946. Professor Emeritus, Harvard University; author, *Charles Sumner and the Coming of the Civil War* (1960); *The Politics of Reconstruction, 1863–1867* (1965); *Liberty and Union* (1978); *Look Homeward: A Life of Thomas Wolfe* (1987); *Lincoln* (1995). SHA president, 1970. [Carol Bleser]

Douglas, Ann (1942–), Ph.D. Harvard University, 1970. Professor, Columbia University; author, *The Feminization of American Culture* (1977); *Terrible Honesty: Mongrel Manhattan in the 1920s* (1995). [Anne Scott]

Drew, Katherine Fischer (1923–), Ph.D. Cornell University, 1950. Professor, Rice University; author, *Law and Society in Early Medieval Europe: Studies in Legal History* (1988); compiler, *The Barbarian Invasions: Catalyst of a New Order* (1970); translator, *The Burgundian Code: Liber Constitu-tionum sive Lex Gundobada: Constitutiones Extravagantes* (1949); *The Lombard Laws* (1973); *The Laws of the Salian Franks* (1991). [Judith Gentry]

Droze, Wilmon Henry (1924–), Ph.D. Vanderbilt University, 1960. Provost, Texas Woman's University; president, Western Piedmont Community College; author, *High Dams and Slack Water: TVA Rebuilds a River* (1965); *Trees, Prairies, and People: A History of Tree Planting in the Plains States* (1977). [Martha Swain]

Duffy, John (1915–), Ph.D. UCLA, 1947. Professor, Louisiana State University; author, *Epidemics in Colonial America* (1953); *History of Public Health in New York City* (1968); *Healers: A History of American Medicine* (1979); *Sanitarians: A History of American Public Health* (1990). [Jo Ann Carrigan]

Dunham, Melerson Guy. Author, *The Centennial History of Alcorn Agricultural and Mechanical College* (1971). [Mollie Davis]

Dye, Nancy Schrom (1947–), Ph.D. University of Wisconsin–Madison, 1974. President, Oberlin College; author, *As Equals and as Sisters: Feminism, the Labor Movement, and the Women's Trade Union League of New York* (1980). [Margaret Ripley Wolfe]

Elliott, William Yandell (1896–1979), M.A. Vanderbilt University, 1920. Professor, Harvard University; author, *Pragmatic Revolt in Politics: Syndicalism, Fascism, and the Constitutional State* (1928); *The New British Empire* (1932); *Television's Impact on American Culture* (1956). [Anne Scott]

Evans, William McKee (1923–), Ph.D. University of North Carolina at Chapel Hill, 1965. Professor, California State Polytechnical University; author, *Ballots and Fence Rails: Reconstruction on the Lower Cape Fear* (1967); *To Die Game: The Story of the Lowry Band, Indian Guerrillas of Reconstruction* (1971). [Betty Brandon]

Fields, Barbara Jeanne, Ph.D. Yale University, 1978. Professor, Columbia University; author, *Slavery and Freedom on the Middle Ground: Maryland during the Nineteenth Century* (1985); coauthor, *The Destruction of Slavery* (1985); *Slaves No More: Three Essays on Emancipation and the Civil War* (1992); *Free at Last: A Documentary History of Slavery, Freedom, and the Civil War* (1992). [Darlene Clark Hine]

Flexner, Eleanor (1908–1995). Author, *Century of Struggle: The Woman's Rights Movement in the United States* (1959); *Women's Rights—Unfinished Business* (1971); *Mary Wollstonecraft: A Biography* (1972). [Anne Scott]

Flynt, James Wayne (1940–), Ph.D. Florida State University, 1965. Distinguished University Professor, Auburn University; author, *Duncan Upshaw Fletcher: Dixie's Reluctant Progressive* (1971); *Dixie's Forgotten People: The South's Poor Whites* (1979); *Alabama Baptists: Southern Baptists in the Heart of Dixie* (1998). SHA president, 2004. [Betty Brandon]

Foster, E. C. (1939–). Professor, Jackson State University; associate editor, *Journal of Negro History* 1978– , president, Association of Society and Behavior Scientists, 1982. [Darlene Clark Hine]

Franklin, Jimmie Lewis, Ph.D. University of Oklahoma, 1968. Professor, Vanderbilt University; author, *Born Sober: Prohibition in Oklahoma, 1907– 1959* (1971); *The Blacks in Oklahoma* (1980); *Journey toward Hope: A History of Blacks in Oklahoma* (1982); *Back to Birmingham: Richard Arrington, Jr., and His Times* (1989). SHA president, 1993. [Darlene Clark Hine, Arnita Jones]

Franklin, John Hope (1915–), Ph.D. Harvard University, 1941. Professor Emeritus, Duke University and the University of Chicago; author, *The Free Negro in North Carolina, 1790–1860* (1943); *From Slavery to Freedom: A History of American Negroes* (1947); *The Militant South, 1800–1861* (1956); *Reconstruction: After the Civil War* (1961); *Racial Equality in America* (1976). SHA president, 1971. [Darlene Clark Hine]

Gaston, Paul (1928–), Ph.D. University of North Carolina at Chapel Hill, 1961. Professor, University of Virginia; author, *The New South Creed: A Study in Southern Mythmaking* (1970); *Women of Fair Hope* (1984); *Man and Mission: E. B. Gaston and the Origins of the Fairhope Single Tax Colony* (1993). [Betty Brandon]

Gatewood, Willard Badgett, Jr. (1931–), Ph.D. Duke University, 1957. Professor, University of Arkansas at Fayetteville; editor, *Controversy in the Twenties: Fundamentalism, Modernism, and Evolution* (1969); author, *Theodore Roosevelt and the Art of Controversy: Episodes of the White House Years* (1970); *Aristocrats of Color: The Black Elites, 1880–1920* (1990). SHA president, 1987. [Rosemary Carroll, Mollie Davis, Elizabeth Jacoway]

Genovese, Eugene (1930–), Ph.D. Columbia University, 1959. Professor, Emory University; author, *The Political Economy of Slavery: Studies in the*

Economy and Society of the Slave South (1965); *The World the Slaveholders Made: Two Essays in Interpretation* (1969); *Roll, Jordan, Roll: The World the Slaves Made* (1974); editor, *The Slave Economy of the Old South: Selected Essays in Economic and Social History,* by U. B. Phillips (1968). OAH president, 1978–1979. [Carol Bleser]

Gilmore, Glenda E. (1949–), Ph.D. University of North Carolina at Chapel Hill, 1992. Peter V. and C. Vann Woodward Professor of History, Yale University; author, *Gender and Jim Crow: Women and the Politics of White Supremacy in North Carolina, 1896–1920* (1996); coeditor, *Jumpin' Jim Crow: Southern Politics from Civil War to Civil Rights* (2000). [Anne Scott]

Gingrich, Newton Leroy (1943–), Ph.D. Tulane University, 1971. Author, *Contract with America: The Bold Plan by Rep. Newt Gingrich, Rep. Dick Armey and the House Republicans to Change the Nation* (1994); *To Renew America* (1995); coauthor, *Gettysburg: A Novel of the Civil War* (2003). Republican Speaker of the U.S. House of Representatives, 1995–1999. [Mollie Davis, Barbara Schnorrenberg]

Glymph, Thavolia (1951–), Ph.D. Purdue University, 1994. Professor, Duke University; author, *A Women's War: Southern Women, Civil War, and the Confederate Legacy* (1997); coeditor, *Freedom: A Documentary History of Emancipation.* [Darlene Clark Hine]

Godfrey, James Logan (1907–), Ph.D. University of Chicago, 1942. Professor, University of North Carolina at Chapel Hill; coauthor, *Europe since 1815* (1947); *Revolutionary Justice: A Study of the Organization, Personnel, and Procedure of the Paris Tribunal, 1793–1795* (1951); coeditor, *Graduate School Dissertations and Theses* (1947). [Elizabeth Jacoway]

Graham, Hugh Davis (1936–2002), Ph.D. Stanford University, 1964. Professor, Johns Hopkins University; author, *Desegregation: The U.S. Supreme Court and the Schools* (1972); *The Uncertain Triumph: Federal Education Policy in the Kennedy and Johnson Years* (1984); *Affirmative Action: Origins and Development of National Policy, 1960–1985* (1989); *The Civil Rights Era: Origins and Development of National Policy 1960–1972* (1990); *Civil Rights and the Presidency: Race and Gender in American Politics, 1960–1972* (1992). [Jo Ann Carrigan, Joanne Hawks, Elizabeth Jacoway]

Grantham, Dewey (1921–), Ph.D. University of North Carolina at Chapel Hill, 1949. Professor, Vanderbilt University; author, *Hoke Smith and the Politics of the New South* (1958); *Southern Progressivism: The Reconciliation of*

Progress and Tradition (1983); *The Life and Death of the Solid South: A Political History* (1988). SHA president, 1967. [Martha Swain]

Gray, Virginia Gearhart (1903–1971), Ph.D. University of Wisconsin, 1928. Archivist, Manuscript Department, Duke University Library; author, "Activities of Southern Women: 1840–1860," *South Atlantic Quarterly* (1928). [Anne Scott]

Green, Fletcher Melvin (1895–1978), Ph.D. University of North Carolina, 1927. Professor, University of North Carolina at Chapel Hill; author, *Constitutional Development in the South Atlantic States, 1776–1860: A Study in the Evolution of Democracy* (1930); *Heroes of the American Revolution* (1932); *Romance of the Western Frontier* (1932); *Democracy in the Old South, and Other Essays* (1969); *The Role of the Yankee in the Old South* (1972). SHA president, 1945. OAH president, 1960–1961. [Betty Brandon, Anne Scott].

Hall, Jacquelyn Dowd (1943–), Ph.D. Columbia University, 1967. Professor, University of North Carolina at Chapel Hill; author, *Revolt against Chivalry: Jessie Daniel Ames and the Women's Campaign against Lynching* (1979); coauthor, *Like a Family: The Making of a Southern Cotton Mill World* (1987). SHA president, 2002; OAH president, 2003–2004. The Jacquelyn Dowd Hall Prize is awarded by the SAWH for the best graduate student papers submitted to the Southern Conference on Women's History. [Elizabeth Jacoway, Anne Scott]

Hamilton, William B. (1908–1972), Ph.D. Duke University, 1938. Professor, Duke University; author, *Anglo-American Law of the Frontier* (1953); *Holly Springs, Mississippi, to the Year 1878* (1984); editor, *South Atlantic Quarterly*, 1957– 1972. [Barbara Schnorrenberg]

Handlin, Oscar (1915–), Ph.D. Harvard University, 1940. Professor, Harvard University; author, *Boston's Immigrants, 1790–1865: A Study in Acculturation* (1941); coauthor, *Commonwealth: A Study of the Role of Government in the American Economy: Massachusetts, 1774–1861* (1947); *The Uprooted: The Epic Story of the Great Migrations That Made the American People* (1951); *Adventure in Freedom: Three Hundred Years of Jewish Life in America* (1954); *The Newcomers: Negroes and Puerto Ricans in a Changing Metropolis* (1959); editor, *Harvard Guide to American History* (1954–). [Anne Scott]

Harris, Robert L., Jr. (1943–), Ph.D. Northwestern University, 1974. Professor, Cornell University, Africana Studies and Research Center; coauthor, *Black Studies in the United States: Three Essays.* (1990); *Teaching African-American History* (1992). [Darlene Clark Hine].

Hedges, William L. Ph.D. Harvard University, 1954. Professor, Goucher College; author, *Washington Irving: An American Study, 1802–1832* (1965). [Anne Scott]

Herd, Shirley M. Taught school in Indianapolis; cofounder with Darlene Clark Hine of Black Women in the Middle West Project; president National Council of Negro Women, Indianapolis Section 1978–1985. [Darlene Clark Hine]

Herring, George C. (1936–), Ph.D. University of Virginia, 1965. Professor, University of Kentucky; author, *America's Longest War: The United States and Vietnam, 1950–1975* (1979); *LBJ and Vietnam: A Different Kind of War* (1994). [Margaret Ripley Wolfe]

Hesseltine, William B. (1902–1963), Ph.D. Ohio State University, 1928. Professor, University of Wisconsin; author, *Civil War Prisons: A Study in War Psychology* (1930); *Ulysses S. Grant, Politician* (1935); *The South in American History* (1943); *The Rise and Fall of Third Parties: From Anti-Masonry to Wallace* (1948). SHA president, 1960. [A. Elizabeth Taylor]

Hewitt, Nancy Ann (1951–), Ph.D. University of Pennsylvania, 1981. Professor, Rutgers University; author, *Women's Activism and Social Change, Rochester, New York, 1822–1872* (1984); *Southern Discomfort: Women's Activism in Tampa, Florida, 1880s–1920s* (2001); editor, *A Companion to American Women's History* (2002); coeditor, *Visible Women: New Essays on American Activism* (1993). [Anne Scott]

Hine, William Cassidy (1943–), Ph.D. Kent State University, 1979. Professor, South Carolina State University; coauthor, *The African American Odyssey* (2000). [Darlene Clark Hine]

Hornsby, Alton (1940–), Ph.D. University of Texas, 1969. Professor, Morehouse College; author, *The Black Almanac* (1972); *The Negro in Revolutionary Georgia* (1972); *The City Too Busy to Hate: Atlanta Businessmen and Desegregation in Southern Business* (1982). [Darlene Clark Hine]

Hyman, Harold Melvin (1924–), Ph.D. Columbia University, 1952. Professor Emeritus, Rice University; author, *Era of the Oath: Northern Loyalty*

Tests during the Civil War and Reconstruction (1954); *To Try Men's Souls: Loyalty Tests in American History* (1959); *A More Perfect Union: The Impact of the Civil War and Reconstruction on the Constitution* (1973). [Darlene Clark Hine]

Jackson, Sara Dunlap (1919–1991), M.A. American University and Catholic University; Honorary Doctorate University of Toledo, 1976. Archivist, National Archives. and Records Administration, 1944–1990. [Carol Bleser, Betty Brandon]

Jacobs, Sylvia (1946–), Ph.D. Howard University, 1975. Professor, North Carolina Central University; author, *The African Nexus: Black American Perspectives on the European Partitioning of Africa, 1880–1920* (1981). [Betty Brandon]

Jennings, Judi (1947–), Ph.D. University of Kentucky, 1975. Founder, University of Louisville's Women's Center; director of the Kentucky Foundation for Women; author, *The Business of Abolishing the British Slave Trade, 1783–1807* (1997). SAWH president, 1988. [Margaret Ripley Wolfe]

Johnson, Guion Griffis (1900–1989), Ph.D. University of North Carolina at Chapel Hill, 1927. Author, *The Social History of the Sea Islands with Special Reference to St. Helena Island, South Carolina* (1930); *Ante-bellum North Carolina: A Social History* (1937); *Volunteers in Community Service* (1967); coauthor, *Research in Service to Society: The First Fifty Years of the Institute for Research in Social Science at the University of North Carolina* (1980). [Anne Scott]

Johnson, Kate Burr. First woman in the country to serve as state Commissioner of Welfare from Morganton, North Carolina; director of the Bureau of Child Welfare of the North Carolina State Board of Charities and Public Welfare, 1919–1921; commissioner of Public Welfare of North Carolina, 1921–1930; superintendent of the New Jersey State Home for Girls, 1930–1948. [Anne Scott]

Jones, Howard Mumford (1892–1980), Ph.D. University of Chicago, 1916. Abbot Lawrence Lowell Professor of Humanities, Harvard University; author, *America and French Culture, 1750–1848* (1927); *Ideas in America* (1944); *The Literature of Virginia in the Seventeenth Century* (1946); coauthor, *Guide to American Literature and Its Backgrounds since 1890* (1953–); *O Strange New World: American Culture, the Formative Years* (1964); *Jeffersonianism and the American Novel* (1967). [Anne Scott]

Kerber, Linda (1940–), Ph.D. Columbia University, 1968. Professor, University of Iowa; author, *Women of the Republic: Intellect and Ideology in Revolutionary America* (1980); *Toward an Intellectual History of Women: Essays* (1997); *No Constitutional Right to Be Ladies: Women and the Obligations of Citizenship* (1998). OAH president, 1996–1997. [Carol Bleser]

Kibler, Lillian A. (1894–1978), Ph.D. Columbia University, 1947. Professor, Converse College; author, *Benjamin F. Perry, South Carolina Unionist* (1946); *A History of Converse College, 1889–1971* (1973). [Carol Bleser]

Klingberg, Frank Wysor, Ph.D. UCLA, 1949. Professor, University of North Carolina at Chapel Hill; author, *The Southern Claims Commission* (1955); *A History of the United States from 1865 to the Present* (1962). [Anne Scott]

Koch, Adrienne (1912–1971), Ph.D. Columbia University, 1944. Professor, University of Maryland; author, *The Philosophy of Thomas Jefferson* (1943); *Jefferson and Madison: The Great Collaboration* (1950); *Power, Morals, and the Founding Fathers: Essays in the Interpretation of the American Enlightenment* (1961). [Judith Gentry]

Land, Aubrey C. (1912–1993), Ph.D. University of Iowa, 1948. Professor, University of Georgia; author, *The Dulanys of Maryland: A Biographical Study of Daniel Dulany, the Elder (1685–1753) and Daniel Dulany, the Younger (1722–1797)* (1955); *Colonial Maryland: A History* (1981). SHA president, 1983. [Darlene Clark Hine]

Lane, Ann J. (1931–), Ph.D. Columbia University, 1968. Professor and Director of Studies in Women and Gender, University of Virginia; author, *The Brownsville Affair: National Crisis and Black Reaction* (1971); *To "Herland" and Beyond: The Life and Work of Charlotte Perkins Gilman* (1990); editor, *Making Women's History: The Essential Mary Ritter Beard* (2000). [Carol Bleser]

Langdon, George Dorland, Jr. (1933–), Ph.D. Yale University, 1961. President, Colgate University, 1978–1988; author, *Pilgrim Colony: A History of New Plymouth, 1620–1691* (1966). [Carol Bleser]

Lee, Charles E. (1917–), Hon. D. Litt. University of South Carolina, 1981. Director South Carolina Department of Archives and History, 1961–1987; president, Society of American Archivists, 1971; president, National Conference of State Historic Preservation Officers, 1985–1987. [Carol Bleser]

Lerner, Gerda (1920–), Ph.D. Columbia University, 1966. Professor, Sarah Lawrence College; author, *The Grimké Sisters from South Carolina: Rebels against Slavery* (1967); *The Creation of Patriarchy* (1986); *ERA and the Politics of Gender* (1990); *The Creation of Feminist Consciousness: From the Middle Ages to Eighteen-Seventy* (1993). OAH president, 1981–1982. [Rosemary Carroll, Mollie Davis, Darlene Clark Hine, Arnita Jones]

Lewis, Helena F. Ph.D. New York University, 1971. Professor, Appalachian State University; author, *The Politics of Surrealism* (1988). [Betty Brandon, Rosemary Carroll]

Link, Arthur (1920–1998), Ph.D. University of North Carolina at Chapel Hill, 1945. Professor, Princeton University; Editor, Papers of Woodrow Wilson. SHA president, 1969; AHA president, 1984; OAH president, 1984–1985. [Anne Scott]

Lippmann, Walter (1889–1974), B.A. Harvard University, 1909. Cofounded the *New Republic*, 1914; assistant to U.S. Secretary of War Newton D. Baker, 1917; one of the authors of President Woodrow Wilson's Fourteen Points; fortnightly columnist syndicated in over 275 newspapers; author, *Public Opinion* (1922); *The Phantom Public* (1925); *The Cold War: A Study in U.S. Foreign Policy* (1947). [Anne Scott]

Lonn, Ella (1879–1962), Ph.D. University of Pennsylvania, 1911. Professor, Goucher College; author, *Desertion during the Civil War* (1928); *Foreigners in the Confederacy* (1940); *The Colonial Agents of the Southern Colonies* (1945); *Salt as a Factor in the Confederacy* (1965). SHA president, 1946. [Mollie Davis, Judith Gentry, A. Elizabeth Taylor]

Ludington, Katherine. National treasurer and director of region one, League of Women Voters, 1920; League of Women Voters National Board, 1919–1933. [Anne Scott]

McCallum, Jane Y. (1877–1957), Suffragist; Texas Secretary of State, 1927; author, *Women Pioneers* (1929); "History of the Texas Woman Suffrage Movement" for *History of Woman Suffrage (1881–1922).* [Anne Scott]

McKitrick, Eric Louis (1919–2002), Ph.D. Columbia University, 1960. Professor, Columbia University; author, *Andrew Johnson and Reconstruction* (1960), *Slavery Defended: The Views of the Old South* (1963). [Carol Bleser]

Marks, Henry S. (1933–), M.A. University of Miami, 1956. Professor, Alabama Agricultural & Mechanical University; member of Alabama governor's staff, 1974; author, *Who Was Who in Alabama* (1972); *Who Was Who in Florida* (1973); coauthor, *Alabama Past Leaders* (1982). [Mollie Davis]

Marks, Marsha Kass (1935–), coauthor, *Alabama Past Leaders* (1982). [Mollie Davis]

Massey, Mary Elizabeth (1915–1976), Ph.D. University of North Carolina at Chapel Hill, 1947. Professor, Winthrop College; author, *Ersatz in the Confederacy* (1952); *Refugee Life in the Confederacy* (1964); *Bonnet Brigades* (1966). SHA president, 1972. [Betty Brandon, Judith Gentry, A. Elizabeth Taylor]

Matthews, Jane De Hart [Jane Sherron De Hart] (1936–), Ph.D. Duke University, 1967. Professor, University of California, Santa Barbara; author, *The Federal Theatre, 1935–1939: Plays, Relief, and Politics* (1967); coauthor, *Sex, Gender, and the Politics of ERA: A State and a Nation* (1990); coeditor, *Women's America: Refocusing the Past* (1999). [Rosemary Carroll]

Matthiessen, Francis Otto (1902–1950), Ph.D. Harvard University, 1927. Professor, Harvard University; author, *Sarah Orne Jewett* (1929), *American Renaissance: Art and Expression in the Age of Emerson and Whitman* (1941); *Henry James: The Major Phase* (1944); *Theodore Dreiser* (1951). [Anne Scott]

Meier, August (1923–2003), Ph.D. Columbia University, 1957. Professor, Kent State University; author, *Negro Thought in America, 1880–1915: Racial Ideologies in the Age of Booker T. Washington* (1963); coauthor, *From Plantation to Ghetto: An Interpretive History of American Negroes* (1966); *CORE: A Study in the Civil Rights Movement, 1942–1968* (1973); *A White Scholar and the Black Community, 1945–1965: Essays and Reflections* (1992). SHA president, 1992. [Darlene Clark Hine]

Mendenhall, Marjorie Stratford (1900–1961), Ph.D. University of North Carolina at Chapel Hill, 1939. Author, "Southern Women of a 'Lost Generation,'" *South Atlantic Quarterly* (1934). [Anne Scott]

Miles, Edwin Arthur (1926–), Ph.D, University of North Carolina, 1954. Professor, University of Houston; author, *Jacksonian Democracy in Mississippi* (1960). [Rosemary Carroll]

Miller, Perry (1905–1963), Ph.D. University of Chicago, 1931. Professor, Harvard University; author, *The New England Mind* (1939); *Jonathan Edwards* (1949); *Errand into the Wilderness: An Address* (1952); *American Thought: Civil War to World War I* (1954); editor, *The Works of Jonathan Edwards*. [Anne Scott]

Morrison, Mary T. R. Foulke (1879–1971), B.A. Bryn Mawr College, 1899. President, Chicago Suffrage Association (1915); recording secretary, National American Woman Suffrage Association, 1915–1916; trustee of Connecticut College, 1937–1971. [Anne Scott]

Murdock, Mary-Elizabeth (1930–), Ph.D. Brown University, 1962. Curator, Sophia Smith Collection, 1970 to 1985; editor, *Catalogs of the Sophia Smith Collection: Women's History Archive* (1975). [Rosemary Carroll]

Myers, Constance Ashton (1926–), Ph.D. University of South Carolina, 1974. Founder, Central Savannah River Area Chapter of the ACLU; cofounder, CCWHP, 1969; author, *The Prophet's Army: Trotskyists in America, 1928–1941* (1977). SAWH president, 1973–1974. [Betty Brandon, Rosemary Carroll, Mollie Davis, Barbara Schnorrenberg]

Nevins, Allan (1890–1971), M.A., University of Illinois, 1913. De Witt Clinton Professor of American History, Columbia University, 1942–1958; author, *Grover Cleveland: A Study in Courage* (1932); *Hamilton Fish: The Inner History of the Grant Administration* (1936); *Frémont: Pathmarker of the West* (1939); *Abram S. Hewitt: With Some Account of Peter Cooper* (1935); *The Ordeal of the Union*, 6 vols. (1947–1960); *Study in Power: John D. Rockefeller, Industrialist and Philanthropist* (1953); *Herbert H. Lehman and His Era* (1963). Founder of the Columbia Oral History Program. AHA president, 1960. [Carol Bleser]

Owens, Rameth R. Ph.D. Florida State University, 1989. Professor Emeritus, Clemson University. SAWH secretary-treasurer, 1986–1992. [Darlene Clark Hine, Margaret Ripley Wolfe]

Owsley, Frank (1890–1956), Ph.D. University of Chicago, 1924. Professor, Vanderbilt University; Friedman Professor of American History, University of Alabama; author, *State Rights in the Confederacy* (1925); *King Cotton Diplomacy: Foreign Relations of the Confederate States of America* (1931); *Plain Folk of the Old South* (1949). SHA president, 1940. [A. Elizabeth Taylor]

Painter, Nell Irvin (1942–), Ph.D. Harvard University, 1974. Professor, Princeton University; author, *Exodusters: Black Migration to Kansas after Reconstruction* (1977); *Standing at Armageddon: United States, 1877–1919* (1987); *Sojourner Truth: A Life, a Symbol* (1996); *Southern History across the Color Line* (2002); editor, *The Narrative of Hosea Hudson: His Life as a Negro Communist in the South* (1979). [Darlene Clark Hine]

Park, Maud Wood (1871–1955), B.A. Radcliffe College, 1898. Head of the Congressional Committee of the National American Woman Suffrage Association. First president, League of Women Voters, 1920–1924. Organized the Women's Joint Congressional Committee, 1924; author, the play, *Lucy Stone* (1939). [Anne Scott]

Perdue, Theda (1949–), Ph.D. University of Georgia, 1976. Professor, University of North Carolina at Chapel Hill; author, *Slavery and the Evolution of Cherokee Society, 1540–1866* (1979); *Cherokee Women: Gender and Culture Change, 1770–1835* (1998); *"Mixed Blood" Indians: Racial Construction in the Early South* (2003). SAWH president, 1986. [Carol Bleser, Joanne Hawks, Darlene Clark Hine, Margaret Ripley Wolfe]

Piper, Linda Jane (1935–), Ph.D. Ohio State University, 1966. Professor, University of Georgia; author, *Spartan Twilight* (1985). [Rosemary Carroll]

Potter, David M. (1910–1971), Ph.D. Yale University, 1940. Professor, Yale University; Coe Professor of American History, Stanford University; author, *Lincoln and His Party in the Secession Crisis* (1942); *People of Plenty: Economic Abundance and the American Character* (1954); *The South and the Sectional Conflict* (1968); *The Impending Crisis, 1848–1861* (1976). AHA president, 1970; OAH president, 1970–1971. [Anne Scott]

Prelinger, Catherine M. (Kitty) (1925–1991), Ph.D. Yale University, 1954. Assistant Editor, Benjamin Franklin Papers; author, *Charity, Challenge, and Change: Religious Dimensions of the Mid-Nineteenth-Century Women's Movement in Germany* (1987); editor, *Episcopal Women: Gender, Spirituality, and Commitment in an American Mainline Denomination* (1992). The Catherine Prelinger Award for nontraditional historians is awarded annually by the CCWHP. [Jo Ann Carrigan]

Robinson, Armstead L. (1947–1995), Ph.D. University of Rochester, 1977. Professor, University of Virginia; director Carter G. Woodson Institute for

Afro-American and African Studies; coeditor, *New Directions in Civil Rights Studies* (1991). [Darlene Clark Hine]

Robison, Daniel M. (1893–1971), Ph.D. Vanderbilt University, 1932. Professor, Vanderbilt University; editor, *Tennessee Historical Quarterly*; author, *Bob Taylor and the Agrarian Revolt in Tennessee* (1935); Tennessee State Librarian and Archivist Emeritus. [A. Elizabeth Taylor]

Rose, Willie Lee (1927–), Ph.D. Johns Hopkins University, 1962. Professor Emerita, Johns Hopkins University; author, *Rehearsal for Reconstruction: The Port Royal Experiment* (1964); *Race and Region in American Historical Fiction: Four Episodes in Popular Culture* (1979); *Slavery and Freedom* (1982). The Willie Lee Rose Prize is awarded annually by the SAWH for the best book in southern history published by a woman. [Carol Bleser, Betty Brandon, Mollie Davis, Judith Gentry, Elizabeth Jacoway]

Ross, Dorothy Rabin (1936–), Ph.D. Columbia University, 1965. Arthur O. Lovejoy Professor of History, Johns Hopkins University; author, *G. Stanley Hall: The Psychologist as Prophet* (1972); *The Origins of American Social Science* (1991). [Mollie Davis]

Rothschild, Mary Aickin (1945–), Ph.D. University of Washington, 1974. Professor, Arizona State University; author, *A Case of Black and White: Northern Volunteers and the Southern Freedom Summers, 1964–1965* (1982); coauthor, *Doing What the Day Brought: An Oral History of Arizona Women* (1992). [Anne Scott]

Rouse, Jacqueline Anne (1950–), Ph.D. Emory University, 1983. Professor, Georgia State University; author, *Lugenia Burns Hope: Black Southern Reformer* (1989); assistant editor, *Journal of Negro History*, 1983–1989. SAWH president, 2001. [Judith Gentry]

St. John, Jacqueline D., Ph.D. University of Oklahoma, 1969. Professor Emeritus, University of Nebraska–Omaha. [Jo Ann Carrigan]

Sanford, Terry (1917–1998), J.D. University of North Carolina at Chapel Hill, 1946. Governor of North Carolina, 1961–1965; president, Duke University, 1969–1885; U.S. Senator, North Carolina, 1987–1993. [Anne Scott]

Schmitt, Hans A. (1921–), Ph.D. University of Chicago, 1953. Professor, University of Virginia; author, *The Path to European Union: From the Marshall Plan to the Common Market* (1962); *Charles Péguy* (1967); *Lucky Victim:*

An Ordinary Life in Extraordinary Times, 1933–1946 (1989); *Quakers and Nazis: Inner Light in Outer Darkness* (1997). [Judith Gentry]

Schulz, Constance B. (1943–), Ph.D. University of Cincinnati, 1973. Professor, University of South Carolina; Cochair, Public History program; author, *A South Carolina Album, 1936–1948: Photographs from the Farm Security Administration, Office of War Information, and Standard Oil of New Jersey Documentary Projects* (1992); *The American History Video Disc and Master Guide* (1992); *Kiplin Hall and Its Families: A History* (1994); *Witness to the Fifties: The Pittsburgh Photographic Library, 1950–1953* (1999). SAWH president, 1992. [Joanne Hawks]

Scott, Joan Wallach (1941–), Ph.D. University of Wisconsin, 1969. Professor, Institute for Advanced Study, Princeton University; author, *The Glassworkers of Carmaux: French Craftsmen and Political Action in a Nineteenth-Century City* (1974); *Gender and the Politics of History* (1988); *Only Paradoxes to Offer: French Feminists and the Rights of Man* (1996). [Barbara Schnorrenberg]

Skemp, Sheila Lynn (1945–), Ph.D. University of Iowa, 1974. Professor, University of Mississippi; author, *William Franklin: Son of a Patriot, Servant of a King* (1990); *Benjamin and William Franklin: Father and Son, Patriot and Loyalist* (1994); *Judith Sargent Murray: A Brief Biography with Documents* (1998); coeditor, *Sex, Race, and the Role of Women in the South* (1983). [Joanne Hawks]

Shaw, Stephanie (1955–), Ph.D. Ohio State University, 1986. Professor, Ohio State University; author, *What a Woman Ought to Be and to Do: Black Professional Women Workers during the Jim Crow Era* (1996). [Darlene Clark Hine]

Silver, James W. (1907–1988), Ph.D. Vanderbilt University, 1935. Professor, University of Mississippi; University of Notre Dame; University of South Florida; author, *Edmund Pendleton Gaines: Frontier General* (1949); *Confederate Morale and Church Propaganda* (1957); *Mississippi in the Confederacy* (1961); *Mississippi: The Closed Society* (1964); *Running Scared: Silver in Mississippi* (1984). SHA president, 1963. [Mollie Davis, Arnita Jones]

Simpson, Amos Edwin. Ph.D. University of California, Berkeley, 1955. Professor, University of Southwestern Louisiana at Lafayette; author, *Hjalmar Schacht in Perspective* (1969); *Death of an Old World, 1914–1945* (1973); *Genesis of a New World, 1945 to the Present* (1973); coauthor, *Henry Watkins Allen of Louisiana* (1964); *The World of Europe since 1815* (1973); coeditor, *Why Hitler?* (1971). [Judith Gentry]

Smith, Hilda L. (1941–), Ph.D. University of Chicago, 1975. Professor of Women's Studies, University of Cincinnati; author, *Reason's Disciples: Seventeenth-Century English Feminists* (1982); *All Men and Both Sexes: Gender, Politics and the False Universal in England, 1640–1832* (2002). [Rosemary Carroll, Mollie Davis]

Spruill, Julia Cherry (1899–1986), M.A. University of North Carolina at Chapel Hill. Author, *Women's Life and Work in the Southern Colonies* (1938). The Julia Cherry Spruill Publication Prize is awarded annually by the SAWH for the best book published in southern women's history. [Judith Gentry, Joanne Hawks, Elizabeth Jacoway, Anne Scott]

Stone, Kathryn (1906–1995), M.A. University of Iowa. National board member, League of Women Voters, 1946. [Anne Scott]

Straub, Eleanor F., Ph.D. Emory University, 1973. Assistant executive director for the American Historical Association, 1973–1977. [Rosemary Carroll]

Strauss, Anna Lord (1899–?). President, League of Women Voters 1944 to 1950. [Anne Scott]

Strickland, Arvarh E. (1930–), Ph.D. University of Illinois at Urbana-Champaign, 1962. Professor Emeritus, University of Missouri–Columbia; author, *History of the Chicago Urban League* (1966). [Darlene Clark Hine]

Sweat, Edward Forrest (1912–1988), Ph.D. Indiana University, 1957. Professor, Clark College; Allen University. [Mollie Davis]

Swint, Henry Lee (1909–1985), Ph.D. Vanderbilt University, 1939. Professor, Vanderbilt University; author, *The Northern Teacher in the South, 1862–1870* (1941). [A. Elizabeth Taylor]

Taylor, George V., Ph.D. University of Wisconsin, 1951. Professor, University of North Carolina at Chapel Hill; author, "The Paris Bourse on the Eve of the Revolution, 1781–1789," *American Historical Review* (1962); "Noncapitalist Wealth and the Origins of the French Revolution," *American Historical Review* (1967). [Anne Scott]

Terborg-Penn, Rosalyn (1941–), Ph.D. Howard University, 1977. Professor, Morgan State University; author, *African American Women in the*

Struggle for the Vote, 1850–1920 (1998); coeditor, *Black Women in America: An Historical Encyclopedia* (1993). [Darlene Clark Hine]

Thornbrough, Emma Lou (1913–1994), Ph.D. University of Michigan, 1946. Professor, Butler University; author, *The Negro in Indiana before 1900: A Study of a Minority* (1957); *Indiana in the Civil War Era, 1850–1880* (1965); *T. Thomas Fortune: Militant Journalist* (1972); *The World of Christopher Columbus: Imperial Spain, 1469–1598* (1991). [Darlene Clark Hine]

Tindall, George Brown (1921–), Ph.D. University of North Carolina at Chapel Hill, 1951. Professor Emeritus, University of North Carolina at Chapel Hill; author, *South Carolina Negroes, 1877–1900* (1952); *The Emergence of the New South, 1913–1945* (1967); *The Persistent Tradition in New South Politics* (1975); *The Ethnic Southerners* (1976); *Natives and Newcomers: Ethnic Southerners and Southern Ethnics* (1995). SHA president, 1973. [Betty Brandon, Elizabeth Jacoway, Anne Scott, Martha Swain]

Toppin, Edgar Allan (1928–), Ph.D. Northwestern University, 1955. Professor, Virginia State University; author, *A Biographical History of Blacks in America since 1528* (1971); *The Black American in United States History* (1973). [Mollie Davis]

Turner, Elizabeth Hayes (1945–), Ph.D. Rice University, 1990. Professor, University of North Texas; author, *Women, Culture, and Community: Religion and Reform in Galveston, 1880–1920* (1997); coauthor, *Galveston and the 1900 Storm: Catastrophe and Catalyst* (2000); coeditor, *Major Problems in the History of the American South* (1999). SAWH president, 1997. [Elizabeth Jacoway]

Turner, Frederick Jackson (1861–1932), Ph.D. Johns Hopkins University, 1890. Professor, University of Wisconsin; Harvard University; author, *The Significance of the Frontier in American History* (1894); *Rise of the New West, 1819–1829* (1906); *The Frontier in American History* (1921). [Anne Scott]

Unterberger, Betty Miller (1922–), Ph.D. Duke University, 1950. Professor, Texas A & M University; author, *America's Siberian Expedition, 1918–1920: A Study of National Policy* (1956); *American Intervention in the Russian Civil War* (1969); *The United States, Revolutionary Russia, and the Rise of Czechoslovakia* (1989). [Carol Bleser]

Vandiver, Frank Everson (1925–), Ph.D. Tulane University, 1951. President Emeritus, Texas A & M University; author, *Their Tattered Flags: The*

Epic of the Confederacy (1970); *Black Jack: The Life and Times of John J. Pershing* (1977); *Shadows of Vietnam: Lyndon Johnson's Wars* (1997). SHA president, 1976. [Judith Gentry]

Voorhis, H. Jerry (1901–1984), M.A. Claremont College, 1928. Author, *The Story of Voorhis School for Boys* (1932); *The Morale of Democracy* (1941); *Out of Debt, Out of Danger: Proposals for War Finance and Tomorrow's Money* (1943); *Beyond Victory* (1944); *Confessions of a Congressman* (1947); *The Christian in Politics* (1951); *American Cooperatives: Where They Come from, What They Do, Where They Are Going* (1961); *Credit Unions: Basic Cooperatives* (1965); *The Strange Case of Richard Milhous Nixon* (1972). U.S. Representative, California 12th District, 1936–1946. [Anne Scott]

Walker, Peter F. (1931–), Ph.D. Vanderbilt University, 1958. Professor Emeritus, University of North Carolina at Chapel Hill; author, *Vicksburg: A People at War, 1860–1865* (1960). [Anne Scott]

Wall, Bennett Harrison (1914–2003), Ph.D. University of North Carolina at Chapel Hill, 1946. Professor, University of Georgia; author, *Growth in a Changing Environment: A History of Standard Oil Company (New Jersey), Exxon Corporation, 1950–1975* (1988); SHA secretary-treasurer, 1952-1985; SHA president, 1988. [Carol Bleser, Betty Brandon, Jo Ann Carrigan, Rosemary Carroll, Mollie Davis, Judith Gentry, Elizabeth Jacoway, Arnita Jones, Martha Swain, Margaret Ripley Wolfe]

Wall, Neva. Administative assistant to the Southern Historical Association, Athens, Georgia, 1965–1985. [Betty Brandon, Jo Ann Carrigan, Mollie Davis, Judith Gentry, Arnita Jones, Margaret Ripley Wolfe]

Wates, Wylma (1928–), M.A. Emory University, 1951. Archivist South Carolina Department of Archives and History 1952–1990; author, *A Flag Worthy of Your State and People: A History of the South Carolina State Flag* (1990); editor, *Journals of the General Assembly and House of Representatives, 1776–1780* (1970). [Carol Bleser]

Weaver, Blanche Henry Clark, Ph.D. Vanderbilt University, 1939. Author, *The Tennessee Yeomen, 1840–1860* (1942). [Martha Swain]

Weaver, Herbert (1905–1985), Ph.D. Vanderbilt University, 1941. Professor, Vanderbilt University; author, *Mississippi Farmers, 1850–1860* (1945); editor, James K. Polk Papers. [Martha Swain]

Weinberg, Gerhard Ludwig (1928–), Ph.D. University of Chicago, 1951. Professor Emeritus, University of North Carolina at Chapel Hill; author, *Germany and the Soviet Union, 1939–1941* (1954); *The Foreign Policy of Hitler's Germany: Diplomatic Revolution in Europe, 1933–1936* (1970); *The Foreign Policy of Hitler's Germany: Starting World War II, 1937–1939* (1980); *World in the Balance: Behind the Scenes of World War II* (1981); *A World at Arms: A Global History of World War II* (1994); *Germany, Hitler, and World War II: Essays in Modern German and World History* (1995). [Judith Gentry]

Weiss, Nancy Joan (1944–), Ph.D. Harvard University, 1970. Dean of Undergraduate Programs, Princeton University; author, *Charles Francis Murphy, 1858–1924: Respectability and Responsibility in Tammany Politics* (1968); *The National Urban League, 1910–1940* (1974); *Farewell to the Party of Lincoln: Black Politics in the Age of FDR* (1983); *Whitney M. Young, Jr., and the Struggle for Civil Rights* (1989). [Margaret Ripley Wolfe]

Wheeler, Marjorie Spruill [Marjorie Julian Spruill] (1951–), Ph.D. University of Virginia, 1990. Senior Research Associate, Vanderbilt University; author, *New Women of the New South: The Leaders of the Woman Suffrage Movement in the Southern States* (1993); editor, *One Woman, One Vote: Rediscovering the Woman Suffrage Movement* (1995); *Votes for Women! The Women Suffrage Movement in Tennessee, the South, and the Nation* (1995). SAWH president, 1996. [Judith Gentry, Joanne Hawks]

Wiley, Bell Irvin (1906–1980), Ph.D. Yale University, 1933. Professor, Emory University; author, *Southern Negroes, 1861–1865* (1938); *The Life of Johnny Reb: The Common Soldier of the Confederacy* (1943); *The Plain People of the Confederacy* (1943); *The Life of Billy Yank, the Common Soldier of the Union* (1952); *Confederate Women* (1975). SHA president, 1955. [Mollie Davis]

Williamson, Joel, Ph.D. University of California, Berkeley, 1964. Lineberger Professor in the Humanities, University of North Carolina at Chapel Hill; author, *After Slavery: The Negro in South Carolina during Reconstruction, 1861–1877* (1965); *New People: Miscegenation and Mulattoes in the United States* (1980); *The Crucible of Race: Black/White Relations in the American South since Emancipation* (1984); *William Faulkner and Southern History* (1993). [Elizabeth Jacoway]

Wilson, Joan Hoff [Joan Hoff] (1937–), Ph.D. University of California, Berkeley, 1966. Former executive secretary of the Organization of American Historians; Distinguished Research Professor of History, Montana State University; author, *American Business and Foreign Policy, 1920–1933* (1971);

Ideology and Economics: U.S. Relations with the Soviet Union, 1918–1933 (1974); *Herbert Hoover, Forgotten Progressive* (1975); *Law, Gender, and Injustice: A Legal History of U.S. Women* (1991); *Nixon Reconsidered* (1994); editor, Papers of the Nixon White House. [Jo Ann Carrigan]

Wittenstein, Kate, Ph.D. Boston University, 1988. Professor, Gustavus Adolphus College. [Darlene Clark Hine]

Woodman, Harold David (1928–), Ph.D. University of Chicago, 1964. Professor, Purdue University; author, *King Cotton and His Retainers: Financing and Marketing the Cotton Crop of the South, 1800–1925* (1968); *New South, New Law: The Legal Foundations of Credit and Labor Relations in the Postbellum Agricultural South* (1995). [Darlene Clark Hine]

Woodward, C. Vann (1908–1999), Ph.D. University of North Carolina at Chapel Hill, 1938. Professor, Yale University; author, *Tom Watson: Agrarian Rebel* (1938); *Origins of the New South, 1877–1913* (1951); *The Strange Career of Jim Crow* (1955); *The Burden of Southern History* (1960); *Mary Chesnut's Civil War* (1981). SHA president, 1952; OAH president, 1968–1969; AHA president, 1969. [Carol Bleser, Anne Scott]

Wright, Benjamin F. (1900–), Ph.D. Harvard University, 1925. President, Smith College, 1949–1959; author, *American Interpretations of Natural Law: A Study in the History of Political Thought* (1931); *The Contract Clause of the Constitution* (1938); *The Growth of American Constitutional Law* (1942); *Consensus and Continuity, 1776–1787* (1958); *5 Public Philosophies of Walter Lippmann* (1973). [Anne Scott]

Young, James Harvey (1915–), Ph.D. University of Illinois, 1941. Professor, Emory University; author, *The Toadstool Millionaires: A Social History of Patent Medicines in America before Federal Regulation* (1961); *The Medical Messiahs: A Social History of Health Quackery in Twentieth-Century America* (1967); *Early Years of Federal Food and Drug Control* (1982); *Pure Food: Securing the Federal Food and Drugs Act of 1906* (1989); *American Health Quackery: Collected Essays* (1992). SHA president, 1982. [Mollie Davis]